Helping Children
Cope With Divorce

Helping Children Cope With Divorce

Revised Edition

Edward Teyber

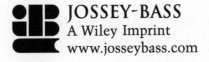

JOSSEY-BASS
A Wiley Imprint
www.josseybass.com

Published by Jossey-Bass
A Wiley Imprint
989 Market Street, San Francisco, CA 94103-1741   www.josseybass.com

Jossey-Bass books and products are available through most bookstores. To contact Jossey-Bass directly call our Customer Care Department within the U.S. at 800-956-7739, outside the U.S. at 317-572-3986, or fax 317-572-4002.

Jossey-Bass also publishes its books in a variety of electronic formats. Some content that appears in print may not be available in electronic books.

Library of Congress Cataloging-in-Publication Data

Teyber, Edward.
    Helping children cope with divorce / Edward Teyber.—Rev. ed., 2nd ed.
        p.   cm.
    Includes index.
    ISBN 0-7879-5554-X
    1. Divorced parents—United States.   2. Children of divorced parents—
United States.   I. Title.
HQ777.5 .T49 2001
306.89—dc21

                                                                            00-012715

Printed in the United States of America
SECOND EDITION
PB Printing   10 9

Contents

For Reed and Ted
and their Grandpa Ed

Acknowledgments

Many friends and colleagues have helped with this work, and I appreciate all they have done. First and foremost, two former graduate students—now colleagues—have shared their expertise and worked with me on every page of this revised edition. I have learned a great deal about children and families from Ronda Reil and Meg Walling. They have shared generously their refined sensibilities and abiding good judgment.

Long-time friends have also given much to this book. I would especially like to thank Faith McClure, Melissa Scarfone, and Margaret Dodds-Schumacher for their support and helpful editing. Thomas Brayton also contributed his time and significant expertise as a family law attorney to this revision.

Alan Rinzler, acquisitions editor for Jossey-Bass, has been a prize to know and work with. His personal commitment to helping children, as well as his reassuring presence, facilitated this work.

Finally, I wish to thank the children and families of divorce I have worked with. They have taught me much. Thanks to all.

Part One

Introduction

Chapter One

You Can Help Your Children Successfully Adjust to Divorce

"What Will Happen to My Kids? I Feel So Guilty!"

This book teaches divorcing parents what they can do to help their children successfully adjust to divorce. The biggest concern for almost all divorcing parents is whether their children will be hurt by the breakup. To be sure, divorce brings painful feelings that are not short-lived; divorce is difficult for every family member to deal with. Children do not understand the changes that are occurring and are worried about what will happen to them. And although parents are usually unaware of this, children also worry about the well-being of their parents, who now seem so angry and sad.

Regardless of who initiated the divorce, most parents are far more distressed by the breakup than they had anticipated. In addition to their own personal distress, they are burdened by guilt over the divorce and by feelings of inadequacy because they do not know how to help their children. However, these and other problems are resolvable. The widespread myth that children's lives are forever blighted is false; parents can take control of this crisis and do a great deal to help their children.

I will be your child's advocate in the pages ahead. I will communicate to you—the concerned parent—what your children may be thinking, feeling, and needing throughout the different stages of divorce. As I help you understand the questions and concerns that divorce evokes for your children, I will also provide practical guidelines to help you respond more effectively. Divorcing parents need specific information and practical guidelines to help with the problems that divorce brings up for children. My goal in this book is to help parents anticipate the concerns that divorce typically arouses for children, understand what these problems mean, and teach parents how they can respond effectively. For example, I teach parents how to explain the divorce to their children, suggest custody and living arrangements that will be in the children's best interest, and provide guidelines to help shield children from parental wrangling. This straightforward approach will make a difficult time easier for both children and parents alike and go a very long way toward helping children successfully adjust to divorce.

In this introductory chapter I first examine the broad social changes that have transformed the American family and led to a soaring divorce rate. The next section summarizes the effects of divorce on children and how children at different ages tend to react to their parents' breakup. The final section addresses the impact of divorce on parents and highlights the different stages of adjustment that parents often go through. In particular, I will show how parents' guilt and distress over the divorce diminishes their ability to provide both the support and the discipline that children need. In contrast to this overview, each chapter that follows focuses on a specific divorce-related problem and provides practical steps to resolve it.

The Changing American Family

As the divorce rate has soared since the 1960s, most of us have either personally experienced or shared with others the disruption of marriage and family. Divorce has become so widespread that well over one million children now go through their parents' divorce every year. How will divorce affect these children? Are there typical reactions or predictable problems that boys and girls will have because of their parents' divorce? What can parents do to help their children cope with the initial breakup, adjust to living in a single-parent family or to moving back and forth between two households, and make the transition to remarriage and living in a stepfamily? The pages that follow answer these questions and many more.

Before we embark on this important journey, however, we need to learn some other things about divorce. In particular, parents need to understand why so many divorces are occurring today. Are people just too selfish to make commitments or care about others anymore? Have people become too lazy or unwilling to work on the problems that exist in every relationship? Unfortunately, divorcing parents are sometimes blamed in these ways, but social demographers and family historians tell us that the explanations for the soaring divorce rate are not so simple.

A Historical Perspective on the Family

Let's take the long view for a moment and see what family historians have to tell us about the high divorce rate in the American family. Researchers have gathered a great deal of historical evidence describing what family life was like in previous centuries. These statistical records and archival materials from the eighteenth and nineteenth centuries show that family conflict and marital instability are not modern phenomena. As far back as the records go, there is unmistakable evidence that family life was fraught with conflict and tensions, subject to dramatic fluctuations, and full of diverse family forms and types. It is a romantic misperception to idealize the family of the past as a safe haven.

The conflict and tensions that have challenged families for hundreds of years have been heightened by recent developments that have changed the fabric of our society and contemporary family life. Urbanization and industrialization in the twentieth century, women entering the workforce during and after World War II, control over fertility through birth control in the 1960s, and the adoption of no-fault divorce have all contributed to the rising divorce rate. These changes have led to a profound shift in the roles and responsibilities that husbands and wives take on, how couples communicate, and how decision-making power is shared in the family. As a result of these far-reaching changes in marital relationships, the divorce rate started rising about 1900, rapidly accelerated after World War II, and doubled between 1960 and 1975. Although the divorce rate peaked in 1980, it has leveled off at a very high rate. One out of two new marriages in the United States eventually ends in divorce, most within the first ten years. Because this high rate of divorce is expected to continue, demographers predict that over 50 percent of children born today will live, at some point, in single-parent families, usually headed by mothers. However, most divorcing parents have given up on a specific partner—not on marriage itself. About three-fourths of men and two-thirds of women eventually remarry, usually within three years after the divorce (60 percent of which will also end in divorce, usually within five years). As a result of the high remarriage rate, about 20 percent of children today are living in a stepfamily.

Too often divorce is misconstrued as a circumscribed or terminal event that ends when the judge drops the gavel. However, divorcing parents soon find that the breakup and legal divorce is but one phase in a series of complex family transitions. In many cases, for example, there is a period of increasing marital tension or overt conflict leading up to the breakup; there may be life in a single-parent household or shared custody arrangement, remarriage and stepfamily formation, birth of new children, and possibly a subsequent divorce. Children and parents alike can struggle or thrive in each successive transition as they cope with the changes that the next phase presents. Divorcing parents face different challenges with their children at each of these successive stages. In the chapters that follow, I help parents anticipate the problems and respond to the concerns that children experience in each new phase of family life.

The Child's Experience of Divorce

The three brief scenarios that follow show typical responses of each family member to the initial breakup. In each situation you will see certain problems beginning to emerge for the children involved. Ask yourself, as you read along, how you would respond if these were your children.

The Abbott Family

Although Jack felt guilty about leaving his wife, Linda, and hurting their two children, he had made up his mind to go. He planned to move into an apartment with his girlfriend by the weekend. "I know this is hard for you," Jack began, and then he abruptly announced that he wanted a divorce.

Linda felt as if she had been kicked in the stomach. "What are you saying? Why are you leaving us? Why didn't you tell me?" Stunned with disbelief, she was almost unable to hear the words he was saying.

Two months later it still seemed to Linda as if her life had fallen apart. Although Jack had originally suggested that they remain friends, Linda was bitter and wanted never to see or speak to him again. She told her daughters that their father had betrayed all of them and they shouldn't have anything to do with him. And, as if humiliating her had not been enough, Jack was going to try to take her daughters away from her, too. Linda simply couldn't believe it. He was actually seeking joint custody of the two girls.

Shortly after the separation, Linda and Jack's daughters' behavior began to change. Thirteen-year-old Marta was angry at everyone and everything. She had sided with her mother and wouldn't see or speak to her father, despite his repeated requests to visit her. Marta blamed her father and hated him for leaving. Yet, even though Marta took her mother's side against her father, she gradually began to distance herself from her mother as well. Marta began to spend little time at home; her grades plummeted, and Linda started receiving reports that her daughter was cutting classes and spending time with older teenagers who missed school regularly.

Unlike Marta, her eight-year-old sister, Ann, wasn't angry all the time. She was sad. Ann felt torn apart inside and was praying that her parents would get back together again. She reasoned that if Marta weren't so angry with Dad, it would be easier for him to move back home.

Ann also felt torn between her parents. She missed seeing her father, and they often talked secretly on the phone. Ann felt guilty, however, and thought, "If Mom knew, she'd think I was on Dad's side. But I want to see Dad. He tells me it's unfair of Mom to make him into the bad guy. But Mom's right. He wouldn't have left us if he really loved us. I don't know who's right; I don't know what to do. I just feel pulled apart." In contrast to Marta, who became "impossible" to manage, Ann directed her conflict inward and began to complain about headaches and stomachaches.

The Baxter Family

When Joan's marriage broke up, her husband moved out of the state without leaving a forwarding address. Joan was left to raise their four-year-old son, Ben, on her own. In the four months after he left, her husband, Jim, sent only two support checks. Joan didn't know how she would make ends meet; her county welfare check wasn't enough to pay for food, rent, and the car payment each month. Joan had a part-time job as a salesclerk, but by the time she paid for day care, there wasn't enough money left to get through the month.

Joan felt overwhelmed by her life. Even her son was out of control. "Ben is driving me crazy," Joan told a relative. "Ever since his father left, I can't control him—he won't do anything I say. It's awful. He fights with me constantly, yet he won't leave me alone for a minute. He throws a temper tantrum when I drop him off at the day-care center, even though he used to like going there. He used to go to bed easily at night. Now putting him down is a battle that takes most of the evening. He wants one more drink of water, one more story, one more light turned on. I don't have anything left to give, and Ben wants more, more, more.

"I've finally given up trying to keep him in his own bed. He wakes up from a nightmare and won't stop crying until I let him climb into bed with me. Then in the morning he still won't obey me. He's just bossy and demanding rather than thankful. I tell you, I just can't handle this boy since his father left. He's ruining my life!"

When his father first left, Ben felt sad and missed him. After the first few weeks, though, Ben just felt angry. He kept thinking to himself, "Why did Dad leave me? I hate him for going away. I don't ever want him to come back." Sometimes Ben felt angry at his mother, too. Maybe it was her fault that his father had left. Ben's feelings were confusing and even kind of scary sometimes. Being angry at his mother could be so scary because Ben was afraid that he might drive away her away, as he believed he had his father. He thought, "If Dad left because he didn't want me, maybe Mom will leave, too! Then I'll be all alone, and there won't be anybody to take care of me." Even though he was really mad, Ben knew it was very important not to let his mother get very far away from him.

The Campbell Family

One month after her thirtieth birthday, Barbara asked Dave for a divorce. Dave wanted to stay together, but Barbara insisted that she needed more out of life than she had. Barbara wanted to go back to school and develop a career that would make her more independent than she had been with Dave. They had married right after high school, and she felt she never really had the chance to become her own person. Although Barbara didn't know exactly what she wanted and couldn't answer Dave's questions very well about "what was wrong," she just knew that what she had shared with Dave wasn't going to be enough.

Six months later, Dave still didn't know what to do with his four- and eight-year-old sons, Danny and Mark, when they visited him at his new apartment. He usually took them to the movies or a park, but nobody seemed to have much fun. And Dave really got frustrated when Danny started crying because he wanted to go home to his mother. He had always felt unsure of what to do when his boys were sad or cried. Barbara had always taken care of those needs, just as she had always fed and bathed and done almost everything else for them. Taking care of children was natural for her. She always seemed to know what to do. In contrast Dave always questioned himself, never quite feeling that he was doing it right.

On top of feeling like a failure as a father, Dave was growing resentful toward his former wife and his children. Dave told a friend, "I spend more than I can afford taking them out to eat and to movies and ballgames, and then they don't even talk to me. And when I take the boys back to their mother, she tells me she resents having to be the disciplinarian while I'm the "tour guide" who just has fun with the kids. Barbara actually told Danny and Mark that the only reason she doesn't take them out the way I do is that I don't give her enough money!"

By the end of the first year, Dave was seeing his sons less and less frequently.

Eight-year-old Mark had been very sad since his father moved out. He was seeing his father fewer weekends now, and their time together just wasn't the same as it used to be. Mark thought that everything would be all right if his parents would just get married again. Mark felt really bad on days when he overheard his mom crying in the shower or in her bedroom. Somehow, he felt, he just had to find a way to keep her from crying. That's when he remembered that whenever he got into trouble, his parents had stopped fighting with each other and paid attention to him. Then they had gotten along better for awhile.

Later that week Barbara got the first note from Mark's teacher that he had been fighting at school.

Even though divorce has become commonplace, it remains very painful, as shown in the typical reactions just profiled. The prevailing theme of these three scenarios is the struggle that each mother, father, and child faces with difficult feelings of guilt and anger, failure and fear, sadness and loss. However, divorcing parents should be reassured that many of the concerns that Marta, Ann, Ben, Danny, and Mark expressed could have been reduced or eliminated if their parents had known what to do. Parents who learn how to respond to their children during and after the divorce can greatly reduce the number of problems the children experience.

The Effects of Divorce on Children

Divorce has become prevalent, but what are its effects on children? Many researchers began studying this question in the 1970s, and they have learned a great deal about children and divorce. One thing researchers have learned is that we must distinguish between children's initial or short-term reactions to marital disruption and their long-term (more than two years) adjustment. Children's long-term reactions vary greatly, depending on how the parents respond to the child during and after the breakup. In particular, *the most important factors that shape long-term adjustment are (1) the amount of parental conflict children are exposed to and (2) the quality of parenting or childrearing competence they receive.*

In addition to these two factors, children's reactions are affected by social or environmental factors such as living in a neighborhood with high crime and violence. Economic factors are an important aspect of divorce, as most single-parent mothers have more economic stress and can provide fewer resources and opportunities for their children following divorce. Economic stress leads to increasing family mobility and an unwanted decrease in kinship networks and family support systems. This becomes especially problematic when it deprives families of grandparents and other kin who can help parents cope in the aftermath of divorce. Further, the stressful impact of divorce is likely greater in Asian, Hispanic, and other ethnic-religious families in which marital disruption is less accepted. With these considerations in mind, let's examine children's initial reactions to their parents' breakup.

Short-Term Reactions

Researchers have found that almost all children are very upset by the initial breakup. When looking back on their childhood, most adults whose parents divorced later describe the initial period of separation (when one parent moved out) as the most painful event in their lives. Children usually do not understand what is happening, even though they may know other children who have gone through divorce. Routinely, children are initially shocked and surprised by the separation, even though it seems clear to the adults that it did not happen suddenly or come out of the blue. Despite the fact that there may have been a great deal of arguing, tension, or unhappiness in the home, children do not want the divorce. Most children do not find relief in it or welcome it in any way unless they have been witnessing physical violence.

During the first year after marital disruption, parents usually see more anger, fear, depression, and guilt in their children. These troubled reactions usually lessen by the second year. To understand children's short-term reactions, however, we must examine how the impact of divorce varies between boys and girls and how it affects children differently at different ages.

PRESCHOOL-AGE. Preschool children (aged three to five) often react to their parents' separation with both anger and sadness. Boys tend to become noisier, angrier, and more restless. They may not play as well with friends and tend to sit alone more often. Boys often disrupt group activities at nursery school rather than cooperate in group activities with other children. Some preschool girls are angry, too, but others become little adults. These "perfect" little girls become overly concerned with being neat and good and may lecture or scold other children the way a parent or teacher would. Both boys and girls at this young age feel sad, cry more often, and become more demanding.

In response to the initial shock of marital disruption, children also regress, that is, act younger than their age; they return to behavior that they had previously outgrown. For example, children may resume sucking their thumbs, carrying a security blanket, asking for a pacifier, hitting their siblings, or needing help to feed themselves. Further, these children feel more insecure. When three- to five-year-old children are anxious, for example, parents observe more nightmares, bedwetting, masturbating, and fear about leaving the parent. As we discuss in Chapter Two, these children often have a very understandable fear. Having seen one parent move out unexpectedly, they are often worried about being left by the other parent as well.

SIX TO EIGHT YEARS OF AGE. Divorce seems to be especially difficult for six- to eight-year-old children, and boys at this age may be more distressed than girls. The primary reaction of these children is sadness. They are sad and weepy and likely to cry openly about the breakup. They usually long for the out-of-home parent, and boys may miss their fathers intensely. At this age, children are especially prone to believe that the departing parent has rejected them. This feeling of rejection and being unlovable results in lowered self-esteem, depression, and all too often a sharp decline in school performance. These children are worried about their parents, have trouble concentrating in school, and often try to prevent the divorce and restore their family.

NINE TO TWELVE YEARS OF AGE. Whereas the primary feeling for six- to eight-year-olds is sadness, it often changes to anger for nine- to twelve-year-olds. These children may be intensely angry at both parents for the breakup or especially angry at the parent who initiated the separation. These children are prone to taking sides with one parent against the other and to assigning blame. As detailed in Chapter Eight, these children are especially vulnerable to becoming embroiled in destructive parental battles in which one parent seeks to blame, harass, or get revenge on the other. Unfortunately, many parents actively enlist children in these toxic battles that are so harmful to parents and children alike.

Not only do they align with one parent against the other but these children express anger in other ways. What do they do? Many single-parent mothers report that it is impossible to discipline their nine- to twelve-year-old sons. In addition, these children may angrily reject their out-of-home father's attempts to spend time with them.

Anger is not the only reaction of these children, however. They are also sad about the breakup, worried about their parents' well-being, afraid about what will happen to them, and lonely. In particular, children at this age feel powerless. They do not want the divorce; they miss their intact families, long for the out-of-home parent, and feel helpless to alter the enormous changes occurring in their lives. Fueled by angry defiance and discouraging feelings of helplessness, school performance drops markedly for about half of the children in this age group. Other symptoms may emerge during this age period as well. For example, many children begin to have trouble getting along with their friends, get into fights with peers, or begin expressing physical complaints such as headaches and stomachaches. And, as I discuss in Chapter Nine, some of these children become so concerned about their parents' well-being that they try to act like adults and meet their parents' emotional needs. They lose their own childhood as they try to take care of their parents' loneliness and depression or solve their financial worries.

ADOLESCENCE. Fewer adolescents experience parental divorce because most divorces occur when children are younger (divorce is most common when children are four to seven years of age). When divorce does occur, however, the responses of adolescents tend to vary greatly. On the one hand, some adolescents may adjust to the family disruption better than younger children. Because they are becoming more independent and removed from family relations, they do not need as much affection and guidance as younger children. Some adolescents cope effectively with the divorce by distancing themselves from tensions in the parental relationship and becoming more involved in their own ambitions and plans for the future. For these adolescents, the main concern is about their future. In particular, they often worry about how the marital failure will influence their own ability to have a good marriage or go to college. Like older school-aged children, adolescents are likely to have problems when they are not free to pursue their own interests but are pulled into "loyalty conflicts" and feel pressured to take sides or choose one parent over the other.

Refreshingly, a few adolescents show a positive developmental spurt in response to the marital disruption. These young people are often helpful to their parents and younger siblings during this family crisis. Their own maturity and compassion can be seen as they participate constructively in family decisions, help with household responsibilities, and provide stable, nurturing relationships to younger siblings. However, this enhancement occurs infrequently, and when it does it is found almost exclusively for daughters and not for sons.

Many adolescents initially feel betrayed by the divorce. Researchers find that about 30 percent of adolescents angrily disengage from the family (more often boys in divorced families and, as we will see later, girls in stepfamilies). They spend as little time at home as possible and actively avoid activities and communication with family members. Serious problems can result if the adolescent's disengagement is accompanied by a lack of parental supervision or monitoring. If so, they are at high risk to become involved with antisocial peers. Delinquency, alcohol and drug use, school failure, and teenage sexual activity often follow.

Other adolescents may become depressed and withdraw from peers and family involvement or lose their plans and ambitions for their own future. It is sad to note that dropping out of high school and being unemployed extend across diverse ethnic groups. As we will see, one of the long-term effects of divorce for some adolescents, especially females, is a diminished capacity to succeed academically and to achieve occupationally during their early adult years.

Gender Differences

In addition to the age differences just discussed, researchers find gender differences in children's reactions in the years following divorce. Although there has been increasing attention to joint custody and father-headed families, about 85 percent of all children of divorce reside with a custodial mother. Studies find that the problems caused by marital conflict, divorce, and life in the care of a single mother may be more pervasive for young boys than for young girls. Boys in single-mother families, in contrast to girls in single-mother families and children in intact homes, tend to have more adjustment problems. Younger boys tend to be more dependent and help-seeking, whereas older boys are more aggressive and disobedient. Compared to girls, boys in single-mother-headed homes also have more behavior problems at school and at home, have more trouble getting along with friends at school, and have poorer school achievement when father is not involved. Two years after the divorce, girls in mother-headed families tend to be as well-adjusted as girls in intact, two-parent homes. In contrast, there tends to be an increasingly widening gap over time between the problematic behavior of boys in mother-headed homes without much paternal involvement and the better adjustment of boys in two-parent homes. This occurs because boys tend to lose their primary identification figure and source of discipline when father moves out and to receive more anger and criticism from custodial mothers than girls do. The evidence of greater difficulty in raising boys after divorce is also found in sibling relationships.

Researchers find more anger and conflict after divorce between sons, and between sons and daughters, than between sisters. This greater difficulty in handling sons after divorce may be one reason the U.S. Census Bureau reports that parents with sons are 9 percent less likely to divorce than are parents with daughters. For fear of not being able to handle a son alone, some mothers may be more reluctant to divorce if they have sons only. These gender differences change as children grow into adolescence, however. As noted earlier, studies suggest that divorce is often harder for young boys than for young girls. When girls reach adolescence, however, conflict often escalates between single mothers and daughters to match the level of conflict between young sons and mothers.

In addition to increasing mother-daughter conflict, adolescent girls are likely to develop problems in dating and romantic relationships, especially if their father has not been actively involved in their lives, their mother has not been able to discipline effectively, and caregivers have not supervised or monitored them closely. Poignantly, they tend to have sex at an earlier age and with more partners than daughters in intact families. Continuing this unwanted theme, they are also likely to marry at a younger age and eventually become divorced themselves. These problems in heterosexual relationships, as well as in greater academic and occupational underachievement for adolescent girls than boys, tend to persist into early adulthood. These gender differences become even more complex as families transition from single-parent, divorced families to stepfamilies. For example, whereas boys tend to adjust positively to the introduction of a responsible stepfather, girls are more likely to struggle with this new addition.

Longer-Term Reactions

Researchers have looked at the long-term effects of divorce on children five to ten years after the divorce, and when children of divorce are in their late twenties and early thirties. The general pattern that emerges across many different studies is that about 25 percent are doing very well, about 50 percent have mixed successes and problems, and about 25 percent are struggling with significant, enduring problems (about 10 percent of children from intact families have similar problems). Many different themes are found in these long-term reactions to divorce, however. Some individuals remain angry with or rejecting of the departing parent; some feel sad and long for a parent who was uninvolved after the divorce; others hold onto unrealistic, idealized memories of the intact family. Some see themselves as needy and having been deprived of a childhood. Others, however, see themselves as stronger and more resilient as a result of the divorce. Understandably, many adult children of divorce have heightened concerns about issues of trust, loyalty, and security in relationships. On average, they also report more loneliness as adults and more marital conflict than the children of intact families.

What does all of this mean to you, the concerned divorced parent? Do your children have to suffer the life-long consequences of your divorce? No, absolutely not! Divorce does not have to harm children or cause long-term problems. The same parenting skills that lead to good adjustment in intact families lead to good adjustment in divorced families. The way you respond to your child during the divorce and the quality of parenting you provide afterward are the most important determinants of your child's adjustment. More specifically, the most important determinants for problems are

- Being exposed to ongoing parental hostilities
- Ineffective discipline
- Losing contact with a parent after the divorce
- Feeling pressured to take sides and choose between their parents
- Being drawn into an adult role and asked to meet their parents' emotional needs.

In contrast, children adjust well if they consistently receive emotional support and effective discipline, maintain secure relationships with their parents, and are not embroiled in parental conflicts. If parents follow the parenting guidelines offered in the chapters that follow, children will make a successful adjustment.

Remember: it is not the divorce itself that causes problems for children, but the way parents respond to the children and the quality of parenting they provide afterward.

Divorce Is Painful for Parents

Although I act as your children's advocate in the pages ahead and focus on what you can do to help your children adjust, I don't forget the parents' difficulties. It may be easier sometimes to recognize or empathize with a child's problems than an adult's. However, when parents feel the support of being understood, it is easier for them to respond in kind and take better care of their children. Before looking further at children's typical reactions to divorce and how parents can best respond, I want to acknowledge how painful divorce is for most parents and the unnecessary guilt they often carry. As we will see, it usually takes far longer for parents to adjust than they had anticipated, and parents often go through a predictable series of stages as they recover from this crisis.

Length of Divorce Process

Researchers have observed wide mood swings, from elation to severe depression, in parents responding to the initial breakup. Parents typically report that diminished work performance, an inability to concentrate, health problems, anxiety, irritability, and sleep disturbances accompany the breakup. Parents also feel insecure in dating at this time, and there is an increased rate of sexual dysfunction in men. Sadly, many parents report increased smoking, drinking, and drug use during this stressful time.

Parents can be reassured to know that the turmoil and disruption brought on by the initial breakup will settle down, but they will not adjust to the divorce in a matter of weeks or even months. One year after the separation is often a low point for parents emotionally; it often takes as long as two or three years for many divorcing parents to regain fully their self-esteem and interpersonal confidence.

Thus parents should not place unrealistic expectations on themselves. Most parents are distressed for a much longer period than they think they should be. Statements like, "I've been separated for nearly a year now, so why do I still feel like crying at the drop of a hat?" are typical of this attitude. Why does it take two to three years for many parents to work through the emotional process of divorce? Many complex issues must be resolved, and some researchers have observed three distinct phases in this divorce process.

STAGE ONE. The initial stage of breaking up is perhaps the most painful period, especially for mothers. This phase includes the wrenching period of increasing conflict, tension, and dissatisfaction in the marriage that culminates in one party wanting out and deciding to divorce (usually the mother) and one party moving out (usually the father). Contrary to the widely held misconception, mothers initiate about two-thirds of all divorces that involve children. These mothers have often agonized over this decision for some time. In contrast, fathers may not experience the full emotional impact of the divorce until later in the process, when mothers may be well on their way toward recovering.

This disruptive period is often chaotic and may cause parents to make poor decisions or act in ways that they regret later. In particular, hurtful interactions between parents occur in this initial stage that can linger and continue to influence the quality of parenting and cooperation that divorced parents can provide years later. This time can be frightening for children because parents sometimes lose their self-restraint and begin to act impulsively. Perhaps one-half of all children see their parents yelling at each other, making ugly threats toward each other, and throwing and breaking things. Tragically, far too many children see their parents hitting each other in their hurt, betrayal, and rage. Common sense and good judgment are most likely to be lost during this stressful, initial stage. For example, children may be inappropriately exposed to their parents' short-term sexual liaisons with new partners, or impulsive parents may act without thinking ahead (for example, by stealing children) and lock hatred and distrust in forever.

This initial stage of marital disruption may last a few months or, in a few cases, it may drag on for a year or two. However, it is damaging for children to witness dramatic parental conflict. Separating parents can do much for their children by shielding them from such scenes. It is especially important during this initial period for parents to exercise restraint and plan arrangements for the breakup as thoughtfully as possible. There will be far less insecurity for children when separating parents can exercise some civility, mutual concern, and a modicum of respect for each other. Even if one parent insists on acting out, children still fare much better if the other parent does not use this irresponsible behavior as license to respond in kind.

In Chapters Two through Four, specific guidelines are given to help parents make plans for their children during this volatile stage. If eruptions have already occurred, however, there are still actions parents can take to help redress their earlier mistakes.

STAGE TWO. As the chaos from the initial breakup settles down, many parents enter a new stage of life transitions. In this second period of trial and error, parents try out new lifestyles and reorganize their lives. Many changes can occur for parents and children during this transitional period that may last from a few months to a year or two. Parents may go back to school, re-enter the workforce, change careers, buy and sell homes, and begin and end new relationships. Children may move to different neighborhoods, change schools, leave friends and make new ones, and go back and forth between two households with differing rules. This uprooting is an unsettling period because parents and children alike must cope with so many changes.

Children adjust better when they have more stability in their lives and fewer changes to deal with. Parents help children cope by providing as much familiarity and predictability in their lives as possible. In other words, children adjust better when parents can keep as many things as possible constant in their lives—school, teachers, church, bedroom, babysitter, playmates, household rules and discipline, and so forth. To emphasize further, children adjust better when parents regulate their daily lives with more predictable daily routines, consistent discipline, and regularly scheduled contact with both parents. When changes must occur, parents can help children by giving clear expectations (and repeated explanations) for what is going to occur and when.

STAGE THREE. The third stage of parental divorce is a renewed sense of stability. This phase happens sooner for some families than others, of course, and children feel more secure as their parents can provide more stability. New love relationships for mothers and fathers settle down, and stable patterns of visitation are established. As the dust settles, some children will be living in single-parent homes, some will be going back and forth between two households, and others will be living in stepfamilies.

Divorce is very painful for most parents, and it may take two or three years to come to terms with the far-reaching changes it brings. Most parents find that the divorce is more distressing, takes longer to adjust to, and changes much more in their lives than they had anticipated. This is usually true for both parents, regardless of who initiated the divorce. As divorcing parents work their way through the three phases of the divorce process, they will adjust better (and parent more effectively) if they can establish support systems with family and friends to help them negotiate these difficult transitions. Mothers often are more effective than fathers at establishing these all-important support systems. One of the most important steps in the parents' adjustment is to come to terms with unrealistic feelings of guilt and blame.

Parental Guilt

As if the divorce wasn't hard enough, guilt feelings only compound the problems. Many parents suffer mightily with guilt over their decision to divorce and, as we will see, it undermines their ability to discipline effectively.

STAYING TOGETHER FOR THE SAKE OF THE CHILDREN. One of the biggest problems for divorcing parents is their own sense of failure because they feel they have let their children down. Almost every parent struggles with guilt about the divorce, even when the other spouse has initiated the breakup. Unfortunately, many parents absorb our society's blame-ridden attitudes toward divorcing parents. The divorcing parent's anguish is often expressed in words such as these: "It's not fair that my children have to suffer because my marriage failed. It's selfish for me to seek a divorce that will hurt my children just to make my life better. Wouldn't it be better to stay married for the sake of the children?"

Should parents stay together for the sake of the children? There are no easy answers to this profound question, of course. Ultimately, each parent must decide what is best for his or her family; what works for one family may not be right for another. For example, the decision to separate or stay together has entirely different effects on children, based on differing circumstances such as these:

Will the children grow up with a calm and responsive divorced parent or have to cope with an irritable or depressed married parent?

Is this a temperamentally easy child who makes friends readily or one who has difficulty with changes or struggles to make transitions?

Will the parent be able to recover from the stress and demands of divorce with some equanimity or remain distressed and unable to parent effectively?

As these contrasting parameters highlight, there are no simple formulas to fit every family. The same decision—whether to part or stay together—will have a very different impact on children in one family context than on children in a different social situation. With this complexity in mind, along with the need to find different solutions for different families, let's see what guidelines the research can provide.

This much is known: it is not in the children's best interests for unhappily married couples to stay together *when this exposes children to chronic marital conflict.* Researchers have consistently found that children adjust better in split homes that function well than in conflict-ridden marriages. More specifically, a harmonious intact family is best for children, but a harmonious divorced environment is better than a disharmonious intact family. However, the evidence is also definitive that a disharmonious divorce, after which the parents continue to battle, is the most problematic environment of all for children. Both divorced and married parents must be willing to share personal responsibility rather than merely trying to blame the other parent for the serious consequences to children of growing up with chronically embattled parents.

Decades of research on family interaction have repeatedly found that children are affected adversely by conflict and turmoil in their parents' marriage. Children are more likely to develop personality and behavioral problems in unhappy, unloving families in which the parents fight continually than in any other kind of family situation.

In other words, *the real issue is not divorced versus intact family structure; it is harmonious versus conflicted family interactions.*

Dysfunctional family relationships cause the differences found in child adjustment, specifically:

- Conflict and negativity between parents, and between the parent and the child
- Aggressive and nonsupportive rivalries between siblings
- Ineffective discipline
- Lack of warmth and family cohesion

Even though the media and popular press have not grasped this core concept, divorcing parents need to recognize this essential distinction between family structure (divorced versus intact) and family interaction (harmonious versus conflicted).

Chronic marital conflict is difficult for all children, but it may be especially hard for boys, who tend to develop behavioral problems as a result. Young boys who grow up in an atmosphere of continuing marital strife are anxious and insecure, but as they become older they often become angry, defiant, and hard to discipline. They are more likely to get into trouble with the police and with school authorities; as young adults, these boys have been found to have a higher arrest rate for criminal behavior. Girls are also affected by ongoing marital conflict, and they too may become more aggressive and disobedient. In many cases, however, they react by becoming anxious, withdrawn, or perfectionistically well-behaved.

A nationwide survey of nearly fifteen hundred children conducted by the National Institute of Mental Health found that children who live with a divorced parent have fewer behavioral problems than those who live with married parents who always fight. This finding goes a long way toward explaining why the most poorly adjusted children of divorce have bitter, litigious parents who continue fighting with each other in court or through the children. Clearly, children living in families where there is ongoing warfare would be better off if their parents would just agree to amicably go their separate ways.

But what about other parents who are simply unhappily married? Divorce is a far more difficult decision when there is no overt hostility between parents and no need to shield children from yelling and loud arguments, demeaning insults, ugly threats, or violence. Do children fare better in quietly unhappy, emotionally disengaged, but intact families than in divorced homes? Unfortunately, research doesn't tell us as much about this more complicated question. Divorce is painful for almost all children in the short run and engenders long-term problems for some. This cold, hard fact must be faced squarely. As noted earlier, most adult children of divorce report their parents' breakup as their most painful life experience. Because the consequences for children are indeed serious, parents should never make the decision to divorce impulsively or in anger. Much soul-searching, consultation with respected others, repeated attempts to address the problems in the marriage, and careful planning for the children must all come first. In weighing the decision to divorce or stay married, however, parents are also balancing the potential costs of deciding to remain unhappily together.

First, children often shoulder a large burden of guilt and responsibility if they feel their parents have stayed together unhappily for their sake. Second, staying in an unhappy marriage may teach children to avoid problems. By providing a role model of passivity in living with disappointment or resignation to having less in life than they want, parents may give children the unwanted message that change is too threatening to risk or that there is nothing you can do to solve life's problems. Finally, parents also have a right to their own happiness, and their lives deserve to be considered as well. Parents may ask themselves this question: If your adult child came to you and asked for your advice, would you tell your son or daughter to stay unhappily married?

Parents may decide that it is not best for them or their families to stay together for the sake of their children after honest efforts have repeatedly failed to resolve marital conflicts. That is not the end of the story, however. With rights come responsibilities, and parents need to make a personal commitment to work constructively in the child's best interest, even when the other parent doesn't. As emphasized throughout this book, the marital relationship can end, but responsible parenting must continue.

UNDERMINING EFFECTIVE PARENTING. When parents do divorce because they are unhappily married, they often struggle with intense guilt. These feelings often are just as strong when the other spouse initiated the breakup. Too often, responsible parents who are devoted to doing the right thing for their children are ruled by unwarranted guilt and self-blame. Parental guilt over the divorce causes unnecessary suffering for many parents, and it contributes greatly to children's adjustment problems.

When parents feel too guilty about the breakup, they may not be able to talk with their children about the divorce, although their children need them to do so. Chapters Two, Three, and Four demonstrate that children adjust better when they receive effective parental explanations that answer their basic questions about why the divorce is occurring and what will happen to them. Unfortunately, most parents do not talk with their children about their concerns because it makes parents feel too guilty to see their children's hurt and anger. Because parents who are ruled by guilt want to avoid the topic, they steer away from their children's questions, worries, or sadness in order to manage their own guilt. As a consequence, children do not receive the explanations they need and have more difficulty coping with the breakup.

Parental guilt also leads to other problems for children. For example, parents who feel guilty about the divorce are overly critical of themselves, which often leads to depression and, in turn, causes parents to withdraw from their children and others. This is especially problematic because self-punitive parents who become depressed are less available to children at precisely the time children feel most insecure and in greatest need of emotional contact with their parents.

Parental guilt also increases problems for children by intensifying conflict between their parents. As emphasized earlier, children are hurt when they are exposed to parental fighting or pressured to take sides between their parents. Divorcing parents need to take steps to insulate their children from whatever acrimony or bitterness may exist in the parental relationship. Guilt plays into this all-important issue of embroiling children in parental conflicts. We have just seen how some parents use guilt over the divorce to blame themselves excessively. In contrast, some other parents try to deflect their guilt and shame over the divorce by *blaming* their former spouses for everything that went wrong in the marriage. These parents rigidly divert all the blame and cannot consider any valid criticisms or recognize their contribution to or shared participation in marital problems. Sharing any responsibility for what went wrong would open the floodgates of their own unacceptable feelings of guilt, failure, and inadequacy. When this defensive stance of blame is adopted, no parental conflicts can be talked about and resolved, and anxious children become insecure adults as they are exposed to unrelenting parental battles.

Most important, guilt undermines parents' ability to discipline children. It is hard enough to discipline children and adolescents in these times anyway; with the breakup it becomes even harder. Perhaps the single most widespread problem in the aftermath of divorce is parents' inability to discipline their children (for example, a mother might say, "If I try to discipline my son, he'll just go live with his Dad!"). When parents feel guilty about the divorce, they find it even harder to take a firm stand, say no, and effectively enforce the rules they have set. Afraid of the child's disapproval, parents become permissive and begin to bargain or plead with the child to behave. Recognizing that they have gained the upper hand in the parent-child relationship, children become manipulative and demanding with parents, aggressive with siblings, and bossy with peers. Clearly, the child develops significant adjustment problems when parents are too guilty or insecure to tolerate the child's protest when they set limits and enforce rules. Chapter Ten examines discipline and the effective childrearing practices parents can employ to help children successfully adjust to divorce.

The following anecdote may help to demonstrate how guilt over the divorce can result in ineffective discipline and cause problems for parent and child alike.

Mrs. Smith

Although Mrs. Smith had been divorced for two years, she still felt guilty about letting her children down. Family finances were much tighter than they had been before the divorce, and Mrs. Smith felt especially bad because she couldn't buy her teenage daughter, Sarah, many of the things her friends were getting from their parents.

Mrs. Smith had started working overtime just to avoid having to say no to her daughter so often. She felt bad whenever she had to say no to Sarah and disappoint her. Although the extra money she earned helped to satisfy Sarah,

Mrs. Smith felt as if she didn't have enough time or energy left for everything else she had to do. And there certainly wasn't any time left for simply enjoying herself. Life had become a grim routine of meeting everyone else's needs, and Mrs. Smith became increasingly depressed by the burden of so many demands. Finally, she followed the advice of a coworker and met with a counselor.

Mrs. Smith's counselor was quick to point out all the ways in which her guilt over the divorce had diminished her own personal life and undermined her parenting effectiveness. In particular, the counselor observed that Mrs. Smith's guilt was hampering her ability to effectively discipline her son. Nine-year-old David had acquired a behavior problem since the divorce (only confirming Mrs. Smith's guilt). He would not obey his mother and had recently been sent home from school for talking back to his teacher. The counselor helped Mrs. Smith realize that David's troubled behavior stemmed from her inability to enforce the rules she had set for him, not just because of the divorce.

In differing ways, Mrs. Smith's guilt was interfering with her ability to take a firm stand and say no to both of her children when necessary. Because she felt that she had hurt David by getting a divorce, she thought she needed to be more understanding and, therefore, more lenient with him. In addition, Mrs. Smith couldn't face David's rebellion when she told him to do something he didn't want to do. This pattern of behavior had evolved to the point where David knew he could say and do almost anything he wanted to his mother and get away with it. The counselor pointed out that once children learn that they can defy a parent, they do not feel a need to be respectful to teachers, coaches, or other authority figures either.

In the next few sessions with the counselor, Mrs. Smith began to reexamine and rein in her guilt about the divorce. As this burden began to diminish, she started to reclaim the control she had given up and stand up to her son's angry demands. With the counselor's guidance, she instituted a "time-out" program of discipline for her son and began to manage him more effectively. Increasingly, as David could no longer manipulate Mrs. Smith, his behavior at home and school took a turn for the better. Similarly, as she learned to tolerate Sarah's disappointment more realistically, Sarah became less needy and pouty and began to act with more maturity. For Mrs. Smith and many other parents, resolving their guilt over letting the children down allows them to discipline more effectively and to have more realistic expectations of themselves.

How can we put realistic limits on irrational guilt and prevent the parenting problems that stem from it? As before, it is important for divorcing parents to separate the *event* (for example, the divorce, the remarriage, the relocation to a new home, the birth of a new sibling) from the *interaction* or way in which parents respond to the event and help children understand and cope with it. We have seen that it does not tell us very much to say that a child is from a nuclear or divorced family. Children can adjust well or poorly in both types of families. Being nuclear or being divorced are not the essential issues. In either type of family there can be mutual respect, support, consistent discipline, effective communication, and an organized household with predictable daily routines. These characteristics of family interaction, regardless of whether the family is intact or divorced, determine children's successful adjustment.

Similarly, threats, loneliness, degrading comments, or competing alliances can exist in intact or divorced homes. These family interaction variables produce unhappy, nonachieving children with adjustment problems. Although this distinction between the event (the divorce) and the interaction (the way parents respond to it) may seem only academic at first, subsequent chapters will show that it largely determines your child's adjustment. Further, the ability to make this distinction gives parents their rightful opportunity to take charge of the divorce process rather than feeling helplessly controlled by it.

In sum, this chapter has emphasized that most of the problems associated with divorce actually are caused by poor parenting: (1) exposing children to ongoing marital conflict and parental wrangling and (2) problematic childrearing practices, especially ineffective discipline. In this context, it is important for parents to realize that children do not have to suffer long-term negative consequences of divorce. Parents can shape their children's positive adjustment by following certain guidelines.

This book gives parents the information they need to respond to their children's questions and concerns and help them successfully adjust to the breakup. These guidelines are not a cure-all, but parents can learn to do much for their children. If parents follow these suggestions, they will often see marked improvement in children who have been struggling with their parents' divorce. This educational program for divorcing parents provides a basic plan of action, and most parents will find they can readily adopt these guidelines for helping their children.

Let's turn now to the subject of children's separation anxieties and the first worry that troubles most young children of divorce—the fear of being left. We will learn what parents can do to allay that fear.

Suggestions for Further Reading

An easy-to-read book, *The Smart Divorce: A Practical Guide to the 200 Things You Must Know,* by S. Goldstein and H. Colb (Golden Books, 1999) provides practical information and "how-to's" on every aspect of divorce—legal, financial, emotional. In such an emotionally charged area, this helpful book is friendly and easy to read.

Surviving the Breakup: How Children and Parents Cope with Divorce by J. Kelly and J. Wallerstein (New York: Basic Books, 1996) is a comprehensive and scholarly book that describes the experience of divorce from the child's and the parent's point of view. Newer books are available (it was first published in 1980) but none are better.

After the Affair by J. Spring (New York: HarperCollins, 1997) helps couples make thoughtful decisions about whether to divorce after an affair or how to go about reconciling, if possible. This informative book also highlights problems for children when parents embroil children in these adult matters.

Part Two

Children's Concerns During the Breakup

Chapter Two

Divorce Causes Separation Anxieties

"If Dad Left, Won't Mom Go Away Too?"

For many children, the biggest concern that the initial breakup brings is the fear of losing their parents. Whereas younger children are afraid that parents may actually leave or physically abandon them, older children are worried that parental love won't be there when they need it. When seen from the child's perspective, this fear is not irrational; it is often based on their real-life experience. Usually without much preparation or warning, children see one of their parents abruptly pack his belongings (it's usually the father) and move away. Thereafter, the departing parent is often seen infrequently and irregularly. This chapter examines how the threat of losing secure parental ties causes separation anxieties (that is, insecurity about being left physically or emotionally) and contributes to many of the problems children experience in the aftermath of divorce.

What Causes Children's Separation Anxieties

Why are three- to eight-year-old children so concerned about the permanence of their relationship with their parents? Shouldn't children who are well-adjusted before the divorce remain secure in their attachment to their parents? Most adults fail to appreciate the extent to which fear of abandonment exists in all children in early childhood. Even up to the age of eight or so, most children have fears that, one way or another, their parents may leave them.

Children's fairy tales that have endured over the centuries reflect this concern. Hansel and Gretel were left in the woods; Cinderella's and Snow White's parents died; Little Red Riding Hood and Goldilocks were sent out into the forest alone; and Wendy tried to take care of Peter Pan and the "lost boys." From *Bambi* to *The Lion King,* and most Disney productions in between, parental loss is the theme of the opening scene. Across the ages, nothing is more central to childhood than children's fear of being separated from their parents and losing their caregivers.

These normative fears of abandonment and loss are greatly exacerbated by the breakup. It seems to children that their worst fear is coming true—these all-important caregivers, the foundation of their universe, might be going away. Children of divorce discover too soon that relationships are not forever and, sadly, too many find that they can indeed be left.

Separation anxieties can be intense and excruciating to experience, for adults as well as children. Perhaps you can recall how you felt when your spouse or a loved one announced he or she was leaving you. That cold, empty, sickening feeling is an adult version of children's separation anxiety. For some adults, even desperate attempts at self-medication through alcohol and drugs fail to soothe the anguish of strong separation anxieties. And think how poorly equipped children are, compared to adults, to understand and cope with such difficult feelings. Thus one of the most common problems that the initial breakup evokes for young children is worry about separation and loss. Children experience these painful feelings of separation anxiety for two reasons. First, these fears result from children's limited concept of time and their undeveloped thinking ability; second, they are caused by children's attachment bonds and emotional needs of their caregivers.

Children's Limited Timeframe

A young child's perception of the world and sense of time is far more immediate and tied to the present moment than an adult's. Because of their limited thinking abilities, children have not yet learned how to project themselves hours and days into the future with the same certainty as adults. Thus when parents say, "I will see you in a few days," young children do not understand what this means and are not reassured about continuing contact. Or, for example, when parents leave children with a babysitter and go to the movies, young children cannot always project ahead several hours and be secure in the knowledge that their mother or father will return. Underneath what appears to be a manipulative temper tantrum to keep mother or father at home may be a fear of being helpless and alone. On the other hand, children can learn to use their tears manipulatively to make parents feel guilty and, in this way, begin to exert too much control over the parent-child relationship. In the pages ahead I will show parents how they can both respond to children's authentic emotional needs *and* remain in charge of the parenting relationship.

In addition, children's "object constancy" is still in an early stage of development. Object constancy begins as the recognition that an object (a ball or toy) still exists when it rolls under the couch and is removed from sight. Later, it is the security of understanding that a departing caregiver will return. And still later in development, object constancy becomes the capacity to be emotionally sustained or soothed just by thinking about the person you love or miss. That is, you can find comfort from feeling emotionally connected to a loved one in their absence, just by remembering or thinking about them without having to be physically present with them. For example, you may have heard an adult say something like this, "My Mother died nearly twenty years ago, but I can still hear her kind voice inside of me, almost as if it was my own voice now. Even though she's gone, it still feels sometimes like we are talking together in my mind." These rich cognitive and emotional achievements have not been fully attained by pre-school-aged children. And for many older children and even adults in crisis, confidence in the constancy of relationships can still be shaken under stress.

Security in the continuity and reliability of relationships can readily be upset when children are under the stress of divorce. This occurs so easily because their object constancy has not yet become a stable cognitive ability or emotional capacity. Before seeing what parents can do to help with this problem, we need to understand separation anxieties better by learning more about attachment.

Attachment Bonds

The second and most important reason children develop separation anxieties is that the breakup threatens their attachment bonds. To understand separation anxieties in children of divorce, we first must know something about the role of attachment in normal development.

From birth, newborns are biologically predisposed ("hard-wired") to form attachment bonds to their primary caretakers. Infants display this attachment-seeking behavior as early as the first few days of life. Babies prefer the human voice to other sounds, for example, and by four weeks prefer the mother's voice and smell to that of others. At two months, they seek their mother's eyes and, to mother's and baby's mutual delight, hold this visual contact. At around three months, babies can recognize details in the human face sufficiently to discriminate human faces from other sights. Because infants' ability to recognize faces is such a great delight, they begin to smile at people at this time. If you think of the pleasure this smile provides parents and the silly antics adults go through to elicit it, you begin to see how parents and children attach to each other.

Between six and nine months, the infant's indiscriminate social smile becomes more selective. Attachment deepens, and the child shows a strong preference for an inner circle of special caretakers. These attachment figures can elicit more delight than others, and they can more readily comfort the infant in times of distress. Reflecting this growing attachment, however, they also engender more distress in the child when they leave. Researchers find that when infants have only their physical needs met but do not receive affection and attention from one or more consistent caretakers, they become depressed, apathetic, and delayed in their development. Simply put, humans need a warm relationship with a loving caregiver in order to thrive.

As toddlers, children use their primary caregivers as a secure base from which to venture out and explore the world. If parents have been emotionally responsive to children, comforting and available when needed, children will be securely attached. When tired, sick, or frightened, these securely attached children are reassured by knowing that they can return to their caregiver's lap for emotional refueling. Soon they want to set off again to resume exploring the world. Rather than fostering the child's dependency, meeting toddlers' emotional needs enables them to leave the caregiver more successfully and to confidently explore the environment on their own.

Researchers find that securely attached infants become more effective problem solvers as toddlers, more enthusiastic and curious preschoolers, and more confident and independent school-aged children, with higher self-esteem. In contrast, children feel insecurely attached when caregivers are inconsistently available or unresponsive to their distress or bids for attention. This *consistent* lack of responsiveness (every parent has bad days) may occur because of parents' ongoing depression, fatigue, lack of interest, or preoccupation with their own problems.

The attachment bonds we form with our parents when we are children are the essence of what is most human about us. From these early attachments develop our later capacities to feel empathy, compassion, and love for others. These attachments also form the basic building blocks of personality and the roadmaps or expectations we carry for future relationships. They give us, for example, our most fundamental sense of whether we are worthy of being loved or don't really matter to others, and whether we will expect others to be trustworthy or to disappoint and fail us. Secure bonds are the greatest source of joy and contentment in childhood but, of course, this door can also swing the other way. They can also be the greatest source of anger and despair when emotional ties are disrupted and caregivers are not available. For children and adults alike, to love and give our hearts is to risk this vulnerability; it cannot be any other way.

Attachment is not a one-way street; parents form their own attachment bonds to young children. For many, these attachments will be the most tender and profound feelings they experience in their lives. These early caregiving years signal the love affair of a lifetime for many parents. When nonparents observe harried parents with tired eyes, stained shirts, and an armful of dirty diapers, they may wonder why anyone would choose to give up their freedom for such overwhelming demands. These skeptical onlookers fail to grasp the power of these early love bonds that often make this the most precious time in life. These early attachment bonds grow and change throughout the lifespan, leaving most parents deeply committed to their child's well-being for a lifetime (and, as many grandparents will attest, to their child's own children as well). Let's look further at how early attachment bonds carry over into later childhood and even adulthood, and how they can emerge as central problems during the divorce.

NATURE OF ATTACHMENT BONDS. The nature of children's attachment bonds and how they express them change as children grow older, but the bonds continue to shape and influence their development. Older children become more independent, and adolescents begin to shift their ties from parents to peers. Even in adulthood, attachment does not wither but remains the central, organizing force in intimate relationships. Throughout life, adults revisit attachment issues; intense love and anguish continue to go hand in hand. At every age, enduring relationships hold the deepest meaning and satisfaction yet leave us vulnerable to hurt, betrayal, and loss. Many divorcing parents, in particular, will struggle for years with the question of whether or not to risk involvement in another relationship and how much of themselves they are willing to invest. No pat answers can be given to such personal questions because the feelings involved are so profound, but as parents grieve and resolve the loss of the marriage, most will choose to love and commit again.

Attachment issues also come to the fore for divorcing parents in the intense ambivalence and distress they experience around the time of the initial breakup. These difficult feelings may last a year or two, or more, after the separation. Even though the attachment bonds to the marital partner have been disrupted, usually they still hold much power. This is revealed, for example, when divorced parents find themselves missing their former spouses, even though they are clear that the marriage was not a good match, or even was harmful to them, and they truly want out. These parents, who genuinely do not want the marriage, are confused by their lingering feelings for their former spouses. At times, they may wonder if they really want to end the marriage and may begin a cycle of reengaging, seeking sexual contact, and then distancing from their former spouses in a way that drives everyone crazy. Such ambivalence is commonplace and often reflects the gradual relinquishing of attachment ties to the former spouse. It is not evidence of still being in love with the former spouse or proof that the decision to separate was a mistake.

ATTACHMENT DISRUPTIONS. Let's consider another way to appreciate the pervasive influence of attachment bonds throughout childhood and adulthood. It is hard for most adults to fully grasp children's complete physical and psychological dependence on caregivers and the life-and-death intensity of children's attachment bonds. It is especially hard for parents to appreciate this continuing need, as preschoolers begin to push parents away ("By my own self"), school-aged children become so capable and independent, and adolescents look so self-assured, at times. However, a closer look at our own adult needs for continuing close relationships may help us be more sensitive to children's attachment bonds and the separation anxieties that result from their parents' breakup.

Take a pen and a piece of paper now, and write down your answers to these three questions:

What was the most stressful personal experience you have had in the last three years?

What was the most distressing experience in your adult life?

What was the most painful experience of your childhood?

The answers most people give to all three questions share a common theme. Most replies for men and women, for each of the three age periods, involve the loss of a primary relationship. Frequently given answers include the death of a parent or loved one, the unwanted termination of a love relationship, or the loss of a friendship or someone important who moved away. Even as adults, our greatest concerns are for the stability and continuity of close relationships. Yet our need for these attachments is far less than children's. I hope this exercise increased your appreciation for the power and importance of children's attachment needs of their parents.

Children's deepest need of us is to provide secure attachment ties. Providing this secure base is the essential task of childrearing. To feel secure in their attachment bonds, children must be confident of their ability to obtain their parent's attention and affection when they need it, not when the caregiver feels like giving it. As

children grow older, of course, they should be able to soothe themselves better, delay their wishes, learn to wait their turn, and function independently for increasingly longer periods of time. When
children cannot dependably elicit a reassuring parental response
when they are distressed, however, the insecurity, anger, or helplessness that may result often becomes a life-long personality trait.

For many reasons, divorce often threatens or disrupts children's attachment bonds. Researchers have found that adults who
grew up in divorced families are more likely to report symptoms of
insecure attachments than are adults from intact homes. For example, adults who grew up in divorced homes were more likely to
be bothered by crying spells, insomnia, excessive worry, feelings of
worthlessness or being unlovable, guilt, and hopelessness. Decades
later, these adults were also more likely to feel afraid and irritable
when alone. These symptoms in adults correspond to the feelings
we call separation anxieties in young children who are distressed
over separation from their attachment figures.

Thus the security of attachment ties is central to children's
short- and long-term adjustment to divorce. However, these attachment bonds need not be threatened by the divorce. Parents
can do a great deal to ensure secure attachment ties for their children in the aftermath of divorce. As emphasized earlier, parents
can provide secure attachments in divorced or intact families, just
as caregivers can engender insecure attachments in divorced or intact families. Before we go on to see what parents should and
should not do, however, parents need to understand better how
separation anxieties are expressed and why the breakup threatens
attachment ties.

How Marital Separation Threatens
Children's Attachments

Some experts suggest that separation anxieties may be the most
painful feelings that children and adults experience in life. Much
of the distress that three- to seven-year-old children experience as
a result of divorce results from their anxiety about feared or actual
separation and loss. As we will see, even if children do not overtly
express worries about being left or losing contact with a sibling or

parent, divorcing parents should still consider the good possibility that they hold these concerns.

When parents decide to divorce, the father usually moves out of the house and establishes a new residence for himself. The day of the move is almost always one of the most difficult times for the divorcing couple. The fact that the relationship is ending becomes a reality after months of just thinking and talking about it. Understandably, both spouses are caught up in their own mixed feelings of anger, sadness, or relief. Parents' own emotional reactions can be so consuming at this point that it's often hard for them to decenter and recognize or fully register what their child may be going through.

Try to imagine the thoughts and feelings that a typical three- to seven-year-old child might have on the day Dad leaves:

> Mom and Dad have been crying and yelling a lot. They seem real unhappy. Mom said Dad was going to move today and he drove away in a big truck. Will I have to move, too? I don't want to go. I want Dad to come back. When will Dad be back? Is Mom going to move somewhere, too? She said we would stay in our house and I could keep my room, but Dad was leaving. If Dad went away, will Mom go away, too? Maybe she'll drive away and leave me here all alone. Are they mad at me? I don't like this. I'm kind of scared.

Most young children have some of these thoughts and feelings in response to their parents' separation. Divorcing parents need to anticipate that young children will become anxious because their secure ties are being threatened. Both young boys and girls express this heightened insecurity through increased bedwetting, a return to thumb-sucking, fear of the dark, nightmares, nail-biting, clinging, and becoming demanding. Over time, these anxiety symptoms can develop into aggressive defiance or childhood depression if the insecurity isn't alleviated.

Because most parents find the idea of deserting their children simply inconceivable, they often have difficulty appreciating their children's separation anxieties and abandonment fears. To varying degrees, however, these fears threaten most young children of divorce. Parents can reassure children about the permanence of their relationship by overtly telling them that they can always count on their parents' love. Parents should reassure children that even though many changes are taking place, they still will be there to take care of the children. We will learn more in this chapter about how to do this effectively. First, however, parents need to be able to recognize patterns of behavior that signal when separation anxieties have been evoked and children are worried about being left.

Problems of Everyday Partings

Parents can be alerted to separation anxieties when children start to have trouble with everyday partings that never bothered them before. Four-year-old Alicia, who bounded out of the car and eagerly ran to the nursery school playground before the breakup, now clings to her mother and cries as she tries to leave. Johnny, who used to be easy to put to bed at night, now exasperates his mother with endless requests for one more story or one more drink of water, or with fears that monsters will come if he is left alone in the dark. The arrival of the babysitter may trigger a temper tantrum that can ruin an evening out for even the most patient and guiltless parent. When divorce or other stressful changes occur, any departure of the parent, even for a brief time, may evoke separation anxieties.

Too often, well-intended adults respond to this kind of behavior with frustration and anger. Although this type of reaction is understandable, it soon becomes part of a negative cycle that exacerbates both the child's and the parent's problems. The frustrated parent may become angry and threaten or punish the child. In response, children may feel pushed away from the parent at the very moment when they most need to feel close. Consequently, children feel even more alone, and their need for parental reassurance becomes even greater. The child's demanding behavior then escalates and further exasperates the parent. Clearly, if the parent does not understand the child's insecurity and need for reassurance at this point, life soon can become miserable for both. Alternatively, the parent can overreact and give the distressed child too much power (for example, by sending the babysitter home and canceling their evening out). If so, children receive the highly problematic message that they can exert too much control over their caregivers.

What's the answer then? There is a more effective middle ground between these two unwanted poles of dismissing the child's genuine distress on the one hand or indulging the child's manipulative demand on the other. Later in this chapter, and throughout the chapters ahead, I will be highlighting parental responses that illustrate this more effective middle ground.

Weekly Visits to Noncustodial Parent

Another situation that commonly evokes children's separation anxieties is the transition between the primary residence and time spent with the noncustodial parent. For example, I met the divorcing parents of a three-year-old girl who could talk all day about the fun she has when she visits her father. On Wednesday her father always arrived to take his daughter home for the night, as per the visitation agreement. However, as soon as they began to leave the mother's home, the child would begin to cry and remain upset for most of the evening. The next day the father would return her to her mother and, once again, the little girl would talk happily about her father and how she wanted to be with him.

How could these parents make sense of their daughter's contradictory behavior? Because their daughter was so reluctant to go with the father, the mother was beginning to wonder what was going on when her child was with him. In turn, the father felt rejected by the child and resentful of the mother because his daughter so obviously chose her over him. At the time I met them, he was becoming less interested in spending regularly scheduled time with his daughter.

After talking with the parents about children's separation anxieties, the parents recognized that their daughter's distress over leaving her mother began just after the father had abruptly moved out of the house. Once the parents understood that her father's initial, unexplained departure had aroused their daughter's fear of being left, I was able to help them talk with their child about her separation anxieties and explain more fully what the divorce meant. Both parents were able to reassure her that, even though they would be living in different houses, they would both always be her mother and father and they would never go away or leave her. With repeated reassurances and continuing explanations, the child soon was able to make the transition from her mother's home to her father's without difficulty.

Explaining the Divorce to Children

For many divorcing parents, one of the hardest things they face is telling their children about the impending separation and divorce. For parent and child alike this is a sensitive topic indeed—and one with important implications for a child's future. The sample scripts and parent-child dialogues provided here will help with these pivotal conversations.

Children are far more likely to develop separation anxieties if they are not prepared for the parental separation. Every phase of the divorce process will be easier for children to cope with if they have been told *in advance* what to expect and when things will happen. All too often children awaken one morning to find that their father is no longer living with them. With limited or no explanation, he is simply gone. Children are told only that their father moved out and that their parents are going to get a divorce.

When a parent moves out suddenly or without forewarning, it is usually shocking for the child and generates much anxiety, even if it seems that the child has not been especially close to or involved with the departing parent. Most of these children experience strong separation anxieties; they do not really comprehend why their father has gone, what their future contact with him will be, or who else will leave.

Parents can tell children about the divorce and begin an ongoing dialogue with them once it becomes a firm decision and parents have settled on a date for moving apart. The best approach is for both parents to sit down together and talk with the children whenever such unity is possible. Also it is usually better to tell children together at a family meeting where everyone is included rather than separately. That way, brothers and sisters can learn to be a source of comfort to each other from the beginning. Sometimes it can be helpful to include a trusted therapist, pastoral counselor, or grandparent in this initial painful discussion, especially if adults' emotions or tempers may be too volatile.

When to Explain

It is important for parents to tell children a week or so in advance of a move. If one parent moves out before a child has been prepared, the unanticipated departure will be highly distressing, and parents will not readily regain their credibility or their child's trust. When parents move apart, they should provide the child with frequent, *regularly scheduled* contact that begins immediately upon the parent's departure. If possible, the nonresidential parent should try to visit or telephone the child every day for the first week or so. It is essential for children to know in advance specifically when and where they will be with their parent again. Visitation schedules cannot be random or casually followed. Parents can give children two identical calendars with the visitation schedules circled (for example, days and nights at Mom's house circled in pink; days and nights at Dad's house circled in blue) and, together, parents and children can hang their calendars in their rooms at both residences. Parents must follow through consistently and adhere reliably to whatever schedule has been established. Predictability is vital to the child's security.

Clearly, separation anxieties are one of the primary sources of adjustment problems in young children following divorce. The best way to alleviate or prevent them altogether is to help children feel more control over the enormous changes occurring in their lives. Parents can best accomplish this by preparing children for what is about to happen and explaining why mother or father is moving out. Both mother and father, together if possible, can prepare their children by

- Telling them what to expect (that is, what is going to happen and when)
- Providing an explanation for the divorce that the children can understand
- Reassuring children of their permanent and continuing relationship with both parents

What to Say

Because children have a difficult time understanding what divorce means, and adults are in the midst of their own personal crisis and distress, parents often find it hard to explain. To help with this problem, this section offers suggestions on how to talk to your children about divorce. Sample parent–child dialogues illustrate how parents can alleviate separation anxieties and other concerns. I encourage you to rewrite and modify these scripts to make them your own and to better fit your personal situation. The words can be spoken a thousand different ways—what is important is the ideas.

1. *Tell children what to expect.* Parents may tell children that mother and father are getting a divorce and will not be living together any more. Children can be told when the departing parent will move out and when they will be able to see him or her. Children should also be assured of their continuing contact with both parents (and receive it). Of course, it is not always possible to be so thoughtful during the crisis of the breakup. However, it is important that parents exercise as much self-restraint and plan as carefully as possible under these trying circumstances. How the breakup is handled initially, both with the children and with the marital partner, will have a significant bearing on how children adjust and on the couple's ability to cooperate in the years following the divorce.

As stated earlier, it is preferable for the mother and father to explain the divorce to their child together. When such cooperation is possible, it communicates to the child the all-important message that both parents will be working together and staying actively involved in the child's life. For example, in the sample dialogues that follow, mother and father alternately speak to their child:

Mother: Daddy and I are not going to be married any more. We are going to get a divorce. We will live in different houses from now on, but we will still always be your Mommy and Daddy. That is never going to change.

Father: I am moving to a new house on Saturday morning. You will live here with Mommy, but you will be staying with me at my new home often.

Mother: You will live with me here, but Daddy will still want to be with you, too. We have arranged for you to be with him every [specify the days], and you will also stay at his house on [days]. Tomorrow, we will all go over to Dad's new house together so you can see your new room there and know where everyone is sleeping every night.

Father: I will miss seeing you every day, but I'll look forward to having you with me on [days]. Also, I will talk with you on the phone on [day and time] between our visits, because we will be missing each other.

Mother: Even though Daddy and I will not be married any more, you will always live with one of us. We will both always love you, and we will work together to take care of you until you are grown up.

Father: This will be a big change for everyone in our family and you will have lots of questions about all of this. What can Mom and I answer for you right now?

2. *Provide an explanation for the divorce.* In addition to letting the child know what to expect, parents need to provide an explanation for why the divorce is occurring. Researchers have found that having an explanation for the divorce that they can understand helps children adjust, but most parents avoid these difficult conversations. One study found that 80 percent of well-educated, upper-middle-class parents gave children no explanations for their divorce! Parents do not talk with their children about divorce for a variety of reasons. Some feel inadequate to respond; they report that they just don't know what to say. Others, immobilized by guilt, do not want to talk about these matters because they will feel too badly about themselves if these conversations make their child feel sad or mad. These parents do not want to evoke reactions in their children that will make them feel worse about themselves than they already do at this difficult time. Still other parents are worried that their own unwanted emotions of sadness or fear will emerge and they won't be able to stop crying. Realistically, it will be painful to talk to children about an impending separation and divorce. Many children and parents alike will later recall this as one of the most difficult experiences in their lives. As difficult as it may be, there is no question that children adjust better when parents give children explanations they can understand and repeated invitations to ask questions about what will happen when and why. If parents find this step too difficult to take on their own, professional assistance from a counselor, pastor, or divorce mediator available through the family law court can help.

Let's look at one kind of parental "explanation" that commonly occurs yet is not at all helpful to the child:

Counselor: How did you and your husband explain the divorce to your eight-year-old daughter, Christina? Tell me what you said to her and the words you used.

Mother: Oh, I don't think we said too much about it. She seemed to figure it out by herself pretty well.

Counselor: How do you know that?

Mother: Well, the day after my husband moved out, I overheard her talking with the girl next door. Her friend asked if her daddy had moved away, and Christina said, "Yeah, my parents are getting divorced." She seemed to know what was going on so I didn't see any point in saying much more. Why just make her upset?

This kind of nonexplanation occurs regularly. When parents don't provide an explanation, however, children will create one of their own. As we will see in Chapter Four, the explanations that children develop by themselves are faulty and cause further problems because children tend to blame themselves for the divorce (for example, "Dad moved out because he's mad at me"). Thus, even though it is difficult to talk to children about divorce, they adjust better when they are given clear expectations for what to expect and age-appropriate explanations they can understand.

One of the most difficult aspects of explaining divorce to children is dealing with the issue of *blame.* In many marital separations, one parent has initiated the breakup, and the other spouse does not want the divorce. The spouse who has been left often feels rejected, hurt, and angry. Too often, that spouse may also feel justified in an effort to enlist the children in blaming the departed spouse for breaking up the family. It is highly problematic for the child when one parent assigns blame for the divorce and communicates that the child should be angry with the parent who has left or should not respect, care about, or want to spend time with that person. Often this blame is assigned by inappropriately providing children with specific details of adult infidelities and sexual relationships. Although tempted to do so, parents should resist this impulse to tell the truth—or the truth as they see it—when this means creating good guys and bad guys and drawing children into competing alliances.

The following explanation for the divorce will help children (1) understand why their parents are parting, (2) communicate that this is an adult decision and that the child is in no way responsible or to blame for the divorce, and (3) alleviate separation anxieties and prevent alienation from either parent.

Father: We loved each other when we got married and when
you were born, but we are not happy being married
anymore.

Mother: Sometimes parents' feelings about each other change as
time goes by, and that is what has happened to us. We do
not feel the same way we used to about each other because we are both different now.

Father: It's hard for us to get along with each other anymore
because some things about Mom make me unhappy,
and some things about me make her unhappy. We have
decided that we want to live apart from now on.

Mother: We want you to know that the divorce is not your fault.
There is nothing you could have done or can do about
it. Divorce is a problem between the adults in the family;
it is between Dad and me.

Father: Even though the way we feel about each other has
changed, our love for you has not changed. We love
you and will be working together to take care of you
until you are grown up. Parents have a very special love
for their children, and that kind of love does not
change. Parents and children never get a divorce.

Mother: It is hard for Dad and me to understand the problems
between us, so I know that it is even harder for you to
understand why we are getting a divorce. You can talk
to us about the divorce whenever you want, and we will
try and answer all of your questions.

Father: This is a whole lot to think about. Are there any questions we can answer for you right now?

3. *Reassure children of their continuing relationship with both parents.* Even if young children are prepared for the marital separation and understand why it is happening, separation anxieties may
still be aroused, and children can feel insecure about their continuing relationships with their parents. Parents can alleviate children's separation anxieties by repeatedly reassuring them that
mother and father will always want to be with them and will never
go away. One way of expressing this is suggested next. The example is written by Dad, but either Mom or Dad could say these
words.

Mom and I do not live together anymore. She has moved to a new home now. Maybe you have worried that since Mom and I do not want to live together any longer, we might not want to live with you. Sometimes boys and girls worry about this when their parents get divorced. I want you to know that we do not feel that way. We will never leave you. Mom and I both love you and will always want to be with you. You will always live with one of us, and we will always be here to take care of you. Have you, or any of your friends, ever had any worries like this?

This message will go a long way toward diminishing the fear of losing parental love that children often experience during the breakup. Remember that children need to discuss these issues many times. Children need to ask the same questions about the divorce—and receive the same reassurances—over and over again. Understandably, it will take many repetitions before children can trust these reassurances because the feelings involved are so profound and the stakes are so high.

Explaining a Trial Separation

The previous dialogues address the situation in which mother and father have decided to move apart and divorce. In many cases, however, there will be an extended period of uncertainty about the future of the marriage. One parent moves out, but the couple may continue spending time together and exploring the possibility of staying together. Such a trial separation also affects children, and parents can consider how to present this ambiguous, transitional period to them.

Parents sometimes wonder, "Will it confuse the children if my spouse moves out but we continue to date?" or "Will it be harder for the children to accept the divorce if we have a trial separation first?" A trial separation is not necessarily better or worse for children than a definitive breakup. Parents may decide to explore spending some time with each other, take a temporary time-out from the marriage, or go ahead and end the marriage. The nature of the separation is less important to a child's adjustment than the way it is presented and how the child is responded to afterward.

Many of the same guidelines for divorcing parents apply to trial separations. Children should be prepared for the parental separation at least several days in advance. It is simply too threatening for children to wake up and find a parent gone or to see a parent move out after a heated argument. In addition, the noncustodial parent and child should have regularly scheduled daytime and overnight visits; telephone contact should begin immediately following the departure. Children's primary fear is of losing access to the parent, which can be assuaged by knowing when and where they next will see the out-of-home parent.

Although children will be deeply concerned about a trial separation, they can cope successfully if their connection to both parents is maintained. When children lose physical or emotional access to either parent, separation anxieties and other symptoms often become enduring problems. The script to follow communicates these important reassurances while realistically presenting to the child what is going to happen and why. Of course, parents must not merely promise to remain involved with children or to be supportive of the other parent's continuing relationship with children. Parents must follow through and enact these reassurances during the years to come. Children don't put much stock in what we say; they believe what we do. This time the words are Mom's; they could be Dad's.

> Dad and I are not happy living together right now. We are going to live apart for awhile so that we can decide whether to stay married or get divorced. Dad will move into his own house for awhile. We will not know for several months whether we will live together again, but we will let you know as soon as we decide. We want you to know that we are not unhappy with you, and we will never leave you or stop loving you.
>
> While Dad and I are deciding whether we will stay married or get a divorce, you will be living with [person's name] at [address]. Dad will still want to be with you, too, so we have arranged for you to visit with him every [days], and you will stay at his home on [days]. You will also be able to talk with him on the telephone when you want, and we will schedule some regular times when you can talk together.
>
> This will be a very big change for all of us. You'll probably have a lot of questions to ask both of us after you have thought about this for awhile. What's the biggest question we can answer for you right now?

The scripts I have suggested may not fit closely with your personal circumstances. Some parents, for example, may be so bitter toward their ex-spouses that they do not intend to support the other parent's continuing relationship with the children. Or sometimes one parent is not responsibly committed to maintaining regular involvement with the children after divorce. These and other situations will be addressed in later chapters because they pose particular problems for children. For now, the point is that clear explanations such as these should be offered to ease the adjustment for children.

What to Do When Abuse Has Occurred

One of the most important things divorcing parents can do for their children is to respect their ties to both parents. Children will be concerned about their ability to sustain physical and emotional access to both of their parents, and it is essential for both parents to help children maintain secure ties. Children have strong attachment needs, and they become highly anxious (and later depressed) if they are uncertain of their ability to be close to both parents. This section, however, looks at one exception to the rule that parents should help children maintain as much involvement as possible with both parents. In a few circumstances, continuing ties expose children to physical or sexual abuse. Although these painful topics are not relevant to most readers and are generally beyond the scope of this book, at times they are an aspect of divorce and must be addressed.

A few marriages break up because one parent is behaving irresponsibly toward a child and the other parent must protect the child from physical or sexual abuse. In other families, abuse that has been occurring secretly may be uncovered during the period of crisis that often surrounds the initial breakup. Myths and misunderstandings are pervasive in this disturbing area of child abuse. Although we often want to turn away from this unwanted topic, we can protect children better by not avoiding it.

Who commits sexual abuse? Contrary to widely held beliefs, it occurs for boys as well as girls and is perpetrated by women as well as men. The most common perpetrator, however, is a stepfather.

One typical scenario is when the mother was molested as a child and has not worked through this betrayal with professional help. Still denying the heartbreaking reality of the betrayal, or unable to face the intolerable shame she suffers over what happened to her, she is vulnerable to choosing men who will repeat that pattern of abuse to them as adults or to their children. Often, it seems, the perpetrator molests the daughter when she is about the same age as the mother was when she was molested. When molestation occurs, alcohol or drug abuse is usually present; both may be. Perhaps the most disturbing fact about child sexual abuse is that in three-fourths of all cases the perpetrator knows the child well and is a family member, close family friend, or member of the extended family. This grim violation of trust may be the most serious long-term consequence for victims of sexual abuse.

Which children are most vulnerable? A common misconception about child sexual abuse is the Lolita myth. Many believe, inaccurately, that the sexually developing, precocious adolescent is most at risk. In fact, however, teenagers are more assertive and can say "no" more effectively. As a result, molestation that began earlier may continue into adolescence, but it seldom begins in adolescence. Instead, the child most likely to be molested is a five- to seven-year-old girl. She is also most likely to be victimized if she is depressed, excessively compliant, and receiving too little affection and attention. Boys are sexually molested as well, but we do not know as much about this because it is less likely to be reported.

How can parents know whether their children are being sexually abused? Many children will speak out directly, and parents should pay close attention; too many parents don't. Thus whenever children tell parents explicitly about sexual contact with an adult, or communicate that they must keep a "secret," parents should not dismiss these concerns but should explore these statements further in order to protect their children. Parents can do this by contacting their pediatrician or family practice physician for further assessment.

What other symptoms or signs may occur? Young children will reenact with dolls or in their drawings and play what has been done to them. Parents should pay close attention whenever children make such drawings or use dolls in sexually explicit play. If this type of play occurs, children may be demonstrating what they have observed on an adult movie channel or pornographic Web site. At times, however, they are acting out inappropriate adult–child contact that they have experienced. Children may also complain of pain or discomfort in their private parts, or they may be very interested in touching other kids sexually, exposing themselves, or wanting others to expose themselves. These are red flags, signaling that the child requires professional assessment.

Myths and denial also surround physical abuse. As with sexual abuse, the biggest problem is that caretakers do not want to believe this could be occurring, so they tend to ignore the signs. The person most likely to physically abuse a child is an emotionally isolated young mother, and the most likely victim is either an early adolescent or a young child about two years of age.

Physical abuse is equally likely for boys or girls and almost always takes place while the parent is trying to discipline the child. Physically abusing families tend to be socially isolated and, in general, highly authoritarian (that is, unaffectionate, noncommunicative, and very strict) in their childrearing. When parents see unexplained marks or bruises on a child, physical abuse may be the cause. As with potential sexual abuse, parents should neither overreact and make accusations nor ignore these signs and assume that nothing is wrong. Again, a responsible first step is to have the child examined by the family pediatrician.

Do litigious parents sometimes make false allegations of physical and sexual abuse to intimidate the former spouse during heated divorce proceedings? Yes, unfortunately, they do. Do parents sometimes ignore signs of abuse, fail to protect their children, and feel terribly guilty later? Yes, unfortunately, this also occurs. In cases in which sexual or physical abuse is occurring, limits must be placed on the child's contact with the abusing parent, for example, by requiring that visits with the child be supervised at all times. Parents coping with these extenuating circumstances need to seek psychological and legal help for themselves and their children.

In addition to deprivation or neglect, another form of abuse is emotional. Again, although continuing close contact with both parents is usually one of the most important reassurances that divorcing parents can offer children, there are important exceptions. For example, researchers have found that young adults find it especially difficult to achieve in school or work or to establish satisfying love relationships when one parent has been repeatedly derogating and shaming. During the chaotic initial phase of breaking up, parents often respond to each other, and sometimes to their children, in emotionally abusive ways. The consequences endure for a lifetime for children whose parents repeatedly yell at them in disgust or tell them that they are stupid, worthless, or bad. If parents have lost control of themselves and said hurtful things like this, they should apologize to their children, tell them it is not true, and take full responsibility for making this mistake. If this shaming recurs and becomes a behavior pattern, parents need to seek help in counseling. Sad to say, these parents are often repeating the hurtful words and phrases to their children, in the same contemptuous tone of voice, that their own parents once said to them.

Children's unprotected involvement with sexually, physically, or emotionally abusive parents engenders anxiety and a shame-based sense of self that can impair them for a lifetime. The primary concern in divorcing families, however, is the long-term problems that result when parents lose control and cannot stop fighting with each other. Although abuse will not be a concern for most divorcing couples, the profound insecurity and the anxiety symptoms found in children witnessing chronic marital conflict is prevalent. Embattled parents are usually reluctant to look at themselves and consider the toxic impact on their children of their own combative behavior. They just want to focus on the ex-spouse and blame him or her for everything. The undeniable fact, however, is that children are highly distressed when they are repeatedly exposed to intense parental conflict and threats. Throughout this book, I stress the serious problems that befall children when parents do not shield them from ongoing parental warfare.

In closing, the basic issue for most parents is the need to reassure children that their all-important bonds to both parents will remain constant. This reassurance can help alleviate the single biggest concern that divorce arouses for young children—the fear of losing their parents.

The next chapter turns to a second cause of problems for many children during the initial breakup: reunification fantasies.

Suggestions for Further Reading

Becoming Attached by Robert Karen (New York: Oxford University Press, 1998) offers a highly readable overview of attachment theory. It will help many parents better understand and respond to their young children.

In her classic, *The Magic Years,* Selma Fraiberg compassionately takes parents into the mind of a child (New York: Scribner, 1959). Parents interested in learning more about child abuse may want to read *When Your Child Has Been Molested: A Parent's Guide to Healing and Recovery,* by K. Hagans (San Francisco: Jossey-Bass, 1998).

Chapter Three

Children Want to Reunite Their Parents

"If I'm Really Good, Maybe Mom and Dad Will Get Back Together Again."

We have just seen in Chapter Two that children become anxious when their parents break up. One way children cope with this anxiety-arousing loss is to deny the reality of the divorce and see what they can do to try and keep their parents together. Although one or both parents may want the divorce, children do not. They don't necessarily talk about it openly, but many children tenaciously hold on to their desire to recreate the original nuclear family for years after the divorce. The reunification wish is often so strong that it may continue, even after one or both parents have remarried and given birth to new children! Similarly, the hope remains despite the realization that the divorce has resulted in less tension at home and a better life for everyone in the family. Many children simply do not want to accept the fact that the marital relationship has ended and that their family, as they have known it, has changed forever.

Reunification fantasies are not just benign childhood wishes. They frequently cause problems. They prevent children from coming to terms with the reality of their current lives and from successfully moving forward in their development. If parents do not give explanations for the divorce that end these reunification fantasies, they often go underground and can cause problems for years afterward. Once parents are certain that they will divorce, they need to tell the children that the divorce is final and that there is nothing the children can do to change this. Doing so, of course, is excruciating for most parents. And—to say it realistically—parents should anticipate that this statement will be as hard for children to hear as it is for parents to speak. However, explanations about the permanence of the breakup are necessary; they help children cope more effectively in the long run. Children will not be able to adjust to the new circumstances of their lives until they are certain that their mother and father will not be married again.

Three Sources of Reunification Fantasies

Why do most school-aged children cling to the hope that their mother and father will not divorce or that, if they do, they will eventually remarry? Why do some children even develop symptoms of illness or other behavior problems in order to get their parents back together? Reunification fantasies can stem from three sources. Each holds a different meaning for children and requires a different parental response.

First, children want to avoid the painful feelings evoked by the breakup. They want to maintain their family as they have known it and to believe that their parents still love and are happy with each other. This response to the initial breakup is almost universal. This first source of reunification fantasies does not tend to cause long-term problems for children, especially if parents provide explanations for the divorce that clearly communicate its finality.

The second source of reunification fantasies is very different and far more problematic for children. In many marriages that end in divorce, a stable parental coalition never formed and, as a result, children in these families could exert too much power. In particular, children often have learned that they can come between their parents, playing one off against the other, and manipulate the closeness in their parents' marriage. These children, who usually become demanding, disrespectful, and difficult to discipline, have been too successful in controlling family relations before the divorce. With the breakup, they often develop further problems as they try to manipulate adult relationships and keep their parents together.

The third and most problematic source of reunification fantasies is when one parent does not want the divorce and enlists the child in convincing the other parent to remain married. Let's explore each of these three types of reunification fantasies more closely.

Normal or expectable reunification fantasies are the most common and the least problematic for children. They are also the easiest for parents to resolve. Such wishes occur for several reasons, perhaps the simplest of which is that they have seen their parents reconcile. Often children have heard their parents threaten to separate, but the threats have never before come true. Further, many children have witnessed temporary marital separations. It makes sense for these children to think that the latest separation can be reversed, too.

Children also develop reunification fantasies in order to deny the reality of the initial breakup. It can be too distressing to acknowledge that the breakup is real all at once, so many children (and some adults) cope by gradually accepting the reality.

Much of the pain that children are trying to avoid springs from the loss of the intact family and the familiarity it provides. Children want their parents to be happy together, in part, because as long as the family stays together children feel safer and more protected. In the previous intact family, children were part of a cohesive family group that gave them their own place in the world. Family membership often bestows a deeply reassuring sense of belonging. Even though there may have been tension and conflict before the divorce, the intact family still provided familiarity and security. After the breakup, the new family structure will be anxiety arousing for children simply because it is different and unknown and because it requires adjustments to new living arrangements, as well as a changing family identity.

Children's reunification fantasies are also fueled by a heightened insecurity about having their basic needs met. Although children's emotional needs increase during divorce, they may not feel as confident that they can rely on their parents to fulfill those needs. Insecurity is further increased because relationships do not seem as stable or dependable as they did before the breakup. This anxiety is exacerbated because children often find that they have significantly less contact with their fathers after the separation. And when children see their parents' distress over the breakup, the reassuring childhood myth that parents are powerful figures—so effectively in command of life—may also end. Perhaps for the first time, as children see their parents' own worries and concerns, they become aware that their all-important protectors have their own vulnerabilities. Children learn, sometimes too early and too completely, that their parents cannot shield them and keep them as safe as they once believed.

For all of these reasons, children do not want to accept that the divorce is permanent, and they hold on to the fantasy that their parents will reunite. As noted before, this is not just a harmless childhood wish. Children use reunification fantasies to ward off painful feelings of sadness and loss at the ending of the family as they have known it. This denial prevents children from accepting the reality of the divorce and moving forward to adapt to their new life circumstances. Parents can help children end these encumbering reunification wishes, as discussed at the end of this chapter.

When Children Exert Too Much Control

In order to understand the second source of reunification fantasies, we must first turn to the topic of "structural family relations" and learn some basic family therapy concepts. *Structural family relations* is an awkward term that is used to describe family interaction patterns and how relationships or groupings between different family members are organized. More specifically, it refers to the relatively enduring patterns of alliances, subgroups, or teams that exist in many families. We will see how structural family relationships shape family communication patterns and the roles that family members adopt.

Among the different structural family relationships, the parental coalition is the pivotal axis of family life and shapes much of how the family functions. In particular, the nature of the parental coalition greatly influences children's adjustment. This is just as true for divorced families as it is for intact families and, as we will see in Chapter Eleven, it applies to stepfamilies as well.

In intact families that function well, the marital relationship is an effective coalition that works together. Both spouses have a loyal commitment to each other such that the marital coalition cannot be divided by grandparents, children, friends, employers, or others. Parents enjoying such an effective coalition will still have differences and conflicts between themselves, of course, and they will be committed to others as well. However, the marital relationship is a stable alliance that cannot be disrupted by others.

In some families, however, there is not a stable emotional bond or working alliance between mother and father. In these families, the primary alliance is between a grandparent and parent, a parent and a child, or within some other dyad. If parents were unable to establish an effective marital coalition during courtship and early marriage, or to maintain it during the stressful period of early childrearing, children will be more likely to have behavior problems, and this marriage is more likely to end in divorce.

Another element in the structure of family relationships is how children try to manipulate closeness in their parents' marriage. Children's response to closeness in their parents' relationship is paradoxical. On the one hand, when parents are physically and emotionally close, children often try to go between them and separate them. On the other hand, when parents break up and divorce, children often try to reunite them.

Parents may observe that, from a very early age, children consistently try to come between them. For example, toddlers sometimes physically separate their parents by climbing between them when they sit down together. Three-year-olds command their fathers, "Don't talk to my Mommy." Four-year-olds may direct parents to stop kissing. Older children often interrupt, talk loudly, or become disruptive whenever mother and father try to sit down and talk together. Children also attempt to play one parent off against the other or try to get one of their parents to side with them against the other parent.

Thus, when children repeatedly succeed in coming between their parents, they often become demanding and difficult to discipline. They develop an exaggerated or unrealistic sense of their own personal power because they can exert too much control over family relationships. Understandably, if their parents divorce, children who could push their parents apart or successfully play one off against the other naturally surmise that they also have the power to bring them back together. These children believe that they can reunite their parents because they have already learned that they can indeed influence what goes on in their parents' relationship.

In contrast, in healthy families that function well, parents are able to maintain their emotional alliance with each other. Even though the parents experience some level of private conflict with each other, children learn that they cannot come between their parents or manipulate teams or "sides" in the family. The parents are in charge of family relationships, not the children. As a result, if parents with a successful marital coalition divorce, their children will not be likely to develop this second and more serious type of reunification fantasy. Because they have not been able to manipulate parental relationships before the divorce, children will be much less likely to develop problems that are disguised attempts to get their parents back together.

Later chapters will examine how parents can work together to establish a successful parental coalition after the divorce, even though they couldn't achieve one during the marriage. For now, however, consider a family in which the child has been able to disrupt the marital alliance.

Charles and Eva

Charles and his wife, Eva, had grown apart over the past few years. They couldn't relate to one another the way they used to, and although Charles didn't quite understand why, it seemed that something always prevented them from being close.

On their tenth wedding anniversary, however, Charles was determined to make the evening different—he was taking Eva to her favorite restaurant. Charles had bought an elegant silver watch and had it engraved as a present for her. He wanted this night to be special for the two of them.

Charles and Eva were excited as they showered and dressed. They were both anticipating a lovely evening ahead—something they hadn't shared in a long time. Charles finished dressing first and went downstairs to get their five-year-old son, Adrian, ready for bed.

"Hey, Adrian, why don't you put your pajamas on early so you'll be all ready for Mrs. Aames when she gets here?"

"I don't like her," Adrian whined. "She's mean and I'm not going to stay with her."

Charles was not in the mood for this kind of nonsense tonight and a loud argument quickly ensued. By the time Eva heard all the commotion and came downstairs, Adrian was already having a full-fledged temper tantrum, and Charles was threatening to give him a spanking. Adrian rushed to his mother for comfort.

"What's the matter, Adrian? Tell me what's wrong."

"I hate Mrs. Aames," Adrian sobbed. "I don't want her to stay with me. I want another babysitter. Will you stay home with me?"

Charles was furious. "You *are* staying with Mrs. Aames tonight and your mother and I are going out. That's the final decision, period, end of discussion!"

"Now wait a minute, Charles," Eva said. "If Adrian really doesn't want to stay with Mrs. Aames, there must be a good reason. We can't just leave him when he's so upset. I'll read him a story and try to put him to bed early. Maybe we can go out a little bit later, after he's calmed down or fallen asleep."

Exasperated, Charles felt manipulated by his son and let down by his wife. It seemed as if something like this happened every time he tried to do something alone with Eva. As he looked at her holding their son, Charles felt angry and alone. Speaking slowly and deliberately, he replied, "Fine. The two of you have a wonderful evening together. I'm going out."

As he backed out of the driveway, Charles wondered whether he could return the watch.

Developing Problems to Reunite Parents

Some of the problems children develop after the breakup may reflect strategic attempts to reunite their parents. For example, sometimes children begin to steal, fight, fail their classes, or become physically ill in veiled attempts to make their parents work together as a couple again. Especially in families without a stable marital coalition, children have learned that mother and father may come together to pursue the common goal of correcting their child's problem behavior. Often, by making trouble, the child actually succeeds in reuniting the parents—at least temporarily.

If the child is in trouble, the family alliances shift away from the parent–child union, and the mother and father become a working partnership again. This commonly occurs in families where the mother and father have repeatedly allowed the child to come between them and disrupt their marital relationship. Let's return to Charles, Eva, and Adrian and see why this is so problematic.

Three years later, Charles and Eva divorced. During the three years, Charles had become increasingly distant and unavailable, and Eva had become more attentive to and involved with Adrian than ever. When the breakup finally occurred, however, Adrian was very upset and became a behavior problem at school. His 3rd grade teacher reported that Adrian was not getting along with other classmates and was doing poorly in his schoolwork. As they had in the past, Charles and Eva came together to meet with the school counselor to discuss Adrian's behavior.

Like most children, Adrian did not want his parents to divorce and did want them to get back together. During the time leading up to the divorce, Adrian had learned that if he got into trouble at school, his parents responded as a team. His poor behavior precipitated what were for him the best moments in the marriage when his parents would talk and work together and show mutual concern. Adrian sensed that if he continued to get into trouble at school, his parents would have to stay together to work on his problems.

When the school counselor suggested to Charles and Eva that Adrian's behavior might be related to the divorce, that reasoning made sense to them. Yet when the counselor later suggested that Adrian's problems were an attempt to reunite his parents, Charles thought the counselor was nuts. He felt like going through the roof as he charged, "How can you sit there and say Adrian's getting in trouble to keep us together when he's the one who's always come between us!"

Eva and Charles spent several more sessions with the school counselor. They talked in more detail about how children may paradoxically try to come between their parents and interfere with their relationship when they are together and then try to reunite them when they part. Gradually, both parents realized that they each had allowed Adrian to exert too much influence in the family by allowing him to come between them so readily when they were married. With this new, shared awareness, it became easier to change this problematic pattern and not allow Adrian to influence their relationship so much after the divorce.

With the school counselor's help, Charles and Eva worked hard explaining to Adrian unambiguously that the divorce was final and that he could do nothing to change that. Gradually, Adrian began to realize that his parents were probably telling him the truth. As he reluctantly came to accept that the divorce was permanent, and that he could not do anything to get his parents back together again, Adrian's behavior problems diminished.

Encouraging the Reunification Fantasy

Many school-aged children consider ways to stop their parents from separating and, years after the divorce, still harbor reunification fantasies. However, there is a different family situation in which these thoughts and fantasies become persistent attempts. In this more serious situation, the parent who has been left actively encourages the children's reunification fantasies. Children caught in this dilemma are almost certain to develop significant emotional problems.

I first learned about this situation from an eight-year-old boy I'll call Johnny. Johnny's mother called the clinic to get help for her son. She reported that he was refusing to go to school, talking back to her rudely, and becoming unmanageable at home.

It became clear during the first counseling session that Johnny was convinced his parents would get back together. Johnny held this reunification fantasy, even though his parents had been separated for several months and his mother was filing for divorce. I asked Johnny's mother if there were any possibility of a reconciliation between her and her husband, and she said no. I asked the mother to say that directly to Johnny. As she began to tell Johnny this, he jumped up onto the coffee table and announced that he was a powerful magician who knew that his mother and father were going to get married again. Johnny became very agitated as he stood on the coffee table; he gestured dramatically and proclaimed that his "magical powers" could make his parents get back together. It was troubling to see this young boy making such a desperate attempt to take control.

At that time I couldn't understand why Johnny's reunification fantasy was so strong. Why did he embrace this reconciliation wish so completely that he was driven to conjuring up magical powers? The answer became clear when I asked Johnny's father to join us the following week to talk about the inevitability of the divorce with Johnny.

In that session I asked Johnny's father to tell him that his parents were going to get a divorce and that, even though Johnny did not want this to happen, there was nothing he could do to change it. The father stammered for awhile and finally offered a vague, watered-down version of what I had suggested. It was easy for Johnny to dismiss such a half-hearted explanation. Only then did it become clear to me that Johnny's father was the one who did not want to give up the reunification fantasy. The divorce had been his mother's decision, and his father was using Johnny as a vehicle to prevent it. As the story began to unfold, it became clear that his father had been telling Johnny that he and his mother were likely to stay married and that Johnny could help make them stay together.

I worked with Johnny's father to help him come to terms with his grief and the unwanted fact that the divorce was inevitable. Finally, for the first time, the father began to share the deep disappointment and feelings of failure that the divorce held for him. Only after he began to deal directly with his own conflicted feelings did he stop encouraging Johnny's reunification fantasies and the inappropriate belief that Johnny had the power to control his parents' marriage. Before long, his father was able to tell Johnny convincingly that the divorce would occur and that Johnny could not change that fact. Although this news made Johnny sad, he also looked visibly relieved and his behavior problems improved markedly. In a six-month follow-up conversation, I was told that Johnny was doing well in school and obeying his mother better at home.

It is highly problematic for children when they are led to believe that they can shape adult decisions to marry, divorce, have children, and so forth. As a result of this false belief, Johnny developed an unrealistic sense of his own power and control. As the "powerful magician," he tried to control his mother and make her remarry his father, but he was also terribly anxious over the prospect of having so much responsibility for his parents. Why did this power make Johnny so anxious and lead him to develop the problems he was having?

First, at age eight, Johnny was far from grown up, and he still had many needs that could only be met by older and stronger adults. He accurately sensed that he could not entrust these needs to adults who could be controlled by a child like himself. Children like Johnny are in a very difficult position: they have to act like adults while still needing to be taken care of as children. Johnny felt more secure, and behaved accordingly, when he could return to being just an eight-year-old boy. As such, he could let down and allow himself to depend on stronger adults to take care of him rather than having to be the one in charge and responsible for his own caregivers.

Second, we have already seen that children hold on to reunification fantasies as a way of avoiding their own painful feelings about the divorce. However, if one parent fosters a child's fantasies about parental reunification, that child is almost certain to develop problems. This use of the child to achieve what the parent cannot—reconciliation—is one example of a larger pattern wherein parents use their children to communicate with each other. When children are used as pawns in parental battles, the effective parental coalition or stable working alliance that characterizes healthy family functioning does not occur. In any type of family that functions well, whether intact, shared-custody, or single-parent families, or stepfamilies, children are not allowed to control adult interactions in this way. There is a clear division between matters that are considered an adult's business or responsibility and those that are considered a child's concerns. In subsequent chapters we examine the significant problems that result when parents allow children to be drawn into adult roles ("parentification") and parental conflicts.

Explaining the Permanence of Divorce to Children

This chapter encourages parents to explain to children that their decision to divorce is unalterable. In order to help children understand that the marriage is truly over, parents can

- Make it clear that the decision to divorce is final, and there is nothing the child can do to change it.
- Explain that Mom and Dad will not reunite or remarry each other in the future.
- Point out that the decision to divorce is strictly an adult decision and children cannot change it because it is not their decision to make.

One effective technique to use in explanations to the child is to emphasize the difference between "adult business" and "child business." This can be done by making a distinction between matters that are adult responsibilities (buying a house, changing jobs, getting a new car, having another child) and matters that children can be involved in with adults (family outings, family vacations, having pets, visiting school friends, assigning household chores). In the first instance, these decisions are adult business and children cannot make them; in the second, the issues involve discussion and input from each member of the family. Divorce is one of the adult issues that children have no control over or responsibility for.

Specific ways parents can talk with their children about their reunification fantasies—and help put them to rest—are suggested in the following sample dialogue.

Mother: You've told me that you wish Dad and I would stay married so that all of us can live together again. I know that sometimes you wish we could have our old family back, just the way it was, and that feeling makes sense to me. You didn't want the divorce, and all of these changes have been hard for everybody. But I have to tell you, that cannot happen. Our decision to divorce is final. We are not going to change it.

Child: Well, maybe you'll change your mind later and want Dad to live with us again.

Mother: I know you would really like it if Dad and I would stay married. Of course you want that; the divorce has made you sad and mad sometimes. But I want to help you understand that our decision to divorce is final; it's not going to change. Whenever you feel bad about the divorce or have questions about it, you can always talk about them with Dad or me. But I need to say again that we are not going to change our minds, and we will not be living together any more. I'm wondering how you might be feeling right now as I'm telling you this?

An alternative script might be:

Father: Sometimes children believe that if they are really bad and get in trouble, or if they are really good all the time, it will help bring their parents back together again. That won't happen because your mother and I don't want to live together anymore. As much as you would like for us to stay married, there's nothing children can do to make their parents stay together. Divorce is an adult decision your mother and I made, and we will not be married or living together again. You know, this is really hard for me to talk about; I feel sad right now. Come sit with me and tell me what you've been thinking about all of this.

It is very difficult for most parents to talk about their divorce so directly and to end their children's wishes to reunite the family so forthrightly. Often these words are as painful for parents to say as they are for children to hear. Parents are encouraged to anticipate or think ahead about their own likely responses during these difficult conversations. By doing so, parents can better manage their own sadness, guilt, and other feelings that may make it more difficult to respond to their children's feelings and reactions. Even though these conversations are hard, parents and children alike adjust better if these topics that everyone wants to avoid can be talked about and made overt. Divorcing parents are working together in their children's best interest when they eschew blame, keep children out of parental conflicts, and provide much-needed explanations such as these.

Suggestions for Further Reading

How to Talk So Children Will Listen: How to Listen So Children Will Talk (A. Faber and E. Mazlish, New York: Avon, 1982) is a marvelous book that teaches all parents how to communicate more effectively with their children and build self-esteem. A few readers may be interested in learning more about family therapy and structural family relations. Interested readers may explore chapters 3 and 5 of S. Minuchin's textbook, *Families and Family Therapy* (Harvard University Press, 1974.)

Chapter Four

Children Feel Responsible for the Divorce

"Maybe If I Had Been Good, Mom and Dad Wouldn't Have Gotten a Divorce."

Many children feel responsible and blame themselves for their parents' divorce. Although it's hard for most parents to imagine that their children could hold such a wildly mistaken belief, many children do. Many young children are concerned that the breakup is their fault and that something they did either caused or contributed to the divorce.

When I am working with children of divorce, I ask them whether they have ever thought that they may have caused their parents to divorce. The majority of children answer yes. I then ask them what they did that caused their parents to divorce. Their answers are always the same: a variation on the theme that they were somehow bad. For example, children regularly tell me, with all seriousness and conviction, that their parents divorced because "I didn't mind my dad enough" or because "my brother and I fought all the time" or because "I wasn't good." Such self-blame can continue in children for years after the divorce and be the source of needless guilt and worry.

Parents can expect this reaction and need to be prepared to dispel the misconception. Fortunately, children's false assumption of responsibility can readily be eliminated through parental explanations and reassurances. Children can be greatly relieved to hear that their perception of their role in the divorce is not true and that they are in no way responsible. This chapter shows how parents can bring the issue of blame out into the open and explain to children that they are never responsible for adult decisions such as divorce. Developing our previous explanations for the divorce further, parents can also emphasize that the breakup is an adult decision—not child business. By helping children understand that the divorce is beyond their control, parents can resolve this false belief and lift the unnecessary burden of guilt and blame that many children carry.

Why Children Feel Responsible

There are several reasons most children up to ten or twelve years of age believe they are to blame for the divorce. First, we have already seen that children are egocentric in their thinking, that is, they tend to believe that the world revolves primarily around them. In children's eyes, much that goes on in their world is happening specifically to them or is caused by them. Second, because of their cognitive immaturity and lack of intellectual development, young children do not have a clear understanding of cause-and-effect relationships. For example, toddlers and preschoolers do not recognize that other people make decisions that affect them and yet are based on motives that have nothing to do with them. Because young children are highly egocentric in their thinking, they experience life as if they are the center of the universe.

As children grow out of early childhood and into the early school years, this self-centered, egocentric thinking is increasingly replaced with a more realistic understanding of the world. Gradually, both the individuality or subjectivity of others and the nature of cause-and-effect relationships are grasped more fully. However, as with the related concept of magical thinking discussed in Chapter Three, the predisposition to consider oneself the cause of events still lingers through adolescence and even into adulthood at times. Adults' tendency to return to this egocentric mode of thinking is greatly increased in emotionally charged situations. For example, upon being told that their biopsy shows a potential cancer, adults can believe irrationally that they have been singled out to receive this punishment for some sin or flaw in themselves. Although it doesn't make sense, the false belief that "I am responsible and to blame for this and I am being punished" may come to the surface. However, whereas some adults may temporarily revert to this unrealistic, egocentric thinking when they are in crisis, children routinely think in this self-centered way. As a result, children often feel responsible for events they actually have no control over, such as the death of a parent or sibling or marital disruption.

Other factors can make children feel responsible for their parents' divorce. Children get angry with their parents at times and wish they were dead, would go away, or would be replaced by other, more idealized, parents. Children misinterpret these commonplace feelings as explanations for how they caused their parents' divorce. When parents divorce, the child's wish that Mom or Dad would leave has come true. Naturally, it is frightening for children to believe that their angry thoughts have actually caused this to happen. Let's examine further the concept of magical thinking.

Magical Thinking

Magical thinking comes about, in part, because children do not fully understand the distinction between fantasy and reality. Parents can often observe their young children trying to discern the difference between their thoughts and actions or asking whether something is "pretend or real." Many children feel guilty because they believe that their angry feelings or bad wishes have caused the divorce. Understandably, children with this false belief become afraid of their own destructive power. Imagine how alarming it would be if you sincerely believed that your inner thoughts or emotions could control adult lives, send parents away, and destroy family relationships. Fortunately, this distorted concept of what has happened, and its accompanying sense of responsibility and blame, can readily be corrected by reassuring explanations from adults.

Naturally, however, because these ideas are so unrealistic or unimaginable to most adults, many parents never think of asking their children whether they think they caused the divorce. A few children might tell one parent that they think they caused the other parent to leave and then apologize for it. In most cases, though, children keep the secret of their blame to themselves. Nevertheless, if you ask children directly whether they have ever felt bad because they caused the divorce, about three-fourths of four-to ten-year-old children will say yes. Many older children and adolescents also share this false belief to a lesser extent. By asking directly about their feelings of responsibility and self-blame, however, parents can offer children a more realistic explanation of the divorce and reassure them that they are blameless.

Parents Blaming Children

As we have seen, most young children struggle with feelings of responsibility for causing their parents' breakup. In a few cases, sadly, parents actually believe that their child is responsible for the divorce! In these families, which may include stepfamilies that break up, one or both parents explicitly blame children and tell them that they are responsible for the parental divorce. These parents might say to their child:

"We broke up because of you."

"None of this would have happened if it weren't for you."

"I left your mother because of you."

"The divorce is all your fault."

It is a tragic mistake to blame children in this way. When children are blamed, their egocentric fear of being responsible is confirmed rather than assuaged by the parent. Such children develop substantial and enduring problems, such as depression, in the aftermath of divorce. In reality, of course, children are never responsible for adult decisions and must not be made to feel they are. When adults suffer with feelings of failure, however, and wish to avoid taking responsibility for their own decisions and actions, it is all too easy to shift this burden onto children. These parents may exclaim, "It's not my fault the marriage didn't work. Jimmy caused all the trouble. He wouldn't mind us and caused so many problems for us that we couldn't have a peaceful home. My husband couldn't stand it and left. Quite frankly, I don't really blame him."

Children, of course, never really control such adult decisions. Parents who have told their children that the divorce was their fault can recover by reclaiming responsibility for their own lives. They can tell their children that these accusations were not true, that they made a mistake when they said this, and they would like to apologize now.

Although some readers may find it hard to believe that parents could accuse their children in this way, such blame occurs regularly. The result is feelings of low self-esteem and even self-hatred in children that are often reflected in chronic depression and a shame-based sense of self. More commonly, however, parents eschew responsibility for their own sense of failure or inadequacy in more subtle ways. For example, some parents shift responsibility onto children by telling them that the divorce was undertaken in the child's best interest. These parents might say, "I thought it would be best for you, Mary, if I left your father." Although far more subtle than overtly blaming the child, such statements again leave the child feeling responsible for something she did not want and had no control over. Whether the child is blamed directly or indirectly, however, the adult's feelings of failure, inadequacy, or guilt are alleviated at the expense of the child. Children who are blamed overtly will believe that they are shamefully bad, whereas those blamed more subtly will feel guilty. In these situations, children develop an exaggerated sense of their own power. They may become anxious about the excessive control over others they can seemingly exert, depressed about their inherent badness, or both.

Children and parents alike adjust far better if parents can reclaim responsibility for their own decisions. This may be hard for some parents to do, but it is the only way to effectively take control of one's life. A realistic and satisfying feeling of personal power follows when one takes responsibility for one's own decisions. In most cases, parents who blame their children for the divorce are much too afraid of the possibility that they have made a mistake or done something wrong. Rather than feeling merely sad or disappointed that the marriage has failed, such parents often fear that the divorce confirms their sense of themselves as being failures in life. These painful, exaggerated feelings of failure, which parents may try to ward off by shunting responsibility onto their children, were often fostered by their own parents' excessive criticism whenever they made mistakes as youngsters. In some cases, these blaming parents were brought up to believe they had to be perfect. As a result of this faulty belief, they may feel unrealistically guilty about hurting their child, disappointing others, or failing to live up to religious mores. In other cases, some blaming parents were indulged as children. They learned early on that they could avoid the consequences of their own behavior by blaming others, and they continue this highly problematic pattern of externalizing responsibility with their own children.

Divorce does not necessarily demonstrate personal failure, of course. In many cases it is a courageous and healthy step forward in life. Many divorcing parents who blame their children need to become more forgiving of themselves and allow themselves to be humanly imperfect. The true measure of people is not how often they stumble or make mistakes but how they recover afterward.

In sum, parents are encouraged to assume appropriate responsibility for their own shortcomings and contributions to the problems in the marriage rather than externalize blame for the divorce onto children. It is important for those who continue to feel that their child is to blame to explore this with a therapist, pastoral counselor, or successful parent whom they trust and respect.

Guidelines for Talking with Children About the Divorce

It is difficult for many parents to initiate conversations with their children about the divorce. Some parents feel guilty and don't want to bring up divorce-related topics; others simply don't know how to broach these topics. In this section, sample parent-child scripts for alleviating blame, along with other guidelines to help parents talk with their children more effectively, are provided.

Sample Scripts for Alleviating Blame

For the majority of families, parents simply need to provide children with an explanation that communicates they were in no way responsible or to blame for the divorce. Several suggestions follow for putting this message into words.

Father: Sometimes when mothers and fathers decide to divorce each other, their children think they caused the divorce. Have you ever had any thoughts like that?
Child: No.
Father: Well, I'm glad you haven't because nothing you said or did caused your mother and me to divorce. You are not

to blame in any way. And if you ever have any thoughts or feelings like that, I want you to come talk to me about them. Would you do that for me?

Or perhaps the child answered yes.

Father: Oh, I see, tell me what you did or how you think you may have caused it. [The child gives an explanation.]

Father: No, that is just not true. You had nothing to do with the reason for our divorce. And it certainly was not because [you were bad, you did something wrong, we were mad at you, or whatever explanation the child provided].

Still another way to respond is to give the child a clear explanation such as this:

Mary, I want you to know that you are not responsible or to blame for our divorce in any way. It's not your fault. You didn't cause it. Remember when we talked about how some things are adult business and some things are child business? Well, divorce is strictly adult business; it's not a child's decision to make. That means it is just between Dad and me, and not you. What do you think about what I'm saying? Have you ever thought about this?

We have now addressed the three primary concerns children have in response to marital disruption: separation anxieties, reunification fantasies, and feelings of responsibility. Parents can be alert for these fears and misconceptions in their children and follow the guidelines suggested for helping children with them. Before going on to other divorce-related issues, I want to address some questions parents often have about discussing these issues with children.

Guidelines for Parent–Child Discussions

Children's separation anxieties, reunification fantasies, and assumption of blame for the divorce all are deeply felt concerns that influence their divorce adjustment. Fortunately, these concerns can be resolved through explanations and discussions between parent and child. However, a single statement made at one sitting is not enough to fully reassure children about the permanence of their continuing relationship together or to convince a child that the divorce is final. The issues for children are too profound and emotionally charged to be resolved so easily. Parents are encouraged to have multiple discussions with their children about each of these topics. Several guidelines for helping parents with these ongoing discussions follow.

What is the best way to approach children? Parents do not need to wait for the child to initiate a conversation. Instead, they can bring up the subjects identified here. As demonstrated in the sample scripts, parents can begin by giving children factual explanations and then engaging them in a mutual, back-and-forth dialogue that draws out the child's own understanding of the divorce. For example, parents might ask children to elaborate on their thoughts and feelings about each topic by saying, "Let's talk some more about the divorce. Tell me again what you think you did to cause the divorce." Once children have fully presented their perception of events, parents can much more effectively clear up their misconceptions.

Unless parents are embroiled in litigation or imposing "loyalty conflicts," most children respond readily to candid questioning. If parents ask direct, matter-of-fact questions, children usually give surprisingly honest and revealing answers. Children share their thoughts and feelings if they have found it emotionally safe to talk to their parents about the divorce. When children do not respond to repeated invitations from parents to talk about the divorce, they usually have good reasons for feeling it is not safe to do so. This reluctance usually stems from two sources: (1) they think it is risky to do so and (2) loyalty conflicts make disclosure unsafe.

RISK. Reticent children have often learned that parents do not really want to hear or cannot accept what they have to say. For example, parents may not be able to tolerate their children's sadness about the divorce or their anger at parents for breaking up or moving out. In order to provide reassurances that genuinely help children, parents can strive to be nondefensive enough to listen to their children's negative reactions without trying to talk them out of their feelings. Children adjust better when parents can tolerate these critical perceptions or hurt feelings that parents, understandably, often do not want to hear. Children will not share further if they hear dismissive parental responses like, "Oh, stop feeling sorry for yourself; you have a lot to be thankful for." They want to share more if they receive affirming responses. Let's contrast some common but ineffective parental responses with better ones:

"Don't be so upset; everything will be fine" versus "I can see how upset you are about this. Tell me, what's been the hardest thing for you?"

"You shouldn't feel that way" versus "That sounds like an important feeling; I'm glad you're telling me about this."

"Why in the world would you think that?" versus "I hadn't thought about it like that before. That's interesting; tell me more about that."

"You have absolutely no reason to feel angry at me after all I've done for you" versus "I can see how angry you are with me right now. Let's keep talking and see if we can work this out together."

"Well, stop it; that's just about enough of that kind of talk" versus "I want to talk with you about this, but you need to be respectful, even when you're mad at me."

"There's nothing wrong; you don't really have anything to be sad about" versus "I'm sorry you've been having such sad feelings and big tears about this; come sit with me and let's be close."

"If that's all you have to say, then it's about time you got a better attitude" versus "You are really sad and mad about all of this. I can see how hard it has been for you. Let's talk together and see if we can find some ways to make this better."

You don't have to agree with your children to listen to them with presence and take their concerns seriously.

Loyalty Conflicts. The second reason children are reluctant to talk with parents is because loyalty conflicts make disclosure unsafe. In these cases, children are covertly or overtly pressured to take sides in parental conflicts. This occurs, for example, when one parent uses what the child has said as ammunition in the battle to get back at the other parent. We will examine closely the significant problems that result from these loyalty conflicts in Chapter Eight.

How do parents know whether their children believe their explanations or whether they are still troubled by a particular topic? Parents can learn to recognize certain signals. For example, if some aspect of the divorce is too upsetting for children to talk about, they often change the subject. To illustrate, Mrs. Brown may say to her five-year-old son, Johnny, "You know, I've been thinking about the divorce and I'm wondering if you have been, too? Maybe this a good time for us to talk together about some of the changes that have been happening in our family?" If Johnny quickly replies, "Look at the pretty bird out on the swing," Mrs. Brown is alerted to the difficulty her son is having talking about or accepting the divorce. This type of response is called avoidance. Most children try to deny unwanted aspects of the divorce but parents can find sensitive ways to bring their child back to the reality at hand.

Mrs. Brown could say, "Johnny, I know that you don't like it when I tell you that Daddy and I are not going to be married any more. But the sad news is that we are going to divorce and that's not going to change. Let's talk some more about what will happen when Daddy and I divorce. What do you think is going to be the worst thing for you when Daddy and I move apart?"

It is possible that Johnny will continue to avoid any discussion of the divorce. For example, Johnny's response to his mother's questions might be: "Be quiet! I don't want to talk about divorce. I want you and Daddy to stay married and live here with me." Mrs. Brown could then reply, "Yes, of course you wish we would stay married. It makes sense to me that you still want Daddy and me to live together, even though we both know that is not going to happen. Let's talk some more about the divorce and some of the things that will change and the things that will stay the same.

Johnny: "What will be the same?"

Mrs. Brown: "Well, one of the things I've been wondering is if you're worried sometimes that Mommy and Daddy won't love you as much or won't be with you as much after the divorce. We've talked about this before, but tell me again what you think is going to happen when Daddy moves out on Saturday?"

Johnny: "Stop it, I don't want to talk about the "vorce" anymore."

Mrs. Brown: "You know, this is hard to talk about. I think we
should make a compromise. We don't have to talk
about the divorce right now if you don't want to, but
we do have to talk about it for a little while some-
time today. You tell me, before you go to bed
tonight, when is the best time for us to talk about
what is going to happen on Saturday when Daddy
moves to his new house?"

Johnny: "Tonight, when you put me to bed, but just for a
minute."

Mrs. Brown: "Sure, we'll talk about these things for a few minutes
tonight when I tuck you into bed. I think that's a
good time to talk, too."

The staging of these parent–child discussions is also important.
Children spontaneously ask questions and make comments if they
feel that their parents are comfortable discussing the divorce.
Whenever possible, parents can also encourage free expression by
dropping other things and responding to children whenever *they*
initiate the conversation or bring up divorce-related issues. When
parents initiate discussions about the divorce, it usually will be most
effective during a quiet and close time. As Johnny has just told us,
bedtime is an especially good opportunity to talk together about
the divorce. For example, the mother or father could rub the
child's back while they talk together about the child's concerns.
Such an affectionate setting helps children express what may be
worrying them. As we have seen, however, parents should not insist on disclosure when children do not wish to talk. These topics
are painful, and it's best if children can have some shared control
over when and how they manage them.

Responding to Sadness

Children need their parents to help by talking with them about all
of the earth-shaking changes taking place. In talking with their children about the breakup, parents want to be prepared to respond

to their children's sadness, anger, and confusion and help them with these feelings. In particular, parents can expect these discussions to evoke sadness in themselves and, especially, in their children. Let's consider this sensitive issue.

Feelings of sadness will emerge throughout the ongoing process of discussing the divorce with children. These feelings often make it difficult for parents to invite children to ask questions or talk about the divorce, and to provide explanations and address children's concerns in the forthright ways suggested here. When talking with their children, parents can acknowledge their own sadness and regrets about the divorce. Parents and children alike need to grieve the loss of the family as they have known it. Seeing the parents' sadness—coupled with the parents' confidence that they will successfully cope with this crisis—shows children that they do not have to be afraid of their feelings and gives them permission to mourn their own loss. Parents can be realistic and acknowledge to themselves, and say to their children, that the divorce is going to be hard and make everyone feel sad sometimes. Sad feelings are OK and can be shared; problems arise when we have to pretend to ourselves, or others, that we are not really feeling what we are authentically experiencing.

Although some parents have difficulty responding effectively to their children's angry feelings, it is children's sadness that many loving and capable parents cannot tolerate. Divorcing parents may want their child to stop feeling sad for many reasons: to avoid their own sadness about the divorce that may seem overwhelming; to keep from feeling guilty for causing their child's unhappiness; or because they feel inadequate to respond and don't know how to comfort their child.

For these and other reasons, many parents have difficulty approaching their children's sadness. This problem becomes increasingly significant over time because the child's sadness does not simply go away. For years after the divorce, children continue to have sad feelings at times about the loss of their original, intact family. How parents respond to these feelings of sadness and loss is an important factor in shaping children's development. Children adjust far better when parents offer a supportive and affirming response to their sadness. Too often, however, divorcing parents avoid these feelings, deny they exist, or diminish their importance to the child by saying something like this: "Come on, what's that look about? You don't have anything to be unhappy about."

Denying Sad Feelings

Others sometimes say Americans "have no soul," by which they mean our culture denies or is afraid of the sad, hurt, or disappointed feelings that are a natural part of everyday life. Too often, it seems, we turn away from these feelings without experiencing or acknowledging them, or even dismiss them contemptuously as reflecting weakness. In reality, however, children often feel sad or lonely during the divorce process, and they need support from grandparents, clergy, neighbors, teachers, and others. Most do not get this emotional support. For example, one study reported that less than 10 percent of children had an adult speak sympathetically to them as the divorce unfolded.

The problem is not that people don't care. Many kind adults see children's distress and care, but they aren't sure whether it is helpful to acknowledge this difficult time or it is better to politely ignore sad feelings. Benevolent adults are also concerned that if they approach these feelings, they might say the wrong thing or somehow make the child feel worse. In most cases, however, children appreciate it when parents and other important adults in their lives can acknowledge that this is a difficult time; then the child does not feel as alone. Adults can do this by simply acknowledging children's sad feelings when they emerge and offering their genuine affection and concern. For example, a scout leader or grandparent might say, "I'm sorry this is such a hard time for you. I know you've had a lot of changes at home, and I hope things are better for everybody soon."

The initial period of marital disruption is highly distressing for most children. It's no mystery why, sadly. The majority of children see their parents lose their temper, make ugly threats and argue loudly, shame and demean each other, and cry. Children also watch one parent move out of the home and are worried about their parents' distress and about what will happen to them. And as we have seen, parents are often unable to respond to their children's sadness because of their own feelings of loss, guilt over the divorce, or uncertainty about what to say or do. As a result, many children do not receive the comfort they need during this difficult transition.

Ineffective responses to children's sadness about the breakup often spring from some form of denial. We have seen that parents usually do this by trying to ignore children's sadness or, if that is not possible, invalidating their feelings by trying to talk children out of them. Let's look further at the most common types of ineffective responses.

Most commonly, parents simply ignore or do not want to recognize the child's sad or hurt feelings. This can occur for many reasons. Often parents may be so caught up in their own distress during this crisis that they cannot step outside their own experience and register what their child is experiencing.

In some families, there is a long-standing pattern of denying feelings, which keeps parents from responding to their children's grief, anxiety, or other feelings. In others, family members may be allowed to feel happy or sad, but no one is allowed to feel a certain emotion, such as anger, which is taboo. Many families have spoken or unspoken rules governing emotional expression—which feelings can be expressed and which cannot. Families also may have covert but clearly understood rules governing at what intensity, and to whom, certain feelings can be expressed. However, some families have an unspoken but clearly understood rule that no one in the family is ever sad or disappointed or that only certain family members are allowed to feel sadness, such as girls or the youngest child. Such a family rule is problematic, of course, but manageable until a family crisis such as divorce occurs. With divorce, feelings become stronger, and the sadness cannot be denied without engendering depression or other symptoms in order to maintain the family rule against sadness.

Sometimes parents want children to be unaffected by the divorce in order to affirm their decision to divorce. Such parents are placing too much control over their own well-being in the child's hands. If the child is sad or weepy, the parent takes this as evidence that breaking up was the wrong course; if the child seems happy, the parent feels the decision to divorce was correct. These parents may try to avert their child's appropriate sadness by trying to cheer him up, perhaps overstimulating him with too many activities in order to keep him busy and "happy." These parents accurately anticipate that if children are allowed quiet, unstructured time, tears will sometimes emerge. However, rather than use this moment as an opportunity to connect deeply with their child, they feel uncomfortable with the authentic emotions expressed. By moving away from these feelings, they move away from their child as well.

Going one step further, some authoritarian parents may invalidate the child's experience more overtly by making statements such as these: "Stop feeling sorry for yourself! You don't have anything to feel bad about. Other people have real problems. You should be thankful for all the good things you have. Knock those tears off or I'll give you something to really cry about." Children subjected to such shaming invalidation may comply with the parental demand and stop looking weepy, but the sadness will go underground and be masked. Situational sadness, an understandable response to marital disruption, then may give way to ongoing symptoms of depression (boredom, inactivity, loss of interests, lack of motivation, and declining school performance) or to agitation (restlessness, unfocused attention, sensation seeking, careless risk taking). As we've seen, a child's sad feelings can be invalidated, or going a step further, be denigrated as well. Boys who are shamed for feeling sadness may be denigrated as weak ("Stop acting like such a sissy; grow up!") whereas girls' emotional needs may be derided as needy or demanding ("Would you just stop crying all the time; isn't this a bit much!").

When children's sadness or longing for the intact family is denied in one of these ways, children do not adjust well. These painful feelings cannot be integrated and resolved because they are not allowed to run their natural course. Children caught in one of these unwanted circumstances soon become uncomfortable with their feelings and, rather than feeling sad or disappointed, they become anxious or confused instead. As children lose touch with their sadness, they also lose touch with other emotions and other aspects of their own authentic experience. These children are, in effect, losing touch with themselves and their own identity. More specifically, they will not be prepared to sort through their own values, spiritual and political beliefs, vocational interests, and future goals as they face the developmental challenge of identity formation in late adolescence. Further, when their legitimate feelings of sadness over the divorce are denied, children do not develop the same capacity for empathy and compassion toward others. In sum, these children may become depressed or more restless and agitated. In addition, by losing the clarity of their inner experience, they often become confused about who they are and uncertain of what they value and enjoy. In turn, they often have more difficulty as young adults in knowing what they like and don't like, and deciding what they want to do with their lives.

But sometimes children may be just feeling sorry for themselves or, more likely, using tears dramatically to manipulate their guilty parents. In other situations, one parent may exaggerate and overreact to a child's sadness as a way to blame or punitively get back at the other parent. In most cases, however, children do not receive the comfort they need because parents feel guilty about causing their child's distress or they feel uncertain and don't know how to respond. However, parents can take several steps to help children successfully manage their sadness and loss.

Responding Effectively to Children's Sadness

Although parents can help in many ways, effective responses to their children's sadness often include the following three-step sequence.

First, parents should *acknowledge* the sad feelings and approach them directly, rather than deny or ignore them in the hope they will pass on their own. When done sincerely, it is remarkably effective to simply acknowledge the sadness by bending over to the child's height, looking kindly into his eyes, putting your hand warmly on his shoulder, and saying, in an understanding tone of voice, something as simple as, "You seem a little bit sad right now."

Second, parents also want to accept children's feelings by *validating* them, not diminishing them or trying to talk children out of them. For example, parents can affirm the child's experience by saying, "Of course you feel unhappy about all of this. You don't want us to go apart; you would like for us to stay together. This divorce stuff is hard, and it makes sense that you're feeling sad about it right now. I think everybody in our family feels this way sometimes; I know I do."

Third, parents can *comfort* their children with overtly spoken affection and approval, not try to "fix" the feelings or press children to be happy when they are not. For example, parents can offer such reassurance by inviting closeness. "Come sit with me; let's be together. What's the hardest thing about the divorce for you right now? Tell me about it so I can understand better."

If parents can approach their child's distress with such acceptance and affirmation, the feelings will run their natural course. The child will not be overwhelmed by his or her feelings or made to feel worse; the child will feel more secure and soon move on to other, happier moods. Responding to their sadness is also one of the most effective way to begin talking with children about their worries and concerns. For example, in response to being asked what they think is the hardest thing about the divorce or what they worry about most, children often express fears of being left, of losing parents or siblings, of being responsible for the divorce, or other issues that parents can address and resolve. The following example illustrates these principles.

Gene

Five-year-old Gene was having the worst Christmas ever. His parents had split up just before Thanksgiving, and his father had moved out of their house and into his own apartment. There had been a lot of arguing and confusion about whom he would spend Christmas with. Finally, they decided that Gene would spend Christmas Eve with his mother and Christmas Day with his father. On Christmas night he would have dinner with his grandparents, Papa and Nana, with whom he had always been especially close.

When his father brought Gene to his grandparents' house on Christmas evening, he told them that Gene hadn't behaved very well and that Christmas hadn't been much fun. His father didn't like how "greedy" Gene had seemed as he raced through his presents, opening them without stopping to appreciate them or thank anybody. A friend of the family who had stopped by to wish them a Merry Christmas jokingly said that watching Gene open his presents was like watching a "shark feeding frenzy." As soon as Gene finished opening all of his presents—which took only a few minutes, even though there were many of them—he started whining, "What else do I get? Isn't there anything else?" Thus his father told Papa and Nana that it hadn't been a very good Christmas with Gene, and he didn't think things had gone much better with his mother the night before.

As soon as he came in the house, Nana could tell Gene was out of sorts and feeling blue. Nana tried to take him by the hand and show him some of her favorite Christmas decorations, but Gene shied away from her. Nana brought out some of Gene's favorite toys—special things that she kept at her house because Gene loved to play with them—but they didn't hold his interest as they usually did. Nana was patient but kept failing in her bids to engage him, and Gene seemed lost as he wandered half-heartedly from toy to toy and room to room.

After following Gene's aimless movements around the house for awhile, Nana could see that he was not settling in and warming up as he usually did. Trying to acknowledge the sadness she saw in his face, Nana suggested, "Is our big boy a little bit sad today? Will you let me hold you in my lap for a minute?"

Gene brushed off her invitation, backed away, and stared down at the floor. Seeing that Gene was feeling miserable, Nana reassured him. "You're sad today, but you don't want me to hold you right now. That's OK. I'll stay here in my chair and just watch you play."

Gene remained distant and restless, and Nana stayed in her chair and watched as he became even more frustrated with whatever he tried to play with. Gene did not maintain his distance for long, however, and a few minutes later he came over to her chair and sat down next to her. Nana gathered Gene up into her lap, held him close, and rocked him quietly. Gene soon said, "I wish Mom and Dad would get married again." Nana appreciated that feeling and said, "Yes, of course you do. It's been sad today because your family wasn't together." Gene nodded, sank more deeply into his grandmother's arms, and they talked some more about the divorce. Before long, however, Gene's face brightened a little as he noticed a familiar toy in the room and asked Nana if they could play with it together. With this transition to a happier mood and shared interaction, Gene became interested in his play again and an especially close evening ensued.

As this case reveals, children may be especially vulnerable to their sadness around holidays and birthdays, and guilty parents can feel uncomfortable with their children's distress and subtly pressure them to feel better. This is what happened to Gene at both his mother's and father's house and, in part, why he was so restless and irritable.

Parents can allow children to be sad and miss things when they are feeling this way, the way Nana did. In these moments, parents can be affirming to children, without trying to talk them out of their feelings or make them feel bad about being sad, missing the other parent, or longing for their old family to be together again. If the parent can be responsive to the child's distress, the sadness will soon run its course and come to a natural close, freeing the child to move on to other interests and activities. If not, many boys eventually channel their unacknowledged sadness into anger and defiance in the aftermath of divorce, whereas girls may become increasingly quiet, compliant, and "perfect."

One of the best ways to prevent these unwanted consequences is for mothers and fathers to (1) accept their children's sad and angry feelings, (2) help them find appropriate ways to share them, (for example, by saying what they don't like in a respectful way rather than hitting or making threats in a mean voice), and (3) comfort them in their distress.

Some parents find it awkward to respond in the affirming ways suggested here, usually because no one has ever responded to them with such understanding. Go ahead and try it anyway, and decide for yourself whether it's good for your child. I think you'll find you are giving your child a gift.

We turn now from children's concerns during the initial breakup to guidelines for parents during the divorce.

Suggestions for Further Reading

Because guilt plagues so many divorcing parents, it may be helpful to read more about this important issue. Although not targeted specifically toward divorce or parenting issues, one useful book is *Imaginary Crimes* by L. Engel and T. Ferguson (Boston: Houghton Mifflin, 1990). *Liberated Parents: Liberated Children* (A. Faber and E. Mazlish, New York: Avon, 1990) is a refreshing book that helps parents understand their children and communicate better with them. These authors write clearly and are true experts.

Part Three

Guidelines
for Parents

Chapter Five

Parental Conflict and Cooperation

*"Do I Have to Be Friends with my Ex to Be a
Good Parent? We're Never Going to Get Along!"*

Researchers have found that in the years following a divorce, the most poorly adjusted children are the ones who are exposed to continuing parental conflict. Children suffer when they witness parental hostilities, when parents criticize or undermine the other parent to the children, and when parents embroil children in parental wrangling by enlisting them to take sides. When angry ex-spouses act in these irresponsible ways, children often develop long-standing problems such as making poor grades, being unable to get along with friends, being defiant toward teachers and other authority figures, and disobeying parents. We can't pretend otherwise: it hurts children when parents undermine each other and say, "Your mother is crazy; you don't have to do what she says" or "You don't have to pay attention to your father; he only sees you on weekends. I'm the one who is really raising you." Because ongoing parental conflict is so problematic for children and because children are exposed to parental hostilities so frequently, we must examine this conflict closely.

Buffering Children from Parental Hostilities

Without question, the single biggest problem for children of divorce is being exposed to continuing parental warfare. Some parents become furious during the divorce process, and many blame the other parent for everything that has gone wrong. Embittered parents who feel justified in their outrage because—from their point of view—the other parent has betrayed or rejected them, often cannot see their own contribution to the problems of the marriage. This insight is necessary if parents are to grow through the experience of divorce or to learn something from all of this pain. It is an essential step in the process of moving beyond the victim stance where exclusive responsibility for the breakup is loaded onto the former spouse. Without the ability to see one's own participation in the problems, anger and blame continue to fuel the chronic parental conflict that is so problematic for children. Parents who allow themselves to grasp how much children suffer when they are embroiled in parental battles will take steps to manage their anger responsibly and to shield children from parental conflict. Let's learn how parents can do this.

Avoiding Chronic Parental Conflict

Married or divorced, parents will have disagreements and be angry with each other at times. If these conflicts are not threatening or pervasive, they are a normal part of human relationships and are not problematic for children. Two people cannot have an authentic relationship if the differences that inevitably arise between them cannot be honestly voiced. Divorcing couples may not have more conflict than happily married couples; sometimes they are just less effective at working out their problems. Divorces between seemingly harmonious couples that seem to come out of the blue usually spring from marriages in which the everyday problems that did exist could never be brought up and addressed. Children do not learn how to resolve interpersonal problems in these superficially harmonious families that gloss over problems rather than address them. In contrast, however, parental conflict that is intense and unrelenting is a very different story. Whether in divorced or intact families or in stepfamilies, it makes children anxious to live with embattled parents.

Erroneously, divorce is widely believed to harm children and inevitably to cause long-term adjustment problems. Researchers have found that, on average, children of divorce do exhibit more problems and have a lower level of well-being than children from intact families. However, research has also shown that the divorce itself does not cause these adjustment problems. They are most likely to result from increased exposure to parental conflict. Let's examine this critical distinction again.

Researchers have found that over 25 percent of the children who have experienced parental divorce are very well-adjusted. Why do these children cope successfully when others do not? The most important reason is that these healthy children either have (1) parents who can cooperate with each other or (2) parents who may not like or trust each other but who do have the good sense to shield children from parental wrangling.

Conversely, researchers have also found that the most poorly adjusted children of divorce have relentlessly embattled and often litigious parents. Most children exposed to ongoing parental conflict do suffer long-term adjustment problems. Thus, the effects of chronic marital conflict must be considered separately from the more general effects of divorce. To be sure, chronic marital conflict is the culprit causing long-term problems for children.

Further, ongoing marital conflict is damaging not only to children in divorced families but is just as harmful to children in intact families. The degree of marital discord is one of the most important determinants of children's adjustment in every type of family. Thus, children in intact families with high marital conflict have more adjustment problems than children in intact families with low conflict; the children have more problems with aggressive and defiant behavior, more emotional symptoms of anxiety and depression, and lower self-esteem than those in low-conflict, intact homes.

The message here is undeniable: divorcing couples must exercise restraint and not fight in front of their children or involve them in parental conflict. Too often, unfortunately, this message goes unheeded. Angry attempts to punish former spouses and to disrupt their relationships with children are commonplace. And many children are exposed to intense scenes of dramatic parental conflict both before and after the divorce. Parental acrimony usually peaks at the time of marital separation, and during this period many children witness bitter and explosive interactions between their parents. One study reported the grim statistic that one-fourth of children in middle- and upper-middle-class homes had witnessed physical violence between their parents at the time of marital separation! Let's look more closely at why marital conflict is so harmful to children.

Parental cooperation, or at least the absence of overt conflict, is essential for children's secure adjustment. Most children will not be able to adjust successfully as long as they are exposed to ongoing parental hostilities. Why are children so affected by threatening and derisive interactions between their parents? Children are frightened when they see their parents shout and threaten each other. Although some older children may try to distance themselves and affect aloof disinterest, they are afraid that harm may befall one of their parents or themselves. Children are intensely concerned about the safety and well-being of their all-important attachment figures and rightly know that they themselves are not secure as long as their parents are threatened. Because they are so preoccupied with the former spouse, however, combative parents cannot see the worry in their children's faces or recognize the anxiety that engenders the sleep disturbances, bedwetting, nightmares, nail-biting, and hypervigilance from which their children usually suffer.

When I am talking with children of embattled parents, I ask, "If I had a magic wand and could grant you any three wishes you wanted, what would you most like to have?" Without exception, their first wish is always, "I wish my parents would stop fighting." Many children go on to ask for the same thing with their second and third wishes as well, saying something like this: "I also wish they would get along better, and, uh, I guess my third wish is that they didn't fight as much." In other words, children cannot imagine wanting anything other than to have their parents stop fighting. Children are frightened when their parents go at each other, often secretly praying that they will stop.

Children have intense worries about their parents' safety and their own well-being. These anxieties worsen as the conflict between them creates stress for embattled parents, thus diminishing their ability to comfort and discipline their children. And, as if feelings of insecurity and loss of effective parenting were not enough, these children also feel *responsible* for parental hostilities. As discussed in Chapters Three and Four, children often believe they are responsible for the major occurrences in their lives, including ongoing parental battles. Further, the issues that parents often fight about exacerbate children's tendency toward egocentric thinking. That is, children routinely listen to their parents fight over them. For example, one parent might derisively yell at the other: "Well I wouldn't have to be so goddamned strict with her if you didn't spoil her so much!" As a result, there is little doubt in children's minds that they are to blame for this unhappiness, even though they do not want it and feel helpless to stop it.

Finally, although chronic marital conflict is destructive for all children, it may be especially harmful to young boys. Researchers have found that, on average, boys are more vulnerable to the adverse effects of family conflict and cannot cope with it as effectively as girls. In most families, girls are more protected from family conflict than boys are, both before the divorce and afterward. Specifically, researchers have found that parents fight more and that their fights continue longer in the presence of sons than daughters.

Managing Parental Conflicts Responsibly

Although parents expect divorce to end their marital problems, they are often dismayed to find that conflict continues in the period following the breakup. In particular, going through a legal battle rather than negotiating a mediated settlement usually intensifies problems over custody, visitation, and support payments. As we will see in Chapter Seven, if parents and their attorneys are adversarial and attempt to win in court rather than negotiate mutually workable arrangements, bitterness and distrust between former spouses escalate, and the hatred often endures for years after the final court decree. This result is a grave problem for children (and parents) who consequently suffer increased stress, unhappiness, and insecurity. A parent who engages in ongoing battles with the former spouse in front of the children can stop participating in this destructive interaction, even if the other parent continues to do so. Parents who are unable to stop their own participation in such warfare, or who are without the restraint to shield children from it, are encouraged to seek professional help for themselves and their children.

Parents can follow three basic steps to establish the most cooperative parenting relationship that is attainable for them in the aftermath of divorce.

STEP ONE: COMMIT TO SHIELDING THE CHILD. The first step toward managing anger and conflict responsibly is to acknowledge the reality that children are harmed by chronic parental conflict and to make a personal commitment to either stop it or to shield children from it. Every divorcing parent should contemplate this fact and try to hold to this resolve as much as possible. Remember, it is the continuing hostilities between parents rather than the isolated problems that inevitably occur that harm children.

This internal commitment to protect children from parental conflict should be made personally and privately, regardless of what the other parent does. Even if one parent continues to behave irresponsibly, this does not give the other parent permission to respond in kind. As we will see, children then lose both of their parents emotionally rather than retain one trustworthy parent who is safe. The concept of an "island of psychological safety" can help parents achieve this goal.

If both parents are vindictive and join the parental battle, children lose emotional access to both. There is no safe shelter from the storm. But if one parent can exercise restraint and refrain from retaliating destructively, children lose psychological access to the other parent but still have emotional contact with the restrained parent. With the support of one parent, these children are sad about the parental conflict but not depressed. Unlike children with two warring parents, these children do not fail in school or act out angrily and defiantly. Although these children are exposed to parental pain and conflict, they also have the support necessary to cope because they have one parent who does not undermine the other or pressure them to take sides. Having emotional contact with this neutral parent allows children to tolerate family turmoil without developing more serious symptoms or enduring problems. Thus, as long as one parent refrains from joining the battle, children retain a much-needed island of psychological safety that is lost when both parents become embattled.

Even though children adjust far better when one parent exercises restraint, maintaining the inner resolve not to lose one's temper or retaliate when provoked is clearly the hard part of Step One. However, it does take two to tango, and if one parent makes a sincere effort to shield children from parental conflicts, family life will improve immediately and significantly for children.

Don't take my word for any of this. Try making the effort and see for yourself what it does for your children. Ideally, of course, it is best if both parents can discuss the harmful impact of ongoing parental conflict and mutually agree to terminate angry conversations when children are present.

STEP TWO: USE HAND SIGNALS TO TERMINATE ESCALATING CONFLICT. Angry former spouses can find ways to manage conflicts between them so that arguments do not escalate out of control. Despite the best of intentions, tempers sometimes flare when certain topics are broached. At these moments conflicts escalate out of control, and children are exposed to hitting and yelling, insults and threats, tears and pain. Divorcing couples can establish a protective mechanism to terminate such unwanted interactions before they erupt, and hand signals are a disarmingly simple but effective method.

On behalf of their children, divorcing couples can mutually agree to abide by the following system. Whenever one parent feels that a discussion with the other is about to escalate emotionally, the parent raises an index finger in the air to signal, "Be still." As soon as either parent gives this signal, the conversation stops immediately. No one gets in the last word. No one criticizes or challenges why the signal was given (for example, by saying, "You always use that signal just to . . ."). Both parties simply stop talking about that topic for five minutes, without further discussion and without exceptions. By giving and following the signal, appropriate controls over escalating emotions have been instituted. After five minutes, parents can mutually decide whether they wish to continue talking about the topic, try talking about something else, or terminate their conversation for the time being and go their separate ways.

However, if one parent fails to honor the agreed-upon signal, the other parent restates one time that the "stop" signal has been given. If the other does not respond promptly and de-escalate, the parent who has signaled restraint should terminate the conversation, as previously agreed upon, and depart.

If both parties agree to use this method, each parent gains needed control over the communication process. Each parent possesses an all-important "stop" button that provides a safe way out of escalating conflicts. Both parents are reassured to know that they have a time-out in which to regroup and gain some emotional distance. When parents feel out of control in the relationship, they are most likely to act in ways that are destructive for children to witness. In contrast, when adults can employ mechanisms such as these to effectively control their own emotions, children feel more secure. Parents will observe a direct relationship between their ability to exercise control over volatility in their relationship and their children's felt sense of safety.

Step Three: Communicate Effectively Using These Guidelines. Many men and women have relatively limited communication skills, and almost everyone is uncomfortable negotiating emotionally charged conflicts in significant relationships. Divorcing couples are faced with a challenging task. They need to make ongoing decisions together about the treasure in their lives—their children—with someone they may dislike, distrust, or even fear. Divorcing parents do not need to become friends, learn to trust each other, or resolve past marital problems. However, they do need to communicate with each other *in a civil manner* about many child-related concerns. Nothing more is needed; nothing less will do. Who will pick up the children from school and take them to soccer games or piano lessons? When will they go to summer camp? How will they handle notes from teachers about meetings and conferences at school? Who will take them shopping for new shoes, and who will pay for school clothes? For many years to come, ex-spouses will have to make joint decisions about their children's daily activities and plans. There are no easy answers, but helpful guidelines are available to structure the difficult negotiations divorcing couples face. Here are ten basic guidelines for effective communication.

1. *Accept responsibility for your share of what went wrong.* Do not assign blame, rigidly resist your former spouse's viewpoint, or insist that your perception of events is the only version of the truth.
2. *Stick to the problem at hand and deal with only one issue at a time.* Do not bring up past problems or expand the current conflict to other topics.

3. *Keep the conflict contained between the two of you.* Do not drag in references to friends or relatives who agree with you. For example, refrain from saying things like this: "Even your mother says . . ."

4. *As a gift to your children, have the dignity to treat your former spouse with respect.* Ask your children, attorney, new spouse, and grandparents to join you in setting this tone. Refrain from provocations. Do not yell, insult, use obscene language, or resort to name-calling, even if the other parent does. Offending the other person will escalate problems and, more important, diminish your stature in your children's eyes.

5. *Stay physically and emotionally engaged with the discussion at hand until it is finished.* Do not withdraw or walk out of the room to avoid conflict without warning your ex-spouse first. Walking out abruptly usually escalates tensions. If you choose to exit, first give the other person one chance to change. Say, for example, "I am invoking the hand signal right now, and you are not responding. If you do not stop talking about this immediately, I am leaving" or "I don't like the demeaning tone of voice you are using. Stop it now and speak to me respectfully or I will leave."

6. *Agree on mutually satisfactory times and places to talk.* For example, volatile couples can meet in a public place, such as a restaurant, where the potential for outbursts is greatly reduced. Do not negotiate under the influence of drugs or alcohol.

7. *Focus only on the problems that need to be resolved.* Do not physically intimidate your former spouse or play on his or her insecurities.

8. *Listen attentively to the other person's point of view.* Do not pretend to listen while shutting the person out and formulating your own rebuttal.

9. *Communicate about specific behaviors without using pejorative labels.* For example, "You were twenty minutes late to pick her up today" is far more effective than "You're always late to pick her up; you're too selfish to think about anyone but yourself." Do not use generalizations such as "you always" or "you never."

10. *Establish a hand signal to terminate conversations that begin to deteriorate into unproductive, escalating conflict.* Do not continue arguing when the other person gives the signal to stop the conversation for five minutes.

By employing these ten rules, divorcing couples can avoid the most common pitfalls of conflict negotiation. Of course, the success of these guidelines depends on both parties agreeing to abide by them as much as possible (no one can be expected to do it right all of the time). A neutral mediator will be necessary if one party is unwilling to cooperate, if one party feels physically threatened, or if emotions are too volatile. A professional divorce mediator is usually available without charge through the family law division of your local county courthouse.

Expressing Parental Conflicts Through the Children

One of the best predictors of how well a child adjusts to divorce is whether the former spouses support each other in their continuing relationship as parents or undermine each other. Although cooperation greatly enhances children's secure adjustment, it is often difficult for parents to achieve. When two people divorce, there is often a great deal of hurt, anger, and distrust between them. Both must cope with difficult feelings such as betrayal, rejection, or failure. As a result, former spouses may continue to vent their anger and bitterness toward each other for years after the divorce.

Unfortunately, one of the most common ways that parental hostilities are expressed is through the children. These hostilities are often acted out irresponsibly by undermining the former spouse's relationship with the children or by disparaging the former spouse to the children. Children develop enduring psychological symptoms and behavioral problems when one parent acts out their hurt and angry feelings toward the other by eroding the other's parenting authority.

Before examining the consequences when one spouse undermines another, let's clarify what I am suggesting by "a cooperative parental relationship after divorce." What can this mean realistically? Do parents still need to love each other, be friends, or even like each other? As emphasized earlier, no they don't. Further, there is no need for parents to pretend to their children that they have positive feelings for the former spouse when they don't. However, parents do need to treat each other with respect and support one another in their relationship with the children. To the extent possible, each spouse should communicate to the children that the other is still their parent, cares for them, and should be respected and obeyed. This step is difficult for some parents to take because they feel so hurt by and angry with their former spouse. As we will see, however, it is in the children's best interest to have the most positive relationship possible with both parents rather than having one parent disparaged as a role model. All of us are human and have problems in our personality and weaknesses in our parenting skills. Thus one can affirm a child's reality-based frustration with something the other parent has done in a way that does not diminish the ex-spouse as a person or parent.

When Parents Undermine Each Other

It is destructive when one parent undermines another with comments like, "Your mother doesn't know what she's doing. Come to me if she tries to tell you what to do" or "Your father's a jerk. Why do you want to see him?" Such comments are not merely criticisms of something the ex-spouse has done, but they disparage the person and the entire role he or she plays in the child's life.

Why is this disparagement so problematic for children? There are many reasons, but one of the most important is that children "identify" with their parents and, in a psychological sense, see themselves as being the same as their parents (for example, love-worthy or unimportant, capable or intimidated). Thus, children are so closely identified with their parents that they often experience their mother's rejection of their father, for example, as their mother's rejection of them. In other words, when parents disparage each other, the long-term effect is about the same as simultaneously demeaning and devaluing the child. Hence the quote, "Fathers (or Mothers) best love their children by treating their Mother lovingly."

Although parents intend only to disparage the other parent, children absorb this contempt as if it were directed against them. This identification is especially strong between a child and the same-sex parent. For instance, it is virtually impossible for a daughter to grow up and feel good about herself as a woman if her father disparages her mother as being "fat" or "stupid." Boys who hear their mother demean their father in a similar way will suffer the same consequences. With this identification between parent and child in mind, consider a typical family scenario in which Bob is undermining Carrie's parenting authority to the children.

Bob and Carrie

Carrie initiated a divorce from Bob several months ago. The two children were living with Carrie during the week and with Bob on weekends. Things had not gone well for Carrie since the breakup. Being a single parent was so much harder than she had imagined; she felt overwhelmed by being pulled in so many directions at once. She was working part-time, taking a few classes toward a college degree, and trying to develop a relationship with a man she enjoyed dating.

All of these demands would have been manageable if not for her two children, who simply refused to cooperate with her on anything. They were impossible, she thought, for her to deal with. In fact, Carrie often felt as if her children had joined in a conspiracy to ruin her life. For example, seven-year-old Bobby would mercilessly taunt Carrie's new boyfriend whenever he came over. Although she repeatedly threatened Bobby and inevitably sent him to his room, he usually found some way to succeed in ruining the couple's time together. Eventually, Carrie's boyfriend did not want to visit her at the house anymore, so she had to pay for a babysitter whenever they got together. Carrie was furious at her son for trying to drive away the most important source of support in her life.

Things were equally bad with her thirteen-year-old daughter, Sara. Sara too had begun calling her mother a "stupid idiot" as her brother did. It was as if her daughter had an uncanny ability to sense what insult would get under Carrie's skin and really hurt her. As was true with Bobby, Carrie could not control her daughter's obnoxious behavior. Carrie's efforts to talk with her daughter and try to understand her were no more successful than her threats, restrictions, and punishments. After months of failure, Carrie felt helpless and gradually gave up even trying to change her children. Feeling that they just "hated" her, she became increasingly depressed.

It was her good friend and neighbor, Jean, who first helped Carrie realize what was going on. Jean had observed that Bobby and Sara treated their mother the worst right after they returned from a weekend with their father. Jean had also overheard a telephone conversation with their father in which the children had laughed at and made fun of Carrie. Jean knew Carrie and Bob had not gotten along well after the divorce and that Bob became especially angry when Carrie started dating, but she hadn't realized that Bob had been encouraging the children's outrageous behavior. Their laughter on the phone made it clear that Bob was thoroughly enjoying the problems the children were creating for Carrie.

"Sure, I've suspected that, but what can I do!" Carrie exclaimed when Jean told her what was going on. "He hates me, and now he has the kids hating me, too. I can't make him stop; he'll just laugh at me. All three of them will probably get together and just laugh at me. I'm so mortified I could die!"

In this all-too-common scenario, Carrie's life is painfully out of control because Bob has undermined her relationship with the children. Although it may not be obvious yet, Carrie's children are hurting as well, and their well-being is in serious jeopardy. They are beginning a lifelong journey down a perilous road of serious problems with self-esteem, intimate relationships, and authority figures such as teachers and future employers.

Let's look first at what is happening to the children and then see what Carrie can do to resolve her problem.

In this example, Bobby and Sara see their mother as someone they can ridicule and dominate. Their father is teaching them that it is acceptable to provoke, demean, and defy their mother. When children are allowed to treat a parent so disrespectfully, this arrogant and grandiose attitude soon will extend to other adults in their lives. Bobby and Sara will probably come to regard some teachers and principals, umpires and referees, camp counselors and scout leaders, as well as coaches, employers, and others in authority with similar disdain. These children are learning that they do not have to treat others with respect or comply with rules and regulations. This antisocial message is serious because it often leads children to behave in illegal, exploitative, or physically abusive ways when they are older. The inability to respect the rights and dignity of others is fostered by vindictive parents who demonstrate that hostility and contempt are acceptable ways of relating to others. If the pattern is not altered, the children's ability to establish mutually respectful relationships may be impaired throughout their lives. In particular, Bobby is at risk to hurt others as he hurts his mother, and Sara will not be able to respect herself or her own body as long as she cannot respect her mother.

Sara and Bobby also lose a role model when their mother is seen as someone who can be discounted. As her daughter, Sara will have to reject her weak and powerless mother and try not to become like her. In doing so, she will lose her most important role model for learning what it means to be a woman. At the same time that Sara tries to push her mother away, she is also likely to adopt the same negative characteristics she has attributed to her mother; she may grow up feeling that she too is a "stupid idiot" or is fat and ugly. Typically, she will select a marriage partner who treats her in the same disparaging manner.

In parallel, Bobby will learn that mothers and wives do not deserve affection or respect. In identifying with his father, he is likely to generalize this contemptuous attitude toward women in general and regard them callously as well. He will have great difficulty developing an egalitarian love relationship with a woman as he matures.

Parents are our most important teachers about relationships. All of us have gained important expectations about relationships from watching our parents' daily interactions for years. From our parents' model we develop "schemas" or road maps for what goes on between two people in close relationships and learn expectations for what people can and cannot do together. How close can we be together? Whose needs can be met, and whose must go unacknowledged? Can we depend on someone else and expect to find them trustworthy? Can we still be cared about when we make mistakes, get help with our problems, and have give-and-take in relationships? Can people have important differences but still remain together or do disagreements inevitably have to force people apart? Can people find ways to communicate about problems and work them out together, or do they have to remain gridlocked forever in anger and blame?

We learn answers to these and many other important questions while growing up in our families. Although we may relearn or alter these schemas as we develop further relationships, these first models are the most important determinants of the satisfaction we find in later relationships. If a parent expresses hostility at the former spouse by undermining the parenting authority of the other, then children like Bobby and Sara will have poor road maps indeed to guide them through life.

When Only One Parent Cooperates

Difficult problems arise when one parent tries to cooperate but the other parent won't. There are no easy answers to this exasperating situation, but guidelines are available that may help. Let's continue the previous illustration.

> Because Carrie's ex-husband, Bob, encouraged their children to disobey and show disrespect for her, both Carrie and her children were suffering from his destructive behavior. Depressed, Carrie felt helpless to change the situation with her children. "I can't stop Bob from ruining my life. He doesn't care how I feel. If I told him to stop, he'd just laugh at me. He never listened to me or did what I asked before the divorce, and he sure isn't going to now."

Carrie, and many others in similar situations, feel helpless and hopeless. This sense of futility is often how they felt while they were married, when they were not respected, listened to, or supported by their spouse. It is terribly frustrating to leave a marriage because of this unfair treatment, only to find that you are faced with the same problems after the divorce. By changing your own responses in these interactions, however, you do not have to live forever with the same problems. Carrie can use this situation as an opportunity to grow out of the old submissive role she had with her husband and learn to respond to him (and their children) more assertively and directly.

How can she do this? Let's consider a progressive sequence of steps, each of which holds the same theme: *the parent stops trying to change the problematic behavior of the other spouse and instead changes his or her own responses in these conflicted interactions.* Said differently, we usually fail in our attempts to change others, but we can exert influence and change faulty interaction patterns by changing our own ways of responding to them. That is the only real control we have.

Initially, Carrie wanted her boyfriend to talk to Bob for her, but this approach would have exacerbated feelings of competition and jealousy. The parent who is undermined needs to speak directly to the ex-spouse about the problem; confronting the issue face to face provides the best possibility of change. Although therapists, new partners, grandparents, and friends may be concerned, their interventions usually fail to rescue the parent, who should do this personally by contacting the former spouse and requesting a meeting to talk about difficulties in their parental relationship. At the meeting, the parents tell their former spouse what they do not like and what they want to change. Parents can clarify as specifically as possible how they are being undermined and why this is making things worse for the children. The former spouses can then be invited to respond.

Surprisingly, the former spouses often have legitimate concerns that can be addressed. However, the parents do not want to enter into an argument about who is right or wrong. Rather, undermined parents simply state again the specific type of comments and conduct that need to stop.

Next, undermined parents need to reassure their former spouses that they will not undermine the former spouse's relationship with the children. For example, a parent might say, "I will not reciprocate by undermining your relationship with the children. I will support you in your role as a parent, and I want you to support me in mine." Often, after being directly confronted and naming the problem behavior or making it overt and being assured that no reciprocal devaluation is going on, some ex-spouses will act more responsibly.

If this first confrontation does not alleviate the problem, the undermined parent then meets with the children and the former spouse together. In front of all concerned, the parent can repeat the request for the former spouse to stop undermining his or her relationship with the children. The parent also asks the children to stop participating in this scheme, even if the former spouse continues to provoke them. Naming the problem and making it overt in this calm but forthright way usually dissolves the destructive alliance between the goading parent and the children. Again, the parent should assure the children and the former spouse that there will be no reciprocal undermining of their relationship.

Sometimes a parent feels physically threatened by the former spouse. If so, a third party can be quietly present (for example, a respected grandparent, mutual friend, or pastor—not a new lover).

Also, these conversations can be held safely in a restaurant or public place where tempers are less likely to flare.

Carrie was able to stop this destructive pattern. She had the courage to confront Bob and her children with the problem. This action, coupled with setting much firmer limits than before on the children's disparaging behavior, largely resolved the situation. In addition, Carrie spoke with genuine resolve when she told her children that they would have to live with their father and visit her on weekends if they continued to be disrespectful. Carrie took control of her life and stopped allowing her former husband to victimize her, but she had to assert her equality for herself. No one else could do it for her. As she claimed her own equal power in the relationship, her children became more respectful. Although Bob did laugh at her and continue trying to provoke the children for awhile, they stopped participating. Carrie resolved this problem by changing herself and her own responses in this toxic situation rather than feeling helpless about her inability to change Bob.

Ending the Marriage

Parents who cannot stop fighting with each other often cannot end their marriage either. Although it is a hateful connection, combative parents keep themselves linked together by remaining emotionally embroiled with each other. For litigious parents, in particular, the former spouse remains the emotional center of their universe, as their worlds are organized around controlling what the other parent is doing and getting back for the injustices the other has wrought. Before they can end their battle and establish a calmer life for their children, they must internally or emotionally end the marriage. This is hard work for everyone and is especially difficult for combative parents. Psychologically ending the marriage entails a great deal more work than just going through the legal process of divorce.

Two people may remain emotionally tied together—in effect, still married—years after the divorce decree. Getting a lawyer, moving out, and signing papers make up the external components of divorce. Someone can go through this procedure, however, and still not really be divorced, just as one can go through a marriage ceremony without becoming married in the sense of making an emotional commitment. Too little attention is given to the fact that the real business of divorcing is internal.

There are several aspects to internally ending the marriage. First, one must grieve or say good-by to the good things in the marriage that will be missed or that once were enjoyed. An inevitable sadness needs to be felt before the marriage can be fully left behind. Some parents grieve for the person who has gone; all parents mourn their unfulfilled hopes and dreams for the relationship. Embattled parents who cannot experience the losses evoked by the breakup or recognize their own contribution to the problems in the marriage may fear that their sadness makes them one-down in the relationship or proves that the ex-spouse has "won" if they are hurt. To ward off such shame, they may be consumed by attempts to punish or control their former spouse and, unwittingly, use their children as pawns in the ensuing battle.

Both partners usually experience some degree of "ambivalence" about ending the marriage. That is, some good things in the marriage are being left behind, along with the problematic things. Some spouses will try to avoid acknowledging these positive aspects of the relationship in order to lessen the guilt over leaving or to mask the shame and reduce the pain of being left. Even deeply embittered couples have shared some good times together, as well as the extraordinary experience of creating a new life and caring for a child. Coming to terms with the reality of the divorce requires parents to acknowledge their contradictory or ambivalent feelings.

To truly end a marriage, parents also need to see their own contribution to the problems of the relationship. It really does take two people to have an argument. When parents begin to see how they share some responsibility for the problems in the marriage and stop putting all the blame for the breakup on the former spouse, they are truly ending the marriage and moving forward to a new life. Family members and well-meaning friends often express their support for one partner by criticizing the other. Such comments are not helpful for either spouse because they heap all the responsibility onto one, making it difficult for parents to learn from this experience and bring something new and better to the next relationship.

Parents cannot psychologically end the marriage quickly, however. The whole process may take several years, especially if it has been a long marriage. If parents can begin the internal work of ending the marriage, however, it will help them gain the emotional distance necessary to establish the most cooperative parenting relationship possible.

Suggestions for Further Reading

Getting to Yes (R. Fisher, Penguin, 1991) will help some couples negotiate conflicts and communicate more effectively. *Necessary Losses* (J. Viorst, Fireside, 1998) can help many parents better understand life transitions such as divorce and come to terms more effectively with the feelings of loss they evoke.

Chapter Six

Children Need Their Mothers and Fathers

"Dad Doesn't Come See Me Anymore. What's Wrong With Me?"

The shared act of conception entitles children to both a mother and a father, but this natural birthright to two parents is lost for most children in the aftermath of divorce. In almost nine out of ten cases of divorce, mothers receive primary physical custody of the children, and fathers are granted visitation rights. For most noncustodial fathers, divorce not only ends their marriage but ends their participation as a parent as well. Fathers tend to see more of their children in the first two years after the breakup but, as years go by, fathers generally see less and less of their children. In particular, fathers are especially likely to give up on parenting when mothers remarry. Researchers find that, in the years following the breakup, only 25 percent of children have weekly contact with their divorced fathers. When fathers remain involved, it is more likely to be with sons than with daughters.

About 20 percent of children see their divorced fathers only once or twice a year; more had not seen their father even once in the preceding twelve months! Why are most fathers so disengaged from their children after the divorce? This chapter examines several reasons, such as the "culture of women" that sometimes exists in childrearing. When the couple's first child is born, a culture of women often gathers to support the new mother and celebrate the birth. Grandmothers and sisters, nurses or midwives, and friends who have already become mothers all share deeply in this great new joy and together teach her how to feed and care for the newborn. Unfortunately, not as many fathers are included in this loving circle that surrounds and nurtures the new mother and her baby. When they are asked to join, many fathers do not allow themselves to accept the help and support being offered. Although our culture is changing, and there certainly has been increasing support for fathering, many fathers still fail to make this life-changing transition in their own personal identity to include the role of caregiver. Rather than being encouraged to participate equally in parenting and being taught how to take pleasure in bathing, diapering, and soothing the baby, many fathers begin to distance from this new caregiving role for which they feel unprepared and inadequate to fulfill.

Many people are not concerned by a father's lack of parenting involvement after divorce; they are only concerned when he fails to make support payments. The cultural norm that women, not men, should take care of children still runs strong. However, the extent of divorced fathers' continuing involvement is an important determinant of children's adjustment. This chapter examines the adverse consequences for children, single-parent mothers, and fathers alike when fathers are uninvolved and suggests ways to help children benefit from a continuing relationship with both parents.

Children Often Lose Both Parents

Chapter Two highlighted separation anxieties and young children's fear of losing their parents through the divorce. No groundless worry, this fear of being left is often realized in the years following the breakup. The long-lasting distress brought on by the breakup and the enormous daily demands of being a single parent often make mothers far less available to their children, both physically and emotionally. The stress of role overload for single-parent mothers, along with most fathers' diminishing involvement in the years following the divorce, combine to greatly diminish the amount of time children spend with an emotionally responsive parent. This loss of physical or emotional access to one or both of their parents causes many of the problems that children of divorce suffer.

Single Mothers Are Overwhelmed

In the first year or so following the marital separation, mothers are often preoccupied with their own personal and financial concerns. Statistics vary, but some studies suggest that custodial mothers lose over one-quarter of their predivorce income. This loss in income is accompanied by increased workloads and residential moves to less-desirable neighborhoods, with poorly financed schools and recreational facilities and higher crime rates. In addition, many mothers are far more distressed by the breakup, and for a much longer period of time, than they anticipated they would be, even if they initiated it. Their efforts to cope with their personal and financial distress may distract them from their children's needs or diminish their parenting effectiveness. Mothers are also struggling with all the new demands of becoming a single parent: dating, losing some old friends and establishing a new support network, and in many cases finding a job and entering the workforce. If the father is not actively involved, she must also take over some of his parenting functions, such as disciplining sons. This task is especially difficult for many single mothers because sons in both intact and divorced families are usually more disobedient toward mothers than fathers.

Mothers without a parenting partner suffer from role overload. They have to do it all. They clean the gutters and mow the yard; take care of the children without breaks or relief; juggle the schedule and get the children to school, scout meetings, and doctors' appointments on time—without being late for work. These mothers "multi-task" about a million things every day. But here is the real rub: children distressed by the breakup and all of the changes occurring in their lives need more from their mothers at the very time their mothers have less to give.

Let's restate this negative interaction between children's heightened needs and single parents' diminished capacity to respond: *At the same time the single mother is trying to adjust to the increasing demands of her new role, children simultaneously are having heightened needs for an organized household, a predictable daily routine, consistent discipline, and emotional responsiveness from parents.* Despite their sometimes heroic efforts, preoccupied and fatigued mothers often do not have the time or energy to meet their children's heightened needs.

To grasp this dilemma fully, let's explore the financial problem further. Divorce precipitates a significant decline in the standard of living for both mothers and fathers. However, the greatest economic decline and stress occurs in mother-headed families in which the father does not assume an active parenting role. Although this statistic is improving, about 25 percent of fathers still fail to make support payments, and another 25 percent make them inconsistently. As a result, these single-mother-headed families are often pushed to the poverty line, and this economic hardship increases the risk of problems for children. Children's nutrition and health, as well as their self-esteem and expectations for success, all suffer when they grow up in poverty. Even for others who fare better, private lessons, educational toys, books, home computers, and other factors in academic success become out of reach. Finally, these demanding role changes and economic hardships become even more difficult to cope with because they occur all at once.

The cumulative result of these stresses is that children receive less adult attention and less-effective parenting than they did before the divorce. What does this mean in terms of specific, everyday behavior? Researchers find that divorced mothers do not have as much time for their children, do not eat dinner with them as often, do not put them to bed at such regular hours, and do not get them ready for school on time as often as they did before the divorce. Divorced mothers also monitor their children less closely than mothers in two-parent families. They know less about where their children are, whom they are with, and what they are doing. Children of divorce often receive less adult supervision than children from two-parent families and are more likely to be home alone or to spend time with their peers. These problems are exacerbated because the quality of care that parents provide also declines. Researchers find that divorced parents communicate less effectively with their children, are more erratic in enforcing discipline, are less affectionate with children, and provide them more disorganized households.

Divorced Fathers Are Not Active Parents

Whereas the emotional unavailability of mothers usually ends after a period of adjustment, divorce all too often means a permanent reduction in the extent and quality of father–child relationships. By the second year after the separation, mothers have generally regained their self-esteem and confidence. They have regained their previous level of competence as parents, and their emotional availability to their children has improved. Unfortunately, this is not the case with fathers. Three years after the divorce, there is little or no father–child interaction in the majority of cases. This finding is troubling because the extent of their fathers' involvement is closely linked to children's adjustment.

Divorced fathers have a continuing personal and financial responsibility to their children, but they often fail to fulfill these obligations. Too often, fathers are blamed exclusively for being too selfish and uncaring to follow through on their childrearing obligations. At times this accusation is true, and it is disturbing when fathers walk away from parenting. But there is more to understanding this complex social problem than one-sidedly blaming men. Divorced fathers who do want to take an active parenting role face formidable obstacles. There are three primary reasons so many fathers become uninvolved parents.

CULTURAL INFLUENCES. The traditional mothering role was institutionalized in the early 1900s by the Industrial Revolution. The transition from an agrarian to an urban society created distinct gender roles that established mutually exclusive and competing power bases in the family. Although fathers were given much more power in the working world, mothers were given an equal but more covert power base in the realm of childrearing. As a result of this rigid sex-role demarcation, many men and women still believe that children belong more to their mothers than to their fathers and that the mother is the "real parent." This gender bias, which was reflected in the long-standing custom of awarding sole custody to mothers and giving alternate weekend visitation to fathers, did not change in the courts until the 1980s.

As a result of these cultural influences, many fathers do not feel they have an important contribution to make to their child's development. Unfortunately, many mothers share this belief. Repeatedly, national surveys reveal that the majority of mothers do not want their ex-husbands to be more involved in childrearing. Researchers also have found that many divorced mothers were prepared to forego child support if they no longer had to be inconvenienced by visits from their former partner! Although this cultural bias is beginning to change, childrearing is still considered a female activity. Mother is viewed as the expert in the realm of childrearing, and father becomes a concerned assistant, at best.

Although women's roles have expanded to include professional achievement and independence, there has not been a reciprocal growth in men's roles to include nurturing and caring for children. If fathers have not been fully involved in the hands-on, daily tasks of feeding, diapering, and bathing since birth, they will not feel very confident or comfortable in the parenting role. In most cases, sadly, they will not know their children as well. With the new demands for more independent parenting after the breakup, they are far more like to feel inadequate and unimportant, and to fall away. Recalling the culture of women that often facilitates the new mother's transition to motherhood, fewer men have enjoyed such support. Further, many men have not benefited from effective role models of emotionally responsive parenting from their own fathers, grandfathers, uncles, or other mentors. They don't know how to assume a responsible parenting role—how to be a capable dad—because, as children, they didn't receive the following from older males:

- Physical affection and comfort when they were distressed
- Support and encouragement for their genuine interests
- Affirmation of their abilities and recognition for what they did well
- Practical help in solving the everyday problems that troubled them
- Firm discipline that didn't shame them

Many fathers never experienced these basic elements of effective parenting in their own childhood, so as adults they don't know how to give their own children what they never received and haven't been taught.

ANGER BETWEEN PARENTS. Continuing parental conflict also contributes to fathers' lack of involvement with their children. As described in Chapter Five, the hurt and anger brought on by the breakup and the hatred fueled by adversarial legal proceedings does not end with the divorce decree. In Euripides' version of the classic Greek myth of Medea, Jason leaves Medea for a beautiful young princess. Contemplating the ultimate revenge, Medea swears, "He shall never see alive again the sons he had from me . . . this is the way to deal Jason the deepest wounds." In line with traditional gender roles, one way for mothers to vent their anger may be to align the children with her against their father. In self-report studies, researchers have consistently found that up to one-half of all custodial mothers report that they actively interfere with or resist visitations as a means of expressing anger. In parallel, of course, fathers' primary means of retaliation is often to withhold financial support.

Both mothers and fathers may embroil children in parental battles by pressuring them to take sides. As we will explore in Chapter Eight, these parents create loyalty conflicts for their children by being overtly angry and disparaging or subtly sad and hurt when children wish to visit or be close to the other parent. Unfortunately, few children of divorce have permission from both parents to be equally involved with the other parent. However, because mothers are usually the primary caretakers before the divorce and, as a rule, children live with their mothers afterward, children tend to be closer to their mothers than their fathers. When pressured to choose between their parents, most children's emotional allegiance initially goes to their mothers. In these circumstances, the father's continuing involvement may, in effect, require his former wife's permission. Feeling powerless and controlled in this situation, many fathers disengage—breaking off ties as they or their ex-spouses remarry and begin new families.

Too often, divorced fathers' absence from parenting has been dismissed as unimportant. There has been increasing pressure to make fathers comply with child support payments, fortunately, but no corresponding interest in involving fathers personally with their children. Most fathers need to be actively encouraged in order to continue their childrearing role after the divorce. Children consistently tell researchers that they want more contact with their fathers and that they suffer socially, emotionally, and intellectually when their fathers are uninvolved. As we have seen, children are egocentric in their thinking and take responsibility for his lack of responsiveness ("There must be something wrong with me or Dad would want to see me"). In this way children usually blame themselves for his departure and suffer a precipitous loss of self-esteem and initiative that is reflected in depression, poor school performance, failure in peer relationships, and sexual promiscuity.

Not only are children deprived when their fathers disengage, but mothers and fathers suffer as well. When fathers commit to their children and invest themselves in these relationships, their lives hold more purpose and meaning. When fathers give up on their parenting role, they are giving up on important parts of themselves as well. The greatest opportunity that life presents for men to express the generative parts of themselves is lost. Similarly lost is the opportunity to rework the disappointing parts and to honor the rewarding aspects of their own childhood. At the same time, without the relief offered by a cooperative parenting partner, mothers' lives are overtaxed by the demands placed on a single parent. Clearly, mother, father, and child all lose when fathers are not active parents after divorce. However, additional obstacles keep many fathers from remaining involved.

TRADITIONAL MALE ROLES. The traditional male gender role also constrains men's involvement with children. Rather than affirming tender feelings and empathic responsiveness, men feel threatened by these qualities and, at times, may even regard them contemptuously. Most men and women do not think of emotional responsiveness to children as masculine behavior. Drying tears, applying bright yellow Band-Aids with dinosaurs on them, brushing teeth, bending over so that you can talk at the child's eye level, preparing lunch, tucking a child into bed, making up a story, and answering a thousand "why" questions when you are tired are not usually considered masculine behavior. This unfortunate socialization limits men's involvement with their children in nuclear families and the custodial arrangements that follow divorce.

This male socialization begins early in life. While they are growing up, most boys in our culture are not invited to try and understand what a younger child might be thinking or feeling in a particular situation, or encouraged to recognize and respond to a younger child's need ("Would you help your little brother get that knot out of his shoe? See how he's trying to tie his own laces but is frustrated because he can't quite get it. Maybe you could sit with him for a minute and show him how you do it or just encourage him as he tries it his own way."). It is uncommon, but very special, to know an adolescent boy who can compete successfully with his peers on the ball field and then come home to help his little brother with his reading.

I recall seeing a four-year-old playing "Daddy" and taking his doll for a walk in the stroller around my neighborhood. I went up to him and asked how his baby was doing today, and he said, "fine." But then he asked if I thought it was OK for him to play this way. Friends at preschool and one of the classroom aides had told him that playing with a doll was girl stuff and that boys didn't do it. So, he asked, did I think it was all right for him to take his baby for a walk?

The sex-role stereotypes we learn as children serve to guide our behavior as parents when we are adults. Although some differences in childrearing practices occur across varying ethnic groups and social class, many parents have been brought up to believe child-rearing is the mother's domain, and the father's contribution is limited primarily to financial support and discipline. In most families, as a result, the vast majority of daily child-care activities are carried out by mothers. One direct outcome of this faulty social-ization is that many fathers do not formulate specific plans for maintaining regular participation in childrearing at the time of marital separation.

When I meet with divorcing parents, I ask fathers, "What con-crete plans or specific schedules have you made to ensure that you will have continuing, regularly scheduled contact with your chil-dren?" Many fathers respond, "I don't know. I guess I haven't re-ally made any plans yet. My wife has mostly taken care of the kids over the years; that's always been her arena. I guess I haven't had a very big role there." In a few cases, sadly, these adequacy concerns may even be aroused for fathers who were effective and involved parents before the divorce. These fathers anticipate that they will be active participants in childrearing and believe they have a con-tinuing parenting responsibility after divorce. However, even men who have been actively involved in the daily routines of child care may feel insecure about their ability to care for their children once they are on their own. A capable divorcing father told me, "When

I was married I could change my daughter's diapers, bathe her, feed her, everything. It was easy and I enjoyed it. My wife was working and I was virtually an equal coparent. But now that my wife's not around, I'm always afraid of doing the wrong thing. It's stupid, I know, but now I can't even do the things I used to do just fine without worrying that I might do something wrong."

Despite such apprehensions, and the rigid sex roles that leave many divorced fathers poorly prepared to assume an active parenting role, fathers need to be encouraged to remain, or for the first time to become, more closely involved with their children. Next, we will see how children often struggle when fathers give up their parenting role.

Adverse Consequences When Fathers Disengage

When divorced fathers do not take an active role in raising their children, boys and girls are more likely to develop long-term adjustment problems. As noted previously, the effects will vary according to the age and gender of the child. In general, however, the effects of fathers' unavailability will be most noticeable in academic, social, and emotional problems, especially depression.

Academic and Social Problems

Research studies have repeatedly shown that children who basically lose their fathers through divorce do not perform as well in many academic or social dimensions as children who have an emotionally available father. For example, children of absentee fathers have lower grades, score lower on achievement tests, and miss school more often. Boys with absent fathers also score lower on standardized intelligence tests such as the Scholastic Aptitude Test (SAT) and the Graduate Record Exam (GRE). Boys whose fathers show little or no interest in their children achieve lower scores in quantitative subjects and math than boys with more actively involved fathers.

To take one example, consider the high school SAT exam, which measures verbal and quantitative skills on a scale ranging from 200 to 800. Boys from intact families with an emotionally distant or unresponsive father, like boys from divorced families in which fathers are absent or uninvolved, tend to score significantly lower on the mathematics section than on the verbal (for example, math 400; verbal, 475). In contrast, this deficit is not found for boys in any type of family structure if there is an emotionally responsive father (for example, math 480; verbal, 475). The lower quantitative score reflects a deficiency in abstract thinking ability. The father's absence tends to diminish this conceptual ability in both boys and girls, but the deficit is more pronounced for boys and is most marked when the father disengaged before the son was five years of age.

In addition to intellectual and academic deficiencies, personality and social problems also trouble father-absent children. Boys without an emotionally responsive father are more dependent and have more difficulty finding their own identity and feeling secure as a boy and later as a man than boys with an emotionally available father. For example, some boys who lose their fathers through divorce may have more trouble making friendships with other boys their own age or competing successfully in sports. These boys may be more immature and only play with girls and younger children. Boys who are older when they lose their father are more apt to react by rebelling against adult authority. These boys become more aggressive and impulsive, and harder to discipline.

The adverse effects of losing their fathers are not greater for sons; problems arise for daughters as well. Girls' problems are most likely to become evident when daughters reach adolescence, however. For example, teenaged girls who have lost their fathers through divorce will have more difficulty in establishing mutually respectful and satisfying love relationships with males. Divorce researchers find, sadly, that father-absent girls approach males more assertively, become sexually active at a younger age, and have more sexual partners than girls whose fathers are active in their lives.

Unfortunately, these problems with heterosexual relations during adolescence carry over into early adulthood and marriage. Later in life, these young women are more likely to have unstable, unsatisfying marriages that end in divorce. Father-absent daughters tend to select marital partners who are self-centered, immature, and unable to respond to their needs and concerns. Their preconception that "men are no damned good" is often confirmed in their choice of marriage partner. In contrast to these problems, one of the best predictors of academic success and professional achievement for young adult women is an affirming and encouraging father.

So we see that long-term intellectual, personality, and sex-role problems are associated with the absence of fathers for both boys and girls. Does this mean that every child whose father disappears after the divorce will suffer these problems? No, absolutely not. These responses reflect averages. We cannot predict the consequences for any one child; there will always be broad individual differences. Some father-absent children have been found to adjust exceptionally well because they have especially competent mothers. Researchers describe these unusually successful single mothers as (1) being emotionally available (2) maintaining firm but sensitive discipline (3) communicating well with their children, and (4) encouraging independent mature behavior in them. By highlighting these four core dimensions of successful parenting, these highly capable single mothers are teaching all of us how to parent more effectively.

There seem to be two types of highly successful single mothers. Some mothers who were traditional wives and were terrified by the divorce became especially capable single parents. While growing up, these mothers enjoyed a strong relationship with their own fathers, who were nurturing and supportive while also setting high performance standards for them. The other type of highly successful single mother was very independent before the divorce. She is especially capable of providing the well-organized, highly structured household that brings children so much security in the aftermath of divorce. Nevertheless, although the absence of the father certainly does not have to yield long-term problems, there is still a compelling need to ensure fathers' part-time parenting participation.

Emotional Problems

When divorced fathers disengage from childrearing, children usually feel sad and angry; many of them eventually become depressed. These three emotional reactions often develop in sequence and merit closer examination.

SADNESS. We have already seen that for children under eight years of age, sadness is the predominant initial response to marital disruption. Most children feel very sad after their father moves out, and this sadness is greatly exacerbated if they don't have consistent, regularly scheduled contact with him. At first this grief may be openly displayed through emotional pleas such as, "I want my daddy. When will my daddy come back?" These children feel weepy, cry frequently, and have a seemingly insatiable need for physical contact and reassurance. Subsequently, if the father stays away, these children become angry in order to reduce or mask their hurt and cope with their sadness. If their angry protest fails, and they are helpless to elicit his response, depression often settles in.

ANGER. Anger is the predominant initial feeling for older children and adolescents, although all children experience both anger and sadness. Eight- to twelve-year-old boys are especially angry after a divorce if their father has left them. If the father disengages and is not an active parent, children experience a painful loss that they do not want and do not understand.

All too often, boys express this anger by driving their poor mothers and teachers crazy. Many single mothers describe life with their provocative and uncooperative sons as a war. Day-to-day living can be miserable for both mother and son, and this battle can continue for years. Some of these mothers feel like the helpless victims of their combative sons—trapped in an escalating negative cycle in which the son becomes angrier, more demanding, less respectful, and harder to manage. In turn, the mother becomes increasingly frustrated and ineffective. In response to his exasperated mother's irritability and criticism, the son becomes even more defiant and disrespectful, and the relationship continues to spiral downward.

Sometimes single mothers seek relief from this miserable situation by trying to keep themselves busy at work or away from home as much as possible. At the same time, however, they often feel guilty about not being good parents or spending enough time with their children. Whenever possible, the best solution to this hostile entanglement between mother and son is for sons to spend regularly scheduled time with an emotionally available father.

The sadness and anger children feel when they lose contact with their father is distressing and evokes further insecurity. In addition, another worrisome reaction is childhood depression.

CHILDHOOD DEPRESSION. Boys and girls of all ages who lose their father through divorce face a profound personal loss. Often this loss of love, which is usually exacerbated by receiving less from an overburdened single mother, dramatically lowers self-esteem and results in childhood depression. This depression can be expressed through different behavioral symptoms and can endure for years.

Childhood depression occurs in response to feeling the loss of love from an important caregiver and consists of two essential components. First, losing a parental relationship may produce a negative self-image in children. Children feel: "I am not lovable; I am not worthy; there is something wrong with me." The second component of childhood depression is a loss of self-efficacy. The child feels helpless and hopeless, no longer competent to do things well or to have an impact. These children perceive themselves as losers; they feel powerless, expect to fail, and are not willing to take on new challenges or activities ("I don't want to try. I can't do it"). Depression in younger children tends to emphasize their loss of self-esteem or being love-worthy; older children tend to suffer more from a critical evaluation of their own abilities, a loss of initiative, and diminished feelings of self-efficacy.

Parents may observe signs of depression in their children in any of the following four categories of behavior.

1. *Emotional.* Depressed children feel sad, look tearful, and cry. The sadness that was evident in their initial response to the breakup does not fade away as it does for most children but continues for at least six months after the separation.
2. *Motivational.* Grades and schoolwork decline, as children fail to complete homework assignments and are not motivated to study. In addition they neglect household chores and are less interested in playing or initiating activities they used to enjoy. The child often says, "I'm bored."
3. *Physical.* Depressed children may lose their appetite or not want to eat as much. Favorite foods are no longer appealing.

Children may feel tired all the time or have vague physical complaints, such as stomach pains, headaches, or just a sick feeling.

4. *Cognitive.* Children may anticipate failure, saying, for example, "I can't do this." They expect failure in any arena—with friends, in sports, or at school.

Children younger than nine or ten years of age tend to have more emotional and physical signs of depression; older children tend to have more of the motivational and cognitive symptoms. The symptoms in these four categories are the overt signs of depression in children, but they are not the whole story of childhood depression.

Children can also be depressed without showing such relatively obvious symptoms. Other kinds of behavior problems can reflect children's attempts to diminish or mask their underlying depression. For example, some children may seek the stimulation of drugs or reckless behavior to ward off the emptiness and boredom of depression. Others may try to escape depression by becoming apathetic and withdrawing into watching TV, playing computer games, or surfing the Internet. Some children's defense against depression is to escape into agitated motion. School-aged boys in particular may try to cope with the loss of their father through agitated, heightened activity that may be an attempt to ward off the sad and helpless feelings associated with parental loss.

Some estimates suggest that as many as 7 or 8 percent of the boys in U.S. public schools are being medicated for hyperactivity—an alarming statistic. These boys are prescribed an amphetamine, usually Ritalin, that helps some children focus their attention and become less distractible and impulsive. This medication is very helpful for the 3 or 4 percent of children—predominantly boys—who actually have attention deficit disorder (this disorder can occur with or without the accompanying symptom of hyperactivity). For these children, who have a neurologically based problem maintaining their focus of attention, Ritalin is a highly beneficial medication. Physicians now often prescribe stimulant medication in a timed-release capsule (Cylert) to diminish side effects. Ritalin helps children with an attention disorder to concentrate more effectively and for longer periods. Increasing their ability to maintain their focus of attention improves their chances of succeeding in school, often helps them get along better with peers because they can attend better to social cues, and makes most hyperactive children calmer and less disruptive to their families.

Lawsuits in many states are now charging that Ritalin is being widely overprescribed to every fidgety child, however. Many disruptive children being medicated do not have a biologically based attention problem. They are warding off the pain of depression or responding to a chaotic or undisciplined family life by escaping into agitated motion. Prescribing Ritalin is an easier way to control them than providing effective discipline and a structured and predictable home environment, and talking with them about how to resolve their feelings of loss. These active and disruptive boys certainly pose a behavior management problem for teachers and parents. However, before deciding that they have a neurologically based attention problem and managing them with medication, it is necessary to discern whether social factors may be causing the disruptive behavior instead. Specifically, it is necessary to assess whether (1) the child recently has suffered an important interpersonal loss, (2) there has been a lack of consistently effective discipline, and (3) the child is living in a disorganized home environment. When these three factors are in play, parents should consider the likelihood that the child is expressing an agitated depression or other behavior problem before accepting a diagnosis of attention deficit disorder, with or without hyperactivity, and beginning medication (virtually nothing is known about the long-term effects on children of stimulant medication). When these three social factors are operating—and in many cases they are—parents can do two things to help: (1) provide firm discipline, more adult supervision, and a structured home environment with predictable daily routines; and (2) provide regularly scheduled time with an emotionally responsive and affirming father. If the father is unable to provide this, an enduring relationship with an uncle, grandfather, or other nurturing male needs to be developed. Children also need to be told that it's not their fault that their father (or mother) does not spend time with them; it's their father's or mother's inability to be a good parent. Otherwise children internalize responsibility and blame themselves for the parental rejection and loss, and usually become depressed.

Gender Differences in Reactions to Divorce

Gender differences are found in every aspect of divorce. In this section, we will examine differences in husbands' and wives' perceptions about the divorce, differences in their parenting styles, and differences between boys' and girls' reactions to divorce and remarriage.

Perceptions of the Marriage

There is usually a poor match between men's and women's descriptions of their divorce. Former spouses do not share perceptions of who initiated the divorce, what was happening in the marriage and in the family before the breakup, or what event precipitated the breakup. Husbands and wives also have different complaints about what was wrong in the marriage.

Women are most likely to complain about men's inability to communicate. Wives wanted their husbands to talk more about themselves and their feelings and to be more affectionate and intimate. Divorced wives also were dissatisfied because of the lack of shared interests and activities. Disturbingly, many women complain of alcohol-related problems with their husbands and of being physically intimidated by them.

Men have a different list of complaints about the past marriage. Husbands' primary dissatisfaction is that their wives were always complaining and criticizing them. Men often depict their ex-wives as carping and nagging all the time. Although both men and women complain of sexual problems, their concerns are different. Men often complain about the infrequency of sexual relations, whereas women are dissatisfied because they wanted more affection. These differences in perceptions continue after the divorce. Mothers' reports of the quality and quantity of fathers' visitation with the children bear little resemblance to fathers' reports.

Another gender difference concerns men's and women's subsequent adjustment to divorce. In the years following the breakup, women often adjust better than men, who are at much greater risk of health problems, psychiatric admissions, and accidents. Women's success occurs, in part, because they are more effective than men in seeking and receiving emotional support to cope with the stresses engendered by the breakup, life as a single parent, and the many changes involved in the transition to remarriage and becoming a stepfamily.

Differences in Parenting

There are also important gender differences in parenting styles between custodial mothers and fathers, each having their own strengths and limitations. Custodial mothers and custodial fathers both seem to be warm and nurturing with younger children. However, mothers have more trouble effectively controlling their children—especially their sons—and with assigning household tasks and establishing expectations for responsible, independent behavior. In contrast, fathers do not communicate with children as effectively as mothers; in particular, they do not talk about themselves and share their own feelings or experiences very well. Children miss this self-disclosure, which allows them to know their parent as a person and to feel closer to them. Although fathers often discipline more effectively than mothers, they do not supervise their children's behavior and whereabouts as well as mothers. Fathers have the most difficulty monitoring the behavior of adolescents, in particular, keeping track of adolescent daughters' activities and companions.

Because mothers often have trouble disciplining their sons effectively, angry control battles frequently result. As a result, relationships between sons and divorced mothers are less close than in intact families. Further, these differences in closeness are found for sons but not for daughters. The lack of closeness between divorced mothers and sons is not just a difficult phase that passes with time, unfortunately, but continues into adulthood.

Boys' and Girls' Reactions to Divorce, Father Absence, and Remarriage

Researchers also find important gender differences for children. Over 85 percent of all children of divorce reside with a custodial mother. The problems caused by marital conflict, divorce, and life in the care of a single mother are more pervasive for boys than for girls. Boys in single-mother families have more long-term adjustment problems than girls in single-mother families and than children in intact homes. As noted earlier, younger boys tend to be more dependent and help-seeking, whereas older boys are more aggressive and disobedient. Compared to girls, boys in single-mother-headed homes exhibit more behavior problems at school and at home, have more trouble getting along with friends, and have poorer school achievement. Two years after the divorce, girls in mother-headed families tend to be as well-adjusted as girls in intact, two-parent homes. In contrast, there tends to be an increasingly widening gap between the behavior of boys in mother-headed homes and boys in two-parent homes.

How do we account for the fact that boys have more difficulty coping with divorce than girls? Researchers have found that, following the divorce, parents (1) give less effective discipline to boys and (2) direct more anger and criticism at boys. Let's examine these factors closely.

LESS-EFFECTIVE DISCIPLINE. Why do boys receive less-effective discipline than girls following divorce? Researchers have found that, on average, parents are more involved in disciplining the same-sex child than the opposite-sex child. That is, daughters tend to be disciplined more by their mothers than their fathers, and sons tend to be disciplined more by their fathers than their mothers. Thus, if the father is not actively involved in parenting after the divorce, the son loses his most important source of discipline. In contrast, because mothers usually retain custody, there is little or no loss of discipline for girls. Mother is there to set and enforce limits for her daughter, just as she has always done, but the father's absence often means that discipline is inconsistent for boys. This loss contributes to their aggressive and disobedient behavior following the divorce. As we explore in Chapter Ten, all children adjust better when parents provide effective discipline.

MORE ANGER. In addition to receiving less-consistent discipline after divorce, boys receive more criticism and anger from both of their parents than girls do. Contributing to the enduring lack of closeness between divorced mothers and sons, these critical responses are especially likely to come from mothers. In addition, parents do not protect boys as carefully as girls and buffer or shield them from conflict. As we saw in Chapter Five, for example, parents expose boys to more parental arguments and conflict than girls. Taken together, these factors contribute to sons' lowered self-esteem and problems with aggressive behavior.

Finally, we have seen that boys and girls feel anxious during the time of marital disruption and try to get adults to respond to their heightened emotional needs. For example, children might express this insecurity by saying, "Can I sit in your lap?" or "Read me one more story" or "Why can't I sleep with you tonight?" However, our culture's sex-role stereotypes tend to deny these needs in boys more than girls. Some fathers fear the dreaded label of "sissy" for their sons. However, these fathers have not learned that boys who grow up to feel more secure in their masculine identity have enjoyed an affirming and affectionate relationship with their fathers.

Until early adolescence, when mother–daughter conflict often increases markedly, there is more childrearing stress for single mothers with sons than with daughters. This tendency may also be true in intact families. The U.S. Bureau of the Census revealed that couples are 9 percent more likely to stay married if they have sons than if they have daughters. Because mothers are more apt than fathers to initiate divorces that involve children, mothers with sons may be less willing to divorce and raise them alone than mothers with daughters. Also, as we have seen, boys in both intact and divorced homes are less likely to obey their mothers than their fathers. Recent brain science has shown that boys are hardwired for more aggression and that they are biologically predisposed toward a higher activity level than girls. These innate factors, coupled with cultural norms that encourage boys to be more competitive and may allow them to be more aggressive, all combine to make it harder for mothers to nurture and discipline a disobedient and disruptive son. Thus *a negative cycle often begins in which sons become more angry toward and demanding of single mothers, and mothers feel increasingly helpless and resentful as their attempts to discipline fail.*

Further evidence of the greater difficulty in raising sons after divorce is found in sibling relationships. Researchers find more anger and conflict between sons, and between sons and daughters, than between sisters. Older daughters in divorced homes often take a teaching-caring role with younger sisters and get along with them better. Perhaps these differences occur because boys, on average, are temperamentally more difficult and because girls are socialized to be more cooperative and empathic. For these and other reasons, however, boys need to be effectively disciplined, to be shown consistency and order, and to be nurtured. Single mothers caught in these negative cycles with sons can often regain control through parenting classes that teach them behavior management skills. These might include using time-out effectively and knowing how to employ natural consequences—techniques that can help them discipline more effectively. Effective parenting skills are essential if mothers raising sons on their own are to feel confident and to take charge. Children do not respect their mothers or their fathers when parents cannot take charge and effectively enforce the rules they set. In turn, children do not feel safe to disclose their concerns or allow parents to comfort them until they are secure that the parent, not the child, is in charge of the family.

These gender differences become even more complex, however. In Chapter Eleven, for example, we will see that boys tend to adjust positively to the introduction of an emotionally responsive stepfather, whereas girls often struggle with this new addition. Further, the gender differences observed between boys and girls change as children grow into adolescence. Divorce is harder for young boys than girls, but when girls reach adolescence, conflict often escalates between single mothers and daughters to match the level of conflict between boys and mothers. In addition to mother–daughter conflict, adolescent girls are likely to develop problems in dating and heterosexual relations if their father has not been actively involved in their lives. Problems are especially likely to develop if parents have not continued to closely monitor and actively supervise adolescent girls. The best solution to all of these problems, for boys and girls at every age, is firm discipline and overtly expressed affection from both their mothers and their fathers.

Fathering After Divorce

Divorce changes the father's parenting role and involvement more than it changes the mother's role. Some fathers who were effective parents before the divorce fall away; others rise to the occasion and become more capable and involved than they were before the breakup. As researchers learn more about children and divorce, it is becoming clear that frequency of visits with father does not predict child adjustment very well, but the quality of parenting he provides does. Long-term adjustment is enhanced when fathers are not just "friends" or "tour guide" parents but maintain a real parenting relationship. That is, they discipline their children, criticize inappropriate behavior, monitor what their children are doing, exert control over who they are with, help them with their homework, and participate in a variety of daily activities. Although some men are effective fathers after divorce, many others struggle with the role of part-time parent. First, we examine several styles of fathering that are common but ineffective and then consider steps that divorced fathers can take to become more effectively involved with their children.

Problematic Fathering Styles

There are many different types of fathers, of course, but problematic fathering often falls into one of three categories. In this section, we will examine the widely known father who is simply irresponsible, a less-well-known father who is immobilized after the breakup, and perhaps the most important problem, the superficial father who becomes only a friend.

THE IRRESPONSIBLE FATHER. Many view the father as the bad guy. His new single life is often romanticized. He is characterized as someone having fun, chasing younger women, and shedding childrearing demands while the mother has to stay at home and deal with her son's anger because the father has left. This scenario certainly occurs sometimes. Some divorced fathers are irresponsible and simply too selfish to fulfill their childrearing responsibilities.

When this is the case, children should be made aware of it. Rather than allowing promises of continuing involvement to be broken, mothers and fathers should tell children that the other parent is leaving and will not be back in any regular or dependable fashion. It is not in the child's best interest to keep unrealistic hopes alive of someday being close to the father (or mother). Although this is a harsh reality to present to children, it should not be avoided. Unfulfilled promises engender lifelong feelings of distrust and disillusion. Although well-intended, it is problematic when the mother tries to protect the father or the children from the consequences of the father's behavior by making excuses or misleading the children by supporting unrealistic hopes and expectations.

In a related fashion, some fathers promise involvement with their children but fail to follow through regularly on their commitments. This pattern of unreliability is often associated with alcohol or substance abuse. Although infrequent contact is easier for children to adjust to than total rejection, inconsistent visiting patterns are highly problematic. Children suffer when they are repeatedly disappointed. Further, young children's egocentric thinking leads them to assume responsibility for their father's unavailability and blame themselves. It is heartbreaking to listen to children tell you it's their fault that their father doesn't see them regularly because, in so many words, they are somehow lacking or unlovable ("There must be something wrong with me or Dad would want to see me"). This type of in-and-out father, who promises a relationship but routinely disappoints, often precipitates depression, low self-esteem, and school failure in children. It is wrenching to watch as children's repeated attempts to elicit his involvement fail.

As noted earlier, when fathers are rejecting or fail to follow through responsibly, mothers and grandparents can communicate to the child that this is a shortcoming or limitation in the father's ability to love and be a parent; it is not a reflection of the child's basic worth or lovableness. It is necessary to have an ongoing dialogue about this painful situation or children will return to this false belief and feel that they are somehow lacking, have some essential defect, or have done something wrong that drove their father away. For boys in particular, long-term relationships with father surrogates must be found, either through organizations like Big Brothers, the YMCA, Boy Scouts, church members or family friends, or especially, uncles and grandfathers. Whenever possible, mothers should try to recruit emotionally responsive men as camp counselors, coaches, karate and guitar instructors, and especially, teachers. Mothers raising sons alone should go to great lengths to select teachers who combine clearly defined rules and regularly enforced limits, warmth and encouragement, and expectations for mature responsible behavior. Permissive or disorganized teachers fail disastrously with these boys.

THE IMMOBILIZED FATHER. For other reasons, a very different kind of father also chooses to relinquish contact with his children following the divorce. Most people are not aware of this counterpart to the irresponsible, abandoning father described previously. Researchers have found another group of fathers who were loving and concerned parents before the divorce but found it too painful to continue their involvement with their children afterward. In some cases, their former wives had aligned the children with her and against him. These mothers cast the father as the bad guy or the enemy and may enlist the children as spies on the father's sexual activities ("Did she sleep over again last night?").

In other cases, these previously responsible fathers are unable to tolerate visiting their children in another man's home, seeing their children on a part-time basis with regular good-byes, or experiencing the children's angry feelings toward them. Rather than continuing to be hurt by these situations, these fathers exit from their role as a parent. The majority of noncustodial fathers who try to remain responsible parents report repeated frustrations and sorrow as a result of the visitation. However, it is especially hard for children to lose a relationship that previously had been good: there are better ways for fathers to cope than withdrawal. A counselor or support group that appreciates the very real obstacles the immobilized father is contending with can help. With support, many of these fathers can manage their sadness and helplessness more effectively and continue to provide the quality parenting they did before the divorce.

Children are faced with a very difficult problem when fathers do not maintain their parental relationship. It is far easier for a child to adjust to a change in the frequency of contact with a parent than it is to adjust to the end of a relationship. The termination of a relationship is akin to a death; children must cope with the sadness and helplessness of their unwanted loss. Psychological problems are far more likely to develop for the child who loses a relationship with a parent, even if others do not believe the departing parent and child were especially close before the divorce. If the father (or mother) does choose to exit, the help of a child psychologist, pastoral counselor, or family therapist can often help the child cope more successfully.

THE SUPERFICIAL FATHER.   The irresponsible father and the immobilized father represent only a minority of divorced men. What about the larger majority of fathers who have become minimally involved in their children's lives? In the aftermath of divorce, most nonresidential fathers develop a friendly, egalitarian, but superficial relationship with their children. Giving up on being a real parent, they try to be just friends with their children and share enjoyable times together. Reluctant to risk disciplining their children, they avoid the conflict inherent in a real parenting relationship and do not attempt to monitor or shape their children's behavior. It's sad to see the opportunity for more significant and formative relationships lost as fathers become just friends. Let's explore why so many father–child relationships become disengaged like this and lose the real meaning and power they could hold.

Perhaps the primary reason so few fathers take an active part in raising their children—both before the divorce and afterward—is their socialization into narrow and restrictive gender roles. Many men question whether they have anything important to offer their children and doubt their competence as a parent. Many men grew up spending little time with their fathers and infrequently talking to them about what mattered in their lives or listening to their fathers share what was important to them. For many, as a result, it feels awkward and foreign to try and respond to the emotional needs of a young child who seems so vulnerable and carries such big feelings. Further, many men and women in our society still believe that children innately belong more to their mothers than to their fathers. This lack of identification with the parental role serves to keep many men from fully participating in childrearing. We have already seen that many new mothers benefit from the culture of women that offers support and information to help them assume the mothering role more successfully. In contrast, few men enjoy this powerful social support that facilitates the transition to parenthood. As a result of these cultural influences, childrearing responsibilities are left primarily to the mother, who is under a different set of even greater social pressures. Following the breakup she is expected to take primary custody of the children, even if she wants to share childrearing more fully or allow the father to assume primary custody. Fortunately, it is often relatively easy to increase the father's involvement and improve family life for everyone.

In one study, therapists met with divorcing fathers for only a few counseling sessions aimed at encouraging fathers' continued parenting involvement. These therapists helped fathers see that they still had an important role to play in their children's lives and much to contribute to their development. Of special importance, the therapists also helped them establish concrete plans and specific schedules for visitation and living arrangements that would ensure regular father–child contact. This short-term counseling was highly successful. Most of these fathers were still actively involved with their children five years later. This high level of sustained participation is very different from the usual low level of father–child contact. With only a few hours of encouragement, coupled with planning weekly schedules for being with their children, these men stayed in their children's lives. The benefits of this involvement were clearly reflected in their children's successful adjustment. The message is clear: mothers, fathers, and children all benefit when fathers are encouraged to be actively involved parents.

Helping Divorced Fathers Become More Involved Parents

Traditional childrearing roles are inadequate. Their failings are most evident in postdivorce family relationships; far too many fathers are too disengaged, and too many mothers are burdened by the overwhelming demands of single parenting. What can be done to provide children with the fathering and mothering they need?

Parents' answers to this question usually cast blame. If you ask a divorced mother why the father is uninvolved in parenting, a typical reply is, "I've done everything I can to keep him involved with the kids, but he doesn't want anything to do with them. He never has. The kids don't really want to visit him either. They only go because I tell them they have to. Actually, they would rather just stay home with their friends."

In sharp contrast, if you ask divorced fathers why they are disengaged, they predictably respond this way:

> She makes it really hard for me to be with the children. It's little things, like being late whenever I go to pick them up or encouraging them to do something "more important" than being with me—like going to a birthday party. I don't think she's ever wanted me to have my own relationship with the kids. Like she told the attorneys, she believes that children just ought to be with their mothers. Even when we were married, she would criticize me when I tried to do something with the kids and tell me the "right" way to do it. And now I get squeezed the other way, too. My new wife resents the money I send and complains that I give in to my ex-wife too easily. She thinks I should be "stronger" and stand up to her more . . . after awhile, it just feels impossible.

Both sides have legitimate concerns, but these radically differing viewpoints reflect poor communication between angry ex-spouses and the inevitable polarization caused by mutually exclusive and competing childrearing roles. Arguments over mothers' and fathers' rights should cease so children can have a dependable relationship with both parents that includes frequent, regularly scheduled, and conflict-free access to both their mother and their father. There are many practical ways to achieve this.

The most loving gift that divorcing parents can give their children is permission to be as close to the other parent as to themselves. Parents need to disentangle their own lingering hostility toward the former spouse from the child's need for a continuing relationship with the other parent. Grandparents can help by not taking sides against their former son- or daughter-in-law. Instead, they can help their grandchildren by discouraging both parents from embroiling children in parental battles and divisive loyalty conflicts. Friends can support the father's role as a parent by emphasizing the importance of his contribution to his children's lives and the importance of his children to the quality of his life. A new woman in a man's life can support his efforts to remain involved with his children and not misinterpret this commitment as a threatening tie to his former wife.

Others outside the immediate circle of family and friends can also help. Counselors and mediators can help divorcing parents make specific plans for custody and access arrangements, beginning at the time of separation, that ensure fathers' active parenting role. Teachers can reach out to divorced fathers by personally inviting them to attend parent–teacher conferences and other school-related activities and by mailing report cards and school notices to both parents. As employers in other industrialized nations already do, employers in the United States must begin to recognize that the most important job for every citizen is childrearing and provide the flexible work schedules that families need.

Family law attorneys have a moral obligation to educate litigious parents about the likely after-effects of the adversarial court process. This includes the substantial financial costs to the family and potential for bankruptcy, the further-diminished capacity for parents to cooperate in the years ahead, and the great likelihood that the final divorce decree will very closely match the pretrial settlement proposals. Family law attorneys also need to discourage clients from fighting over children in court whenever possible. They should seek mediated settlements whenever possible and impress upon clients that whenever one parent "wins" in court, the children lose, not the former spouse. Judges may examine their own sex-role biases and recognize that children belong equally to their mothers and their fathers. Parenting plans and schedules have to be tailored flexibly to fit the differing circumstances of each family, but they need to ensure that both parents have an active parenting role.

Many fathers recognize and welcome their continuing responsibility to care for their children after divorce. Some fathers who were not especially involved before the divorce can use this family crisis to change and take a more significant role in their children's lives. The crisis of divorce certainly holds much pain, but it also holds the potential for change. Without the concerted efforts suggested earlier, however, many fathers will not be able to maintain an effective parenting role on their own. The crisis surrounding the breakup provides an opportunity for everyone to change and begin working together to ensure that children have both a mother and a father in the aftermath of divorce.

Suggestions for Further Reading

Still a Dad: The Divorced Father's Journey (S. Prengel, Mission, 1999) captures the experience of being a part-time father and offers encouragement and practical advice to divorcing fathers. *The Single Parent Resource Book* (B. Noel, Champion, 1998) and *The Single Parent's Almanac* (L. Foust, Prima, 1996) help mothers and fathers find the resources they need to cope effectively in the aftermath of divorce.

Chapter Seven

Custody, Mediation, and the Courts

"What Kind of Mother Am I if My Kids Miss Their Dad When They're Spending Time with Me?"

There are two principles to guide parents in determining access arrangements: (1) provide continuity in a child's relationships with both parents and (2) shield children from exposure to marital conflict. With these two goals in mind, parents can establish many different kinds of parenting plans, each with its own strengths and limitations. In most cases, mediation is a far better way to negotiate custody arrangements than litigation. Nevertheless, because custody and access arrangements may be decided in court, I'll begin by briefly reviewing the history of these arrangements.

The History of Custody Determination

In earlier times, surprisingly, the law favored fathers as exclusive custodial parents and only later shifted in favor of the mother. The present confusion over custody arrangements arises from another shift, as the legal system attempts to find a new middle ground for determining shared responsibility. Custody adjudication is still in a period of flux. The traditional means of deciding on custody matters continue to change, but definitive guidelines for today's parents have not yet fully emerged.

Throughout the eighteenth and nineteenth centuries, American and British judges awarded custody solely to the father. This preference was grounded in the economic reality that fathers were better able to provide for the children financially. Court decrees came to romanticize the father's benevolent role by including such assertions as, "Only a father's special love for his children can provide. . . . "

Economic and social changes began to influence this legal bias at the beginning of the twentieth century. By 1900 the United States had shifted from a farming nation to an industrial society. As the labor force became mobile and moved from the farm to factories in the cities, the support provided by an extended family of grandparents, uncles, and aunts was lost and replaced by a more isolated—and vulnerable—nuclear family. Gender roles became more distinct and polarized, as fathers became the primary wage-earners in the factory, and mothers became the primary child-care providers in the home. At this point the mother's importance in nurturing and caring for children began to be revered, just as the father's had in the previous century.

By 1900, mothers were seen as possessing an inherent nurturing ability (maternal instinct)—an orientation toward children that made them more effective than fathers in bringing up children. The idea gradually evolved that children suffered irreparable damage if separated from their mothers during the formative tender years of early childhood. This "tender years doctrine" then emerged as the legal basis for supporting the mother as the preferred custodial parent.

From 1900 to the mid-1970s, the legal preference for maternal custody prevailed, and the father was viewed as a breadwinner with no direct childrearing role. Mothers were granted custody of children, and fathers were issued alternate weekend visitation rights, required to make long-term alimony payments to mothers, and provide child support to "the family."

These arrangements did not work well. They discouraged fathers from taking an active, part-time parenting role and overloaded mothers with the demands of single parenting. Further, it became clear that when fathers did not have an active relationship with their children, they were less likely to keep up child-support payments, placing an additional economic burden on mothers and children. These failings, along with the growth of the women's movement, the growing recognition that the "tender years" doctrine is a social bias rather than a biological predisposition, the adoption of no-fault divorce in most states, and research findings on the positive effects of father's involvement have all led to a new era in custody and access arrangements.

The current transition has been to replace the tender years doctrine with "best interests of the child" statutes. Although it is difficult, if not impossible, for courts to determine objectively what is in a child's best interest, this approach has supported fathers' more active role in childrearing and has addressed the earlier concern that bias in favor of the mother constituted sex discrimination. In the 1980s, these factors led courts toward joint custody arrangements as a potentially better answer to the complex and often painful issues of custody determination.

Joint legal custody and more equally shared parenting plans have solved some problems and created new ones. These plans have provided a beneficial new middle ground that encourages both parents' participation in raising their children. However, joint custody and equal access arrangements are no panacea for the significant problems that divorce arouses. Joint custody will not work for many families, especially if parents are combative. Later in the chapter we will evaluate the pros and cons of this frequently misunderstood arrangement, as well as the effects on children of other custody and access (visitation) schedules.

Throughout this book I make suggestions for divorcing parents based on well-documented research on children and divorce. We now know a great deal about the different factors that cause healthy versus problem-ridden adjustment to divorce. In contrast, much less is known about the effects of different custody and access arrangements on children. Some research in this area has been completed, and further studies are under way, but important questions about the effects of different plans are only partially answered. In this section I want to share the information and guidelines that are now available, but readers should know that there is less factually supported information in this area than in others covered in this book.

There are no easy answers to the profound dilemmas of custody determination when the stakes are so high. Parents must begin this process knowing that the most thoughtfully constructed parenting plan will be imperfect and have limitations. Nor is there an established formula for divorcing couples; what has worked well for one family may cause problems for another. Thus parents need to tailor specific plans to fit their own individual circumstances. As years go by, parents need to be flexible and revise these plans to meet the changing needs of their children. A divorce mediator usually can offer parents a great deal of help in establishing effective parenting plans and resolving custody disputes.

Finally, the language used in child custody statutes is problematic and often threatens parental power and identity. The terms *custody, visitation, sole custody,* and even *joint custody* connote ownership of children and reflect the adversarial court process from which these terms have been derived. For example, children do not leave their homes with their mothers to visit their fathers. His children are equally at home at his house; they are not visitors who really belong to their custodial mothers, as this language suggests. In 1991, British courts acknowledged the power of language to invalidate a parent's role and discarded these weighted terms. Instead of making custody and visitation orders, British courts now use more neutral terms and make a "contact order" and a "residence order." American courts are also changing, and terms such as *residential parent* instead of *custodial parent* and *access parent* instead of *visiting parent* are coming into use in most states. There is great significance in this choice of language.

Joint Legal and Physical Custody

Around 1980 many states began enacting legislation that encouraged frequent and continuing contact with both parents. "Joint legal custody," in which children have a primary residence but parents share responsibility for making important decisions, is often the preferred arrangement. Joint custody is a beneficial new approach that works well for most cooperative parents, and it can succeed if parents, who may not get along well with each other, are able to shield children from parental conflict. Too often, however, courts have applied this arrangement erroneously to embattled couples, for whom it fails disastrously.

Joint custody has also been widely misunderstood. The principal misunderstanding about joint custody is the confusion between *joint legal custody* (shared responsibility for important decisions regarding children) and *joint physical custody* (visitation or access schedules). Joint custody does not mean a fifty-fifty split in which former spouses are bound by law to equally share the time spent with their children. Nor do children have to move between two homes on alternate weeks, or for alternate six-month stays, or any other rigid enforcement of equal time. Joint legal custody simply legally defines both parents as having equal power and authority in making decisions affecting their children (for example, education, medical care, religious affiliation, general welfare). By giving parents this equal role, joint legal custody validates both the father's and the mother's continued parental role and encourages both parents to remain actively involved in the children's lives.

Within this joint legal framework, parents can then make any physical custody plans (access arrangements or visitation schedules) they wish. Some parents may wish to fully share child care on a fifty-fifty basis; most do not. Again, although many different coparenting arrangements are possible, the guiding principle in all determinations should be (1) continuity of child–parent relationships and (2) protection of children from exposure to parental conflict.

Patterns of Coparenting Arrangements

Among the different kinds of coparenting arrangements, researchers have found that residential parents with primary physical custody (either sole legal custody or joint legal custody) are more satisfied with living arrangements than noncustodial or outside parents with whom the children only visit. When some type of shared parenting arrangements have been made, and children spend a significant amount of time in both households, the arrangement usually falls into one of three different patterns of coparenting.

First, about one-fourth of divorcing parents maintain the mutually supportive and nonconfrontational coparenting relationships that are so advantageous to children and to parents. These parents are able to work together in the child's best interest, and they successfully isolate their problems with each other from their functions as parents. These cooperative parents also make plans for their children, discuss children's problems, attempt to enforce similar rules between households and, most important, back up each other's parenting. Joint legal custody and some type of shared parenting arrangements are ideal for these harmonious couples. These parents disprove the widely held myth that an unworkable marriage can only result in an unworkable parenting relationship.

Second, the majority of shared parenting couples are disengaged from each other but not combative. These parents seldom talk to their former spouses and do not attempt to coordinate activities and rules between households. To their credit, however, they manage the logistics of visitation with little conflict, and children do not see their parents argue or undermine each other. In most cases, these parents have made plans to exchange the children at times and places in which they do not have to see each other or interact (for example, at school but not at home). Children often adjust well in these families, even when parents may go a year or longer without speaking to each other. Research suggests that parents are more likely to be successfully disengaged from each other—in effect, parallel parents—if children are older. It seems to be harder for parents to achieve this neutrality if children are under the age of six.

Coparenting arrangements are ideally suited for cooperative parents and usually work well for disengaged parents with little communication or conflict. In the third category, however, about one-quarter of divorced couples remain gridlocked in high levels of bitter, ongoing conflict that continue to be toxic for parents and children alike. Shared parenting arrangements pose significant problems for their children. These parents do not cooperate or communicate well and, what is more important, their wrangling spills over into their parenting. They argue in front of the children when they make exchanges, threaten to go back to court or take the children away from each other, criticize or undermine the other parent's relationship with the children, sabotage his or her attempts to visit, pressure children to take sides or carry messages between embattled parents, and so forth. These parents often vent their competitiveness, hostility, and high need for control through litigation, and their children suffer mightily as a result. About 15 percent are embroiled in ongoing court battles, and they have the most poorly adjusted children of divorce. Research suggests that family size may be one factor related to higher levels of interparental conflict. Parents find it easier to avoid conflict if they have only one child, but discord seems harder to avoid if they have three or more children.

Shared parenting plans engender distress in the children of embattled parents. Researchers have found that the more days children share with embattled parents the more likely they are to be described by their parents as depressed, withdrawn, and uncommunicative. They are also more likely to have somatic symptoms such as headaches, stomachaches, and sleep disturbances. Parents also reported acting-out symptoms, such as aggressiveness. What parenting plans are better suited for parents who cannot stop fighting?

Shared parenting arrangements should not be established in these families. Instead, sole legal custody and primary physical custody should be given to the parent who provides the children with the *least contested access* to the other parent. In other words, courts now give preference to the parent who is most willing to allow ample and unconflicted visitation to the other parent (known in the legal system as "friendly parent" provisions). If neither parent is more cooperative, the guideline is to give primary physical custody to the parent with more effective parenting or childrearing skills.

The courts usually rely on psychological evaluations to make both of these determinations. If neither parent is evaluated as more adept at childrearing or better at facilitating the child's relationship with the other parent, two options can be followed. Children can be placed with the same-sex parent and given flexible visitation schedules with the other parent. This often works well with older children, especially teenagers who usually prefer to live in one residence and with the same-sex parent. Or sole legal and primary physical custody can be given to each parent in alternate years. This allows both parents to remain involved, but they do not have to cooperate or interact about decisions for the child. Alternate-year transitions will be disruptive for some children, of course, but far less problematic than leaving them exposed to their parents' continuing battles.

I encourage most cooperative parents, as well as disengaged parents who can manage their distaste for each other responsibly, to establish joint legal custody with some type of shared parenting arrangements, although not necessarily equal-time visitation schedules. Joint custody serves the goal of working for the best interest of the child. It helps assuage children's sadness and their feelings of powerlessness by increasing access to both parents.

When parents can provide continuity of relationships without exposing children to parental power struggles, many different physical access plans can be successful. Often, divorcing parents become too focused on the number of hours the child spends with each parent every week and miss the bigger point that the access schedules themselves are less important than the degree of tension and parental conflict in children's lives. That is, the interparental attitude of cooperation or hostility is far more important to children's adjustment than the specific schedule established, which will need to be revised regularly anyway. Grandparents, attorneys, or new partners shouldn't be allowed to make parents lose sight of this or to become invested in winning or getting even. With this in mind, let's review the different visitation or access schedules that are possible.

EQUAL TIME. Some divorcing parents want to share equal time with their children and are committed to following through with this responsibility over the years. Although the courts have now made this option available to many, most parents do not choose this fifty-fifty split; if the father (or mother) is willing to accommodate his work schedule and wants equal time with the children, however, the request is often granted. The three primary types of equal-time arrangements are (1) split week or alternate weeks, (2) alternating years, and (3) shared home. When a court makes an equal-time order, split week or alternate weeks is most common.

SPLIT-WEEK AND ALTERNATE-WEEKS ARRANGEMENTS. A common equal-time arrangement is for the child to alternate between the parental homes. Younger children may split each week with three and one-half days at each home. Children eight years and older usually want to reduce the number of transitions and prefer to alternate every other week. One concern with this access schedule is the potentially negative effects on young children of repeated separations from their primary caregiver. However, children form multiple attachments when they have several responsive caregivers.

Because children can form secure attachment bonds to more than one caregiver, a separation from one parent is not so stressful when followed by a reunion with the other. The strength of this shared access arrangement is that it allows children to maintain a close relationship with both parents.

The drawbacks of this arrangement are the increased number of transitions and reduced day-to-day consistency in the child's life. Some robust children can flexibly cope with the transitions that accompany equal-time arrangements; others find them too disruptive and require the stability of a primary residence. Parents want to tailor access arrangements to fit the varying temperaments and personality styles of each child (and remember that their child's needs will change over time).

When will the split-week arrangement fail, and when will it succeed? This arrangement is best for harmonious couples. Because it requires more parental cooperation, it should not be adopted if it will increase children's exposure to parental conflict. Joint physical custody and equal-time arrangements are problematic for children when parents cannot refrain from arguing with each other, when they regularly criticize the other parent to the children, or when they pressure children to take sides or choose between parents. That is, shared parenting arrangements will not succeed unless angry ex-spouses can separate the marital dimension of their relationship from the parental dimension, manage their conflicts responsibly, and shield children from parental wrangling. Also, in order for split-week arrangements to succeed, the child must have the flexibility to make frequent transitions and adjust to two different households. Children vary widely in their ability to do this. Some can do it readily; others cannot.

Too often, combative couples have been encouraged by courts and mediators to adopt joint physical custody to end their battle—to the detriment of their children. If parents cannot agree to interact without conflict, equal-time arrangements are problematic for children. If tensions between parents remain high or children are exposed to ongoing litigation, sole legal custody and primary residence should be given to (first) the most cooperative parent, (second) the most capable caregiver, or (third) the same-sex parent. Too often, the difficult decision on a primary residence has been avoided by establishing an equal-time arrangement. Although this keeps parents from feeling they have "lost," it does not work very well for children.

In order for the split-week or alternate-weeks arrangements to succeed, parents need to live near each other, and the child must continue to attend the same school. The split-week arrangement does not usually work as well for children under seven or eight, who often feel confused; they can't quite grasp their place or where they belong. Better suited for school-aged children, this equally shared visitation arrangement will make sense to eight- to thirteen-year-olds because they are oriented toward fairness. In harmonious divorces, it is usually helpful to let children participate in choosing the pattern of movement between the two parental homes rather than imposing a visitation schedule on them. This suggestion follows from the general principle that, as children grow older, parents should give them more control over access arrangements whenever possible.

Older children usually benefit from being able to participate in decisions about living arrangements—it empowers them. In families with high parental tensions and loyalty conflicts, however, this involvement only engenders further anxiety for children. Children never want to be put in the wrenching position of having to take sides or risk hurting or alienating a parent by expressing their preferences. Empowering children by including them in discussions about access plans only helps when parents have made it safe for children to express what they really want. Finally, most adolescents need a safe harbor, and they usually choose a primary residence. By mid-adolescence, many of these teenagers will wish to live with the parent of their same gender, and parents are wise to heed this preference.

Alternate-Year Arrangements. If parents cannot live near each other, they may establish an alternate-year(s) arrangement for school-aged children. For example, the child might live with the mother the first year or two and then move to the father's home for the same period. Because it is less disruptive to friendship networks, most children prefer to alternate between parental homes every two years. Although children have to change schools every year or two, adjustment is easier for some children than losing a primary relationship with one parent. Each year, children should have frequent and regularly scheduled time with the parent they are not living with—for example, at Christmas and spring breaks, and eight to ten weeks each summer. As before, some resilient children cope well with this plan; others cannot maintain or reestablish friendships.

Although the alternate-year arrangement does not require as much interparental contact as the split-week–alternate-week schedule, the parents need to be able to cooperate—or at least remain neutral or disengaged from each other—for this plan to work. Joint physical custody and equal-time, shared-visitation arrangements work best when former spouses support each other as parents; they fail when they increase children's exposure to parental battles. In addition, they do not work for children who are shy, who make friends and warm up to new situations slowly, or who need more stability and routine in their lives (for example, a child with a learning disability or attention deficit disorder). Further, what works for a child at one stage often will not work at another—parents need to be prepared to make ongoing modifications.

Parents are often more familiar with the split-week and alternate-week schedules than the alternate-year schedule. Next we'll examine the case study of Robby, which illustrates how the alternate-year arrangement can work well for some families.

Robby

One day Rob returned home from work to find that his wife, Clair, and his seven-year-old son, Robby, had packed their things and moved out. Clair had left a note saying she was sorry but she couldn't stay in the marriage any longer, and it was just too painful to leave any other way. She informed Rob that she was moving back in with her parents in a nearby city and taking their son with her, and she would call him soon. Rob exploded in outrage. Nothing on earth was going to stop him from getting his son back.

The next six months were confusing and painful for everyone. Rob and Clair actually had moments when reconciliation seemed possible, but Clair was becoming increasingly interested in having her own life, and Rob could not forgive her for walking out like that. Things were tough for Robby, too. He was very upset about moving away from his father and often felt sad and tearful. Even though it was hard for Clair to see Robby miss his father so much, she still believed that young children should live with their mothers, and her own parents were supporting this view. Rob disagreed wholeheartedly, to say the least, and believed Robby should be with him. He had always been an involved parent, and after Clair's destructive exit, it was very clear to him that he could provide much more stability in Robby's life than Clair. For the divorce settlement, both parents had hired lawyers and psychologists to argue that each was the better parent and should have primary physical custody of Robby.

Although the attorneys advocated strongly for their respective clients, and strategically highlighted the personality and parenting flaws of the other parent, the judge realistically assessed the family situation. Despite Clair's troubling departure, both she and Rob were fit parents who could provide Robby with loving homes. The judge hoped to keep both of these well-intended parents in their child's life and thought joint legal custody with an alternate-year, shared visitation schedule could succeed. Although both parents initially felt they were "losing" with this arrangement, Robby stood to gain the most. The judge suspended the adversarial hearings, which would soon destroy any possibility of Rob and Clair ever working together for Robby, until they attempted to resolve their dispute through a court-ordered divorce mediator.

After six sessions with the mediator, both parents relinquished their opening positions and agreed to a shared parenting plan. They agreed to share joint legal custody of Robby, which met Rob's need to be guaranteed that Clair, or her parents, would never be able to take his son away. Robby's mother would have primary physical custody of him the first year, and he would be enrolled in a local school where his mother lived. Robby would spend two weekends a month (pick up Robby after school on Friday and return him to school Monday morning), Christmas vacation, spring vacation, and eight weeks in the summer with his father. After one year, Robby would move back to his father's home, enroll in school there, and have the same visitation schedule with his mother that he had with his father. At the end of this two-year period, they would meet again with the mediator to evaluate the plan and modify it as necessary.

Although the rules were a little different at his mother's than at his father's house, Robby knew what was expected of him at each home. Robby's parents were also able to let him know that they loved him and wanted him very much. Although Rob remained angry at Clair for leaving him and trying to take Robby away, he knew that Robby loved his mother and missed her when they were apart. Rob would certainly never trust Clair again, but they were able to separate their hurt and distrust toward each other from their parenting relationship with Robby. As a result Robby adjusted securely. The sadness and withdrawal that were evident in Robby's behavior when his parents separated went away as he saw he could remain close and involved with both of his parents.

After trying one year with each parent, Robby did not want to switch schools again. To Rob's and Clair's credit, they made it safe for him to say what he wanted and put his needs ahead of their own. Although Robby loved being with his Dad, he asked if he could live in one home with his Mother so he could stay close to his friends. Rob was able to accept this huge disappointment and remained actively involved with Robby for the next three years maintaining the previous visiting schedule. When Robby was thirteen, however, he again asked for a change. He now wanted to move back to his Dad's house in order to attend the same high school for all four years. This was heartbreaking for Clair, but she could see that now, as a teenager, Robby really wanted to be with his Dad. Thanks to his parents' flexibility, Robby was a well-adjusted young man, still close to both of his parents, when he graduated four years later.

SHARED HOUSE. Some media attention has been given to the situation in which children remain in the same house, and their divorced parents periodically move in and out. This visitation arrangement is not suitable for most families on a long-term basis and is so rare as to hardly bear mentioning. Unfortunately, however, this situation has been used at times to ridicule the concept of joint custody. This prejudice reflects the widespread confusion over *joint legal custody* (which encourages both parents' continuing role in the child's life) versus *access schedules* (which vary flexibly).

Finally, a frequent concern of parents about all of these different equal-time and shared parenting plans is whether children will have difficulty adjusting to two households with different rules and schedules. Several studies suggest that by the time they are school age, children can adjust well to alternating between dissimilar parental homes as long as there is consistency *within* each home. In order to succeed with any of the shared parenting plans described, parents can follow these guidelines:

- Cooperate and support each other concerning the children or at least be able to shield children from parental tensions.
- Establish a predictable schedule for alternating between residences that children can count on and plan for (some older

children can have more flexible schedules, but dependable routines are usually best).

- Establish as much consistency of the rules as possible within each of the two parental homes.

Children adjust well when there are clearly defined but different rules between the two households on such practices as bedtimes, mealtimes, and acceptable behavior. Children have difficulty when the rules and expectations are not clearly laid out and reliably enforced by each parent in each respective home. Remember, lax discipline is common and is especially problematic for children of divorce.

Primary Physical Custody to One Parent

Parents can also establish joint legal custody without adopting the equal-time living arrangements just described. In the large majority of families, parents choose to have the mother retain primary physical custody and the father to take a part-time parenting role. Many different living arrangements are possible when one parent (either father or mother) assumes primary physical custody.

Paternal Custody

In recent years, increasing attention has been given to fathers who seek custody. However, the increased number of men who seek primary custody reflects the increased number of divorces, not an increased percentage of fathers seeking custody. Almost nine out of ten children of divorce still end up living with their mothers, but when fathers seek primary physical custody, they obtain it about half the time. Fathers who seek primary physical custody are more likely to be the parents of school-aged and adolescent children than of preschoolers and younger children.

What are the effects on children of living with their father? Researchers have found that children living with their custodial fathers are as well-adjusted as those living in their mothers' custody. Just as with mothers, child adjustment depends on (1) the father's ability to parent effectively (that is, to provide nurturance, effective discipline, and an orderly household routine) and (2) his ability to support the child's relationship with the mother.

Perhaps the most important research finding about maternal versus paternal custody is the interaction between custodial status and gender of the children. Although only a few studies have been conducted, researchers have consistently found that school-aged children tend to be better adjusted when they live with the same-sex parent. Both boys and girls have more problems with aggressive behavior and lower self-esteem when they are living with the opposite-sex parent. However, sons in father-custody homes are also less communicative and affectionate, perhaps as a result of less exposure to female expressiveness. On average, however, boys tend to adjust better than girls in father-custody homes, and girls tend to adjust better than boys in mother-custody homes. If both the mother and the father want primary physical custody and equal-time, alternate visitation is not satisfactory, parents should consider this same-sex advantage, along with other variables noted in this chapter. A continuing relationship between a child and the same-sex parent seems to be very important.

Although parents should consider this same-sex advantage in their custody deliberations, it is not the key dimension. A more important finding is that, regardless of which parent has primary physical custody, *child adjustment is determined by the parenting ability of the primary caregiver.* In both mother- and father-custody families, children of both sexes are best adjusted when parents are affectionate toward them, set and enforce clear rules, and encourage communication. These effective childrearing practices are clarified in Chapter Ten.

Maternal Custody

Most divorced fathers do not seek primary physical custody or equal-time arrangements, and over 85 percent of children live with their mothers in the years following the breakup. Most parents still want the mother to have primary physical custody and the father to establish a schedule for being with their children. However, many of these parents can establish joint legal custody to validate the father's role and encourage his full parental participation and financial support after the divorce. Within this joint legal custody framework, the mother has primary physical custody and parents establish a schedule for the father to be with the children that fits their circumstances. Useful guidelines are available to help parents establish these parenting plans.

General Guidelines for Living Arrangements

Clearly, widely differing custody and visitation arrangements are available, and parents' task is to sort through them and determine the arrangements that best fit their family. Whatever parenting plans are agreed upon, their success ultimately depends on how they are implemented—not the specific number of hours the child spends with each parent. This section provides important guidelines that will shape the success or failure of whatever plans have been adopted.

Regularity

Although spontaneity and informality are often appealing, they do not work well in custody matters. A clear-cut schedule that provides specific details regarding when the child will be with each parent is essential. Why? Schedules minimize parental conflicts because they empower fathers to tell their children when they will see them next without first having to check with mothers, and they ensure that mothers know what will happen without having to ask fathers about their plans. However, parenting plans must also have some flexibility to meet the changing needs of children and parents. Parents may wish to include a provision in their divorce decree establishing that the parenting plan will be reviewed periodically and that the agreement can be changed with the consent of both parents.

Most children function best within a consistent and predictable daily routine, and this regularity is especially important in the aftermath of divorce. Children are more secure if they know with certainty and in advance which parent they will be staying with each day and when and where they will see the other parent next. The access schedule that parents agree on should be carefully presented to the children so they clearly understand when they will be with each parent. Parents can help children remember when they will be with the other parent by drawing the schedule for them on their own calendars, which they can hang in their rooms at both residences. Whenever the agreed-upon schedule cannot be met, children should be notified in advance of the changes.

Unpredictable visitation schedules are highly problematic; children need dependability. So when four-year-old Susie says, "Daddy, I miss Momma; I want to go," it's best if the father can respond, "I know you miss Momma sometimes when you come to stay with me. It would feel good to be with her now. But today is Wednesday and that is our time together. Let's go look at your calendar together and you can see that Momma will pick you up tomorrow morning at 8:00 A.M. You can be with her then and tell her how much you missed her. Would you like to draw a picture for her now and give it to her in the morning? She always loves your drawings, you know."

Consistency and Familiarity

Parents want to keep as many factors as possible constant in their child's life during and immediately after the parental separation. Change is stressful. Teachers, babysitters, family friends, and school companions all provide an important source of continuity and stability for children while they are coping with the changes at home. Parents should do what they can to avoid changes in a child's routine and environment. New schools and neighborhoods are sometimes necessary after divorce, but they demand further adjustment and accommodation. Whenever possible, parents should minimize changes in children's lives and know that familiarity and stability are comforting.

In addition, children require their own sense of place. Children benefit from having at least one space in each parent's home that belongs only to them. At the very least, this space can be a box or shelf that is reserved just for their things. Parents can further enhance the children's sense of belonging by putting their name on their shelf, room, bed, closet, or cubby and keeping it just for their use.

Frequency

If the mother has assumed primary physical custody, the more time the father spends with the children, the better (unless this exposes children to more parental hostilities). Research studies show that more frequent time with the father is associated with greater intimacy in father–child relations, greater satisfaction for the child during visits, and more effective control over the children by their fathers. Ideally, fathers will see their children every week, including overnight stays, so he can be involved in the real parenting activities of homework, discipline, mealtimes and bedtimes, and so forth.

Visitation works best when it is frequent, regularly scheduled, and conflict-free. The historical visitation pattern of alternate weekends should be avoided because it is not enough time for the parent and child to know each other or have a real parenting relationship. Visitation days for noncustodial fathers usually do not work very well. It is stressful for fathers to handle children for eight hours in an artificial setting in which father and child do not know what to do with each other. Children of all ages emphatically tell researchers they are frustrated and dissatisfied with this limited contact. Time spent with noncustodial fathers should include regularly scheduled overnight stays and weekends. This arrangement is essential because it allows noncustodial fathers to include children in daily activities such as cooking dinner, doing homework together, and sharing bedtime routines. Longer visits permit these real-life interactions and prevent the unsatisfying emphasis on entertainment that characterizes visits between most noncustodial fathers and their children. (Joint custody works, in large part, because this entertaining mode of visitation stops.) Much is lost when fathers become just friends. Fathers need to tough it out and wrestle with the daily conflicts inherent in a real parenting relationship—exerting discipline and control, monitoring children's activities and behavior, interacting with their teachers and friends, wiping tears and putting on Band-Aids, reading together at bedtime, and so forth. Finally, children benefit from telephone contact and e-mail correspondence between visits (for example, Dad calling every Wednesday night at 8 P.M.).

To illustrate, one schedule that works well for many divorced families is for the noncustodial father to have the children live in his home two long weekends each month, beginning after school Thursday and ending Monday morning when he drops the children off at school. He may also schedule a dinner or, preferably, one overnight stay during the weeks he doesn't have the children. (School-aged children love it when parents make the time to visit them at school during the week, volunteer in their classroom, or attend field trips or school outings.) Parents may alternate holidays such as Thanksgiving, Christmas, and birthdays. By coordinating work and vacation schedules, parents can arrange extended time periods with the children, such as two weeks at Christmas, a week at spring break, and several weeks in the summer. With less time, children and fathers do not really know each other and, too often, their relationships become friendly but superficial. As a result of this mutually unrewarding and often awkward contact, many father–child relationships wither in the first two years after the breakup.

Finally, with rights come responsibilities. Noncustodial parents seeking significant time with their children need to follow through and provide this parenting themselves. Children should not be taken away from their primary caretaker only to be cared for by grandparents, day-care workers, or others. Noncustodial parents who wish to have more extensive time with their children should receive it. However, in turn they must be willing to alter their work schedules, career goals, and time spent in other relationships in order to provide this parenting personally.

Child's Control over Access to Parents

The more control children can exert over when they see their parents, the better they will cope. Children who can bicycle, walk, or take a bus to the other parent's home, *when they want to,* are most satisfied with visitation arrangements. As we have seen, divorce brings about feelings of helplessness in most children, which lowers their self-esteem and sense of self-efficacy. If children can exert some control over the visitation schedule, they are empowered to cope more effectively with the divorce. Although parents cannot always give children the access schedules they want, parents should listen to what they would like and try to accommodate their preferences as much as circumstances allow.

In most divorcing families, the father moves out of the family residence, and the mother obtains primary physical custody of the children. Because of economic constraints, many fathers initially move back to their own parents' home. Fathers without custodial living arrangements often move three to five times within the first five years after separation, with disastrous effects on visitation.

Whenever possible, departing fathers should plan their initial move carefully and establish a more permanent residence. Visitation for noncustodial parents can also be enhanced if, at the time of the initial breakup, the noncustodial parent actively involves children in making a new home together so that they feel included rather than left out. For example, they may help arrange father's furniture, hang pictures, and decorate their new rooms together. Fathers should establish their new homes near their former wives (within the same school district) so it is easier for children to see him, maintain the same peer friendships, and retrieve belongings without involving the other parent. Too many parents are shortsighted and fail to heed this important guideline. Only children who have such easy bicycling or walking access to both of their parents' homes say they see each parent "almost enough."

Comings and Goings

Transitions from one parent's home to the other's for visitation, which require children to regularly leave one parent for the other, can be difficult times for every family member. Let's approach this topic thoughtfully. The parent who is being left can have many different reactions: sadness at seeing the child leave, anger toward the former spouse as old conflicts are aroused, or relief over the temporary respite from parental responsibilities. Whatever their feelings, parents who are left behind want to reassure children that they will be fine while the children are gone and that they want the children to enjoy their visit with the other parent without worrying. Parents who are being left can also say they are pleased that the child has this opportunity to spend time with the other parent, and they will be very happy to see the child again on Tuesday at 4:00 (be specific about day, time, and place). In other words, *many children need spoken permission to leave the custodial parent without worrying about their parent's well-being in their absence and to feel close to the other parent without guilt.* In most circumstances, if you show confidence about visiting, your child will have confidence, too. In contrast, if your children repeatedly witness your tears or sense your fear or loneliness about their departure, they are apt to develop an anxiety disorder.

The parent the child goes to visit should not necessarily expect the child to feel close to or be especially happy to see him or her at first. There often needs to be a warming-up period for getting to know each other again. The first night of a visit is usually the most difficult for children, and parents should not be upset or feel rejected if a child is testy or shy. Avoid planning a flurry of activities to entertain the child. Instead, the best way to negotiate a child's initial visit is to ease the transition for both parent and child by planning low-key, shared activities. For example, parent and child can prepare dinner together, take an after-dinner walk or bicycle ride, play board games together that allow the opportunity to talk together casually, and end the evening quietly by reading bedtime stories. Although children may protest at first that they only want to watch TV or play computer games, they soon welcome the more personal contact of reading together, playing catch, walking the dog, or other shared activities that make it possible to talk together easily.

Parents and children who see each other infrequently risk losing the potential for a meaningful relationship. Often it is awkward to begin visits after a parent and child have been apart, and it may be especially hard to end them. To avoid this initial awkwardness or ending heartache, some parents overstimulate children with too many artificial activities. "Disneyland daddies" or "tour guide parents" entertain their children—and the activities are unfulfilling for all. Instead, parents can actively seek ways to join children in their interests and to find ways they can be emotionally present with them. Also, children are relieved if parents can openly acknowledge their difficult feelings about comings and goings and communicate that it's acceptable to have them. For example, a father might say, "It must be a little bit hard sometimes to leave your Mom and come stay with me. I know how much you miss her, and you haven't been here with me for awhile. Let's think for a minute about what we might like to do together tonight and both come up with some suggestions. What sounds good to you?" The best way to join with your children is to support their genuine interests and find ways to participate in the activities they enjoy (for example, playing chess or Ping-Pong, riding bikes or going swimming together, making puzzles or origami, and so forth).

Parents and children both need quiet time in shared activities that allow them to find each other again. Further, parents and children often do not become as close as they could because they do not talk together well. In particular, if children happen to express problems, mothers sometimes reassure or suggest a solution too quickly, and fathers sometimes dismiss their concerns as unimportant or exaggerated worries, saying, for example, "That's no big deal." More trust could develop if parents did not try to fix or dismiss their child's concerns so readily and instead invite further discussion and listen more closely. Parents can let the child know they are taking them seriously and want to hear more about this issue by asking open-ended questions such as, "That does sound like a problem, and I can see you've been thinking about this. Tell me more about it so I can understand better."

Noncustodial parents can also establish family traditions that facilitate more important conversations between parent and child. For example, parents can set up weekly councils or meeting times to discuss family plans or make decisions that affect everybody. Children find comfort in the predictability of having the same bedtime ritual every night. For example, everybody gathers in the same place at 8:30, washed and brushed, to listen to parents reading favorite short stories, going through a chapter book, or reading about a vacation place the family plans to visit. After this shared focus has been established, quiet time for more significant conversations that children initiate often follows naturally. Without such efforts to create opportunities to talk, listen, and know each other more authentically, relationships become superficial and visitation drops off. Fathers who want to foster this emotional connection with their children but who don't know how to provide it because they never received it themselves can find help. The capacity to develop more meaningful relationships with your children can be learned from therapists, pastoral counselors, parenting courses, and support groups such as Parents Without Partners.

For starters: fathers, share more about yourself. Tell your child something about your own childhood that was fun and exciting; another time, disclose something that was scary, disappointing, or a problem for you. Another day, share something you have been thinking about that is important to you now, and see for yourself if your child is eager to know more about you and your life.

Age of Children

I will suggest some visitation schedules that can be arranged for children of different ages, but I want to emphasize that many other options are available. The schedule that works well for some children may be a disaster for others.

Frequent shorter visits for a few hours every other day are better than a few longer visits for infants and young toddlers, who need such regular contact with their primary caregiver. During these visits, however, fathers must want to be actively involved in feeding, bathing, soothing, and changing the baby. Even though the mother, grandmother, or new wife may be able to do these things more skillfully at first, fathers should not give in to their own fears of inadequacy or to the other adults' preference for a female caregiver. This only serves to keep fathers from learning how to care for their very young children. If fathers allow others to continually correct them or take care of their babies for them, they will never learn to feel like an equal parent who can competently care for their child. Fathers need to set limits with well-intended helpers and say, "No, thank you; I'll do it," or they will never feel comfortable taking care of their children. It is essential that noncustodial fathers spend time alone with their baby or very young child. The attachment bonds that form in these early caretaking activities are the foundation for a lifelong relationship. It's the adventure of a lifetime. Don't miss out on any of it.

Children under four years of age should not be separated from their primary caretaker for very long. A separation of two or three days is a long time for young children to be away from their primary caregiver. An overnight visit with the noncustodial parent every third or fourth night or on the weekend, bolstered by a telephone call every other night, works well for many families. Preschoolers, in particular, need familiar routines and consistent schedules.

School-aged children can succeed with longer separations, can handle more flexible schedules, and usually want more time with both parents. Many children six to seven years old and older can comfortably alternate between living in the mothers' and fathers' homes every third or fourth day. Extended weekends and overnight stays during the school week usually work well. Access schedules must be arranged to accommodate school and other activities with as little disruption as possible.

Preteens can handle longer visits, and they want more control over where they stay and when they are with each parent. As children reach mid-adolescence, by age fourteen or fifteen in particular, they often choose to live with the same-sex parent. Parents should anticipate this preference and, rather than fight a losing battle, accommodate it when possible. A time-limited preference, it usually passes in about two years. In general, adolescents should be important participants in determining visitation plans and living arrangements. It is empowering for them to do so. Their preferences should be considered carefully and responded to as much as possible.

Taking Charge

Parents should expect children to test limits and push boundaries within the new family arrangements. Children are often angry after the breakup and are harder to discipline. They attempt to play one parent against the other. Eight- to eleven-year-old boys, in particular, are often angry. At times, they seem to be experts in finding ways to punish their parents and can quickly make many noncustodial parents feel guilty or unwanted and lose interest in visiting.

Following the breakup, some children proclaim, "I don't want to see you." These threats are especially successful in distancing noncustodial fathers who already may feel rejected, guilty, or insecure with their children. Or when one parent disciplines or enforces limits, children routinely threaten to leave and go live with the other parent. Many divorced parents feel disempowered by their children and become one-down in the parent-child relationship as they seek to please or bargain with children. Grave consequences can ensue when children gain the upper hand and parents give children too much power and control.

Valid complaints from children should be heard, but they should not have the power to decide whether the parent–child relationship will continue. Except in extenuating circumstances, parents should not let children choose whether to spend time with the noncustodial parent or to have a continuing relationship. The continuity of relationships is presented to children as a fact, a given.

Although angry and hurt feelings should be discussed, and solutions to real problems in the relationship sought, they should not be used to jeopardize a parental relationship. Too many fathers overreact to their children's angry rejection and give up their parenting role altogether, whereas too many mothers give up their resolve to have children follow rules and respond respectfully. Becoming grandiose and cynical, children suffer lifelong consequences when they are allowed to exert too much control over adults and given the power to drive a parent away.

Finally, we have seen that children are almost certain to develop long-term adjustment problems if their parents continually battle each other in court. The two issues that most frequently bring about legal battles are child support payments and the visitation schedules we have been discussing. Next, the final section examines these two problems and encourages parents to use a divorce mediator and settle their differences outside the courtroom whenever possible.

Resolving Disputes Through Mediation

The two traditional but ineffective ways that people respond to conflicts could be characterized as "fight or flight." A more constructive way to resolve most disputes is through mediation. In almost all states, the law empowers parents by giving them the opportunity to work out their own custody or parenting plans with the help of a neutral mediator. If the two parents can agree on a custody plan, the judge will almost always accept it. If parents will not mediate or cannot agree during mediation, attorneys will argue for each parent and, almost inevitably, further wound and embitter exspouses. At the end of this painful and expensive legal proceeding, the judge will decide their fate for them. While so much of the divorce process feels out of parents' rightful control, mediation offers many parents the opportunity to decide their own destinies. Let's look more closely at what mediation is and is not.

Mediation is a noncombative way for divorcing couples to resolve their disputes during and after divorce. A skilled mediator is a neutral professional with knowledge of family law, child psychology, and negotiation techniques. The mediator helps divorcing families clearly define the issues in dispute and reach agreements that are in the best interests of the family. The mediator does this by guiding the communication process so that a rational discussion can take place, everyone has a chance to be heard, and conflicts are discussed one at a time. The mediator does not take sides, assign blame, or make decisions for divorcing couples. Instead, the mediator tries to help parents understand the needs of children, reach agreements that are in the children's best interests, and establish the most cooperative parenting relationship that is possible for these two parents. The mediator may offer suggestions and help couples develop parenting plans, but the final agreement is up to the parents.

Mediation is not marital counseling or psychotherapy. The mediator focuses on helping couples reach their own agreements, and, unlike the attorney, does not represent one party. The purpose is not to help divorcing couples reconcile, trust each other, or become friends. Mediation aims to help families resolve divorce-related issues and reach successful parenting agreements. Similarly, mediation is not a substitute for an attorney. Most parents still wish to have an attorney help them understand the law, make informed agreements, ensure that their rights are protected, and write up or review the final agreement. Many parents also try to have their respective attorneys negotiate an out-of-court settlement that is acceptable to both parties.

Like joint custody, mediation is not a panacea; it presents its own problems and limitations. The process does not work for everyone. Although participants do not have to like or trust one another, they must be willing to work together in good faith to try to find solutions that will be fair to all family members. When one party "wins" settlements, further conflict and litigation usually follow, creating more problems for children.

Mediation is likely to fail in three situations: when either of the parents is (1) physically violent, (2) addicted to drugs or alcohol, or (3) highly dependent on the child for happiness and security. If one parent gives in and signs on to a custody plan he or she doesn't really believe in, the parent usually brings it back to court later or undermines it. The success of mediation also depends on whether the attorney's attitude toward mediation is "Let's try to resolve it out of court" or "Just go through the motions, and I'll get you what you want in court."

Some cases must be settled in court (for example, a spousal abuse victim who cannot negotiate on even footing with an intimidating ex-spouse, even with the help of a skilled mediator). For the majority of families, however, mediation is by far the best alternative for resolving the complex problems divorce creates. When parents settle disputes in court, the acrimony and distrust that already exists between parents is greatly exacerbated by the adversarial court process. The resulting hatred often endures for decades—to the detriment of both the parents and the children. Children suffer greatly when they see their parents fighting in court, and they are hurt by the parental hostility that remains years afterward.

In addition to emotional benefits for parents and children alike, mediated settlements are far less expensive than court battles. It is sobering for family court observers to watch two parents fight in court until one goes bankrupt. With no money left to pay further legal bills and a family in financial crisis, a compromise is reached. Routinely, the divorce settlement and custody plan then adopted is virtually indistinguishable from the initial plan that was presented long before the ruinous litigation began. Keep in mind that most judges determine alimony and child support payments by simply viewing the computerized guidelines on the software program that is up and running on their desk.

Finally, mediated agreements are usually more flexible than court-ordered solutions because they can be changed by mutual consent rather than by filing with the court. Divorcing parents are forewarned to make sincere efforts to resolve their disputes through mediation before embarking on the adversarial court process.

The two most common arenas of dispute after divorce are child custody arrangements and child support and alimony payments; mediation can play a constructive role in helping parents resolve these disagreements.

Child Custody Disputes

Sometimes one parent wants to renegotiate custody or visitation arrangements that already have been handed down. Parents are most likely to seek custody changes (and to make threats about going back to court) when their ex-spouses remarry. It is easier to establish joint legal custody or equal-time visitation arrangements *at the time of the initial divorce decree* than it is to change sole custody declarations later on. Although the court may respond favorably to subsequent requests by the noncustodial parent for greater access to the child, often the court will not be willing to hear the case again unless proof of compelling circumstances can be shown.

When parents disagree over custody and visitation arrangements, the court often encourages or even mandates parents to try and resolve their differences through a divorce mediation program. As emphasized earlier, these mediation programs are often effective in resolving disputes in a way that minimizes distress for children. Polarizing court battles, as well as the stresses associated with psychological evaluations, often can be avoided. It is one thing for parents to fight over money and property in court; it is highly disruptive for children when parents are fighting over them. The adversarial court process dramatically increases parental hostilities, which translates directly into adjustment problems for children.

Statistics vary, but about 15 percent of divorcing parents are unable to either compromise with each other or end their legal battles. They continue to fight in court over custody of the children and sometimes try to bar the other parent from seeing the child. In some cases, responsible parents are taking the protective stance needed to place necessary limits on another parent's inappropriate involvement. In more cases, however, parents are playing out their own angry control battles with each other through the children. At times, when parents cannot successfully mediate a settlement or engage in repeated litigation, grandparents may be acting behind the scenes to fuel the conflict rather than endorsing good judgment.

When one parent tries to win sole custody, however, children usually lose, not the other parent. Litigious parents who are embroiled in continuing legal battles over their children have the most troubled and maladjusted children of divorce. If court battles over custody and visitation ensue, children should enter therapy to shelter them from continuing parental conflict.

Frank and Brenda

Frank hated his former wife, Brenda, and thought she was a "worthless mother." Their nine-year-old son, Carl, was having behavior problems at school, and Frank saw this as further evidence of Brenda's failure as a mother.

Carl's fourth-grade teacher described him as "a very angry little boy" and was concerned because Carl was so defiant and had such little respect for his teachers.

Frank complained to Brenda that she didn't know how to manage Carl properly. He had a long list of things he wanted Brenda to correct in the way she raised both Carl and their daughter, but Brenda was prepared to die before she would listen to one word of his advice. She had divorced Frank to escape his constant criticism and control, and she certainly was not going to submit to his attempts now. She was finally out from under his thumb, and Brenda wasn't going to let Frank undermine her again.

Brenda realized Carl was having serious problems at school, and she was having a hard time controlling him at home. It was an excruciating dilemma. Brenda was determined not to let Frank take over, blame everything on her, and tell her what to do but, at the same time, she had a sickening feeling that something was terribly wrong for Carl.

As he had a million times before, Frank called Brenda to talk about the guidelines he wanted her to follow in raising the kids. Brenda interrupted him before he could finish and said he could handle Carl his way when Carl was with him but she would do what she thought best when Carl was with her. The argument escalated when Frank charged that Brenda was obviously an "incompetent mother" and that "his" children were suffering from the consequences of Brenda's inadequate parenting. If Brenda wouldn't follow his advice, Frank threatened, he would go back to court to prove what a "shitty mother" she was, gain custody, and raise them the "right" way with his new wife. Brenda shouted one last insult before hanging up the phone.

Five days later, Brenda returned home from work to find two unwanted letters. One, from Frank's attorney, told her that Frank would follow through with his threat to take her back to court. The other letter, which was even more upsetting, was from Carl's teacher. She wanted to discuss the need to remove Carl from her class. The teacher's note said Carl had been a discipline problem all year but, in the last few days, he had become unmanageable and was taking away from her ability to manage the rest of the class.

Neither Brenda nor Frank realized it was the continuing conflict between them, and watching his father deride his mother, that was the source of Carl's behavior problems. As long as Brenda and Frank had continued to fight, and Carl had continued to observe his father responding so contemptuously toward his mother, Carl would have remained a serious behavior problem. In addition, if Frank and Brenda had battled in court for custody, Carl would have felt responsible for his parents' conflict, and his aggressive behavior problems would have escalated. Fortunately, Frank and Brenda's attorneys both supported a sincere attempt at mediation. A skillful mediator was able to dissuade Frank from bringing this conflict back to court and helped Frank grasp that Carl acted out more when he watched Frank demean Brenda. Frank still remained critical of Brenda and never really gave up his attempts to control her, but he did stop insulting her. Brenda also got help from a parenting support group. She became better at setting limits with Frank and emotionally disengaging from his critical intrusions. More important, she became more effective at demanding a respectful attitude from Carl. The tension subsided for everybody as soon as the court date was dropped, and Carl's behavior at school began to improve.

Child Support Disputes

Noncompliance with child support payments is the other issue that brings parents to court, increasing the likelihood of child adjustment problems. Mandatory child support guidelines now are in effect in most states. Many states tie child support, to some degree, to the percentage of time the noncustodial parent has the children. As a result, some custody disputes are viewed by the custodial parent as a device to decrease child support payments rather than as a genuine desire to spend more time with the children. As we will see next, this issue may be resolved in mediation.

How should a mother respond if the father does not fulfill his financial responsibilities? She should neither protect her former husband by hiding this fact from the children nor use this as a weapon to distance the children from him. On the one hand, the financial hardship that results from a father's noncompliance can be presented realistically to children. On the other hand, mothers may not want to refuse visitation privileges as a way to obtain money. Although some courts support mothers who deny contact until support payments are made, this approach often creates further problems for children. Children in this situation are likely to lose whatever relationship they may have had with their father, become further embroiled in parental hostilities, and become more vulnerable to a range of adjustment problems.

A more effective way to secure child support payments is for the mother to resolve this problem through adult channels and direct negotiation with the father. The first approach, of course, is to discuss support payments with the father personally. Second, when a direct request fails, mothers should initiate meetings with a family court mediator to resolve the problem. Most county courts and community mental health agencies have mediation counselors trained to work with these problems. Ironically, some delinquent fathers are responding to the feeling that they have no personal relationship with their children. Because visits with their children are infrequent and unsatisfying, some fathers feel used and resent their financial obligations. Some of these fathers can be brought into financial compliance if the mother becomes more supportive of his continuing relationship with the children. Some noncomplying fathers will begin making child support payments reliably when they have freer access to their children.

A third approach is required for irresponsible fathers who do not want to spend time with their children or contribute to child support. If mediation fails, the mother should then go to court to obtain child support payments (and request any attorney fees and all back payments). The family law division of the district attorney's office prosecutes aggressively for noncompliance with support payments by withholding wages and attaching liens on property.

As we saw earlier, courts at one time awarded mothers sole custody of children, long-term alimony, and child support payments. Over one-half of all divorced fathers failed to make these payments, however, and the courts did little to enforce payment. Around 1980, this pattern began to change in most states. Now courts often award mothers smaller alimony payments over a shorter period of time because divorced mothers are expected to enter the workforce. In contrast, courts have become stricter in enforcing child support payments; they often order wage deductions when dead-beat dads do not comply. Fortunately, mothers today are more likely to get the legal and financial support they need than they were in the past. As much as possible, however, children should be buffered from these negotiations.

Susan and Larry

Finances had been the biggest problem for Susan and her three children since the divorce. Although Susan had gone back to work, sold the house, and moved to a low-rent apartment, she still didn't have enough money each month. There was one reason for this: her former husband, Larry, paid less than one-third of the child support the judge had ordered. Some months he sent nothing; other months he sent part of the payment, but Susan could not remember the last time the full amount arrived on time. Without his financial support, Susan could not feed, clothe, and shelter a family of four.

The Christmas holidays brought Susan's financial problems to a head. When she realized that her budget could not be stretched to buy even a few modest presents for her children, she knew something had to change. Susan scheduled an appointment with a divorce mediator through the family law division of the county courthouse and told Larry he could meet her there or in court, whichever he preferred. Larry arrived (ten minutes late) for the first mediation session.

The mediation counselor said she wanted to begin the session by hearing how each of them saw the problem. She asked Susan to begin by telling Larry, as specifically as possible, what she saw as the problem and what she wanted to change through mediation. In a cool and factual manner, Susan articulated the hardships caused by Larry's failure to make the support payments reliably. The mediator then turned to Larry, "That's how Susan sees the problem. Will you tell your side of it now?"

Larry exploded: "You never *let* me have anything to do with the children! You criticized everything I ever did with them. If I tried to change a diaper, you hovered over me giving directions as if I was about to make some horrible mistake. When I tried to feed the baby, you told me I gave her too much food, too fast. When I tried to fix the children a sandwich, you'd say I was getting in your way in the kitchen. It seemed as if every time I was alone with one of the kids, you would come in and tell me to do something different. You felt threatened whenever I got something good going with them. You always had to be the boss in charge of everything. And doing things right meant doing them your way! I finally gave up fighting you for them—you were going to make them *your* children no matter what I did. But you still expect me to pay for it all. What a nice arrangement for you. Go to hell!"

Susan continued to try to explain her good intentions, and Larry only continued his barrage. The mediator soon regained control of the session, however, and made it clear that angry ventilation was unacceptable here. The mediator did help both parties to feel heard, however, and this soon changed their tone. As things calmed down they began to talk more constructively about their children. At the end of the session, both Larry and Susan agreed to keep meeting and scheduled the next week's appointment.

Susan never agreed with Larry's perception that she kept the children to herself or disrupted his relationship with them. However, she did follow the mediator's suggestion and told Larry she would sincerely try not to criticize or direct what he did with the children in the future, and she would actively support his relationship with them. The mediator also suggested a new visitation plan that gave Larry regularly scheduled time alone with the children, including overnight stays. Larry said it was hard for him to be with all of the children at once, so new arrangements were made for him to see the children one or two at a time on occasions. In turn, Larry agreed to make the full child support payment on time each month. Susan accepted this plan but meant it when she said she would file a noncompliance grievance with the family law court and have his wages garnished the next time he was late or sent a partial payment.

Although I have offered many different suggestions in the preceding pages, there is no ideal parenting plan that will work for every child. Each divorcing couple must work out arrangements tailored to fit their child and their family's needs. Parents need to be flexible—prepared to modify plans as children grow and circumstances change. The fundamental guideline in all custody and visitation arrangements, however, is to balance children's need for a continuing relationship with both parents with children's need to be shielded from ongoing parental conflict. In most cases, one of the most helpful things parents can do for children is to keep their problems with each other from becoming legal battles. Resolve disputes through a neutral mediator whenever possible. Children adjust better when mediation replaces litigation.

Suggestions for Further Reading

Does Wednesday Mean Mom's House or Dad's? (M. Ackerman, New York: Wiley, 1997) and *Mom's House, Dad's House* (I. Ricci, New York: Fireside, 1980) have helped many divorcing parents work out the practicalities of shared custody and other visitation plans.

Whenever possible, mediation is a far better alternative than litigation. Parents are encouraged to examine *The Divorce Mediation Handbook: Everything You Need to Know* (P. James, San Francisco: Jossey-Bass, 1997). However, even the most cooperative parents need to be informed of their legal and financial rights. *Divorce and Money* by V. Woodhouse and V. Collings (Nolo.com, 1996) is highly recommended.

Part Four

Childrearing After Divorce

Chapter Eight

Loyalty Conflicts

"Why Should I Let Them Go? He Never Spent Time with Them When We Were Married!"

Children suffer from loyalty conflicts when they feel pressure to choose between their parents. Divorcing parents want to give children permission to be close and involved with both parents at the same time. In the majority of families, however, parents give children the message that they must take sides with one parent at the expense of closeness with the other. The mother may subtly communicate, in facial expression or tone of voice, that she is hurt or disappointed when her son expresses eagerness to visit his father. Or the father may be more overt. He may say, "Fine, if you miss your mother so much, just go live with her! The two of you can have each other as far as I'm concerned." Sometimes parents communicate these loyalty conflicts to their children overtly, but usually they do it indirectly, without being aware of it. Loyalty conflicts, conveyed directly or indirectly, are wrenching for children because closeness with one parent means being disloyal to the other.

Children want to be close to both parents and are distressed when they feel pressured to choose one over the other. The stronger the press for children to take sides and choose, the greater their conflict and the more tenuous their adjustment. Loyalty conflicts engender long-term problems for children, and they are especially likely to occur when parents remain gridlocked in angry control battles. In this chapter, we will see how parents can reach for a higher standard of ethics and give children clearly spoken permission to love and feel as close to the other parent as to themselves.

Effects of Loyalty Conflicts on Children

In thirty years of clinical practice, I cannot recall one child of divorce with significant, long-term adjustment problems who was not struggling with loyalty conflicts. Children are placed in an impossible bind when they feel pressured to take sides or choose between their parents. Children cannot make this choice without great inner conflict. They want a relationship with both parents and feel torn apart inside when they are pulled in two directions by their parents.

Loyalty conflicts can be a problem for children of all ages but nine- to thirteen-year-olds are especially vulnerable to parental pressures to take sides. At these ages, children are especially prone to rigid all-good and all-bad moral judgments. Because they cannot integrate their mother's and father's separate versions of "the truth," they readily accept implicit parental invitations to choose sides and join one parental camp or the other. When children are pulled into these loyalty conflicts, they often become insufferably moralistic and judgmental of the other parent.

Understandably, parents want to be assured of their child's loyalty during the crisis of marital disruption. A secure, loving bond with the children is especially comforting when ties with the spouse are unraveling. It is understandable for parents to feel hurt or even threatened sometimes by their child's interest in the other parent, especially when that ex-spouse has caused so much pain. However, if parents act on these feelings by subtly pressuring children to choose them over the other parent, children are faced with an unsolvable dilemma. It doesn't have to be that way. Parents can help their children greatly by giving them direct, spoken permission to love and care for both parents at the same time. Parents who can do this are truly working in the best interest of their children, and they will be rewarded with more secure children. The following illustration is a typical family scenario in which loyalty conflicts are occurring.

Mary and Jim

Mary and Jim had been divorced for eight months. Their middle son, David, developed a serious symptom during the breakup—a peptic ulcer. Mary called the psychological clinic to request help for the twelve-year-old after their doctor explained that peptic ulcers were a psychosomatic illness brought on, in part, by emotional tension.

During the initial therapy session with David and his mother, the therapist learned that Mary did not really support David's desire to spend time with his father. Mary described how much she worried when the children were at their father's home. Jim was a hunter who owned guns and, even though he kept them locked up, Mary did not trust that he supervised the children as closely as necessary. Mary was afraid Jim wasn't careful enough and there would be an accident someday.

The therapist believed Mary's concern about the guns needed to be taken seriously, but she also wondered whether a broader issue of divided loyalties was being expressed through Mary's anxiety about the guns. The therapist decided to meet together with mother, father, and all three children to see how other family members were reacting to the divorce, to assess the children's safety, and to explore her guess about loyalty conflicts.

At the second session, the therapist quickly learned that her hypothesis was correct. As she walked into the treatment room to greet the family, she noted how their seating arrangement reflected the family's alliances. Mother and father sat across the room from each other. The youngest child, the daughter, sat next to her mother; the older son sat next to his father. In the very center of the room, not one inch closer to mother on the left or father on the right, sat David.

The therapist immediately began to bring the loyalty conflicts out into the open by asking, "What are the teams in this family? Who goes with whom?" Like most polarized families, each family member knew exactly what the teams were. Mother and youngest daughter were together; father and oldest son were allied; David was precariously in the middle, trying to be on both sides at the same time. Although many families can identify allied teams or subgroups of family members (for example, the Big Kids and the Little Kids, the Girls and the Boys), these more benign subgroups are much less rigid and exclusive than the alliances were in this family.

The therapist continued to focus on the source of David's loyalty conflicts by asking him, "How does your mother feel when you want to visit your dad?" David replied, "I think she feels bad." The therapist asked, "Do you feel close to your mom and like to spend time with her?" David answered candidly by nodding in agreement. The therapist then asked, "How does that make your dad feel?" David again answered with the forthright clarity that children often have about family matters, "I think it makes him mad sometimes."

The therapist's technique of helping David state his predicament had a strong impact on his parents. If she had suggested to the parents that they were subtly pressuring David to choose, they would have disagreed strongly. When they heard David's answers to the therapist, however, they were shown convincingly how each of them was giving David the message that he should be close to one but not the other. It became evident to all that David was not free to enjoy a relationship with both of his parents.

Like most parents, once Jim and Mary saw how the conflict between them was hurting their child, they began to work constructively with the therapist on this problem. In a short time, the parents were able to say to each other that, even though they did not like or trust each other, they could see it was in their children's best interest to stop exerting subtle pressure on the children to choose between them. They were also able to say to each other *in front of the children* that they would not make the children choose between them and that they would like the children to have a good relationship with the other parent.

David's ulcer improved after these conversations. Soon he was having fewer stomach problems, and at the six-month follow-up session his ulcer was virtually cured. Before therapy, David was literally being eaten up inside by the stress of being torn between his parents, both of whom he loved and needed. He had been walking on eggshells in his efforts to be close to one while not losing the other. When his parents stopped making David choose between them, the tension leading to his ulcer abated.

Why Parents Make Their Children Choose

Some parents recognize that their former spouse is just as important to their children as they are. These parents are not threatened by the children's need for the other parent and support that relationship. At the other extreme are parents unwilling to acknowledge how important the other parent is to their children and demand exclusive loyalty from them. Most loyalty conflicts fall somewhere in between these two extremes. Many parents who exert loyalty conflicts are not fully aware of how they are communicating to their children that being close to the other parent is disappointing or hurtful to them.

There are six common reasons why parents may intentionally or unwittingly impose loyalty conflicts on their children. These are discussed in detail in the sections to follow.

Anger Toward the Former Spouse

The most common source of loyalty conflicts for children is parental anger and blame toward the former spouse. As the Greek story of Medea teaches us, the most effective way to punish or retaliate against the other parent is to take their children away. The consuming anger and vindictiveness that may be aroused by the divorce seems justified when it is rooted in the feeling of having been betrayed or humiliated by the one who left. When this shame-driven hatred continues for years after the divorce, parents often are using it to defend against their own intolerable feelings of being inherently unlovable or having been abandoned. Such parents rigidly cast blame in order to deny any shared responsibility for the marital failure and bolster their own wounded self-esteem. Unfortunately, some attorneys, therapists, grandparents, and friends fuel this blaming stance and exacerbate problems for children by supporting the one-sided view that, in effect, the divorce was perpetrated by an unscrupulous person against a helpless victim.

Traditional sex roles are also the source of much parental anger after divorce. Some mothers feel justified in claiming exclusive loyalty because they are angered by their former husband's "new-found interest" in the children and shared parenting after the divorce. From their point of view, their husband's lack of parental involvement before the divorce left them unsupported in their childrearing role. These mothers, understandably, may feel as if the children really do belong to them because they have done so much more to raise them. Such mothers may think to themselves, "I'll be damned if I am going to let him take them now. He never had anything to do with them before!" In parallel, of course, these fathers are often angry as well. They counter that their former wives always complained they didn't do enough for the children but, whenever they tried, their wives interfered in some way or criticized them, no matter what they did. There is usually some truth to both sides. No one can win this argument, of course, but the children lose when parents act on angry feelings by placing loyalty conflicts on children.

Competitiveness Between Former Spouses

Children caught in divisive loyalty conflicts may have parents who competed with each other throughout the marriage. Because child-rearing is the greatest area of shared involvement for former spouses, the child's affection or loyalty provides the principal arena for continuing the competition. Sad or hurt feelings from the breakup often fuel the wish to get the better of the former spouse. The faulty belief in this competitive battle is, "If our son cares more about me than he does about you, it proves I am a better parent." As parents realize the child is the one who really loses in this contest, they may find it easier to back off from their own participation in it. Only then can embroiled former spouses begin to address what they really need to do—emotionally disengage from each other and begin the internal work of psychologically ending the marriage.

Seeking Validation

The child's positive feelings toward the former spouse can arouse unfounded guilt in parents over their decision to divorce. It is painful for parents to see their children feeling sad or longing for the other parent. All too often, parents regard their children's troubled feelings about the divorce as evidence they should have stayed married. These parents are managing their own guilt by trying to dissuade the child from missing or wanting to be with the other parent. The mistaken notion is, "If my child does not want to be with my ex, then my decision to divorce was correct."

These parents can find better ways to resolve their guilt than by engendering loyalty conflicts. To illustrate, suppose your child says, "I miss Daddy." Resist the inclination to invalidate the child's feelings by countering, "But you were just with him over the weekend." Instead, try saying, "Of course you miss him, and he misses you too when he's not with you. Would you like to give him a call and say hello when he gets home from work tonight?"

Parents may engender loyalty conflicts to validate their decision to divorce in a second way. When two people divorce, there is almost always some ambivalence about the breakup. Even though the problems in the relationship outweigh the rewards, some loving feelings may remain for the ex-spouse. Many parents are threatened by these lingering feelings because they fear that continuing to care about or miss their former spouse at times means they should not have divorced. If so, the child's wish to be close to the other parent may be threatening because it arouses the parent's own unacceptable, positive feelings. Demanding the child's primary loyalty is an ineffective means of managing one's own conflicted feelings.

Finally, parents may also need their child's favor in order to validate themselves as good parents. Some adults hold the faulty belief that they are better parents if their child loves them more. It can be deeply gratifying to be the most important person in the whole world to your child. Parents may enjoy those alternating phases of childhood when they are their child's favorite and the child wants only one parent to bathe and dress her, read to her, or put her to bed. However, when parents' needs for their children's approval becomes too strong, it diminishes their ability to be effective parents. In particular, it is impossible for parents to set limits and enforce rules when they are threatened by their children's disapproval. Parents who need their children's approval can easily be manipulated. Better, parents can validate themselves as good parents by doing what they believe their children need, not what their children want. In other words, parents should focus on doing what is in the child's best interest rather than what will win the child's approval in the moment.

Exerting Control

Some parents pressure children into loyalty conflicts out of their own need to exert excessive control over their children's lives. When parents are overly controlling, typically, everything must be done their way and they must be in charge of every facet of their children's lives. These parents want the best for their children and are confident they know what that is. To their continual dismay, however, the children's relationship with the former spouse is one arena beyond their control.

Ultimately, one parent cannot determine what the other parent does with the children. For example, parents often disapprove of what the former spouse allows the children to do at his or her home. Rules and routines usually vary between the two households, and these differences can be presented to the children as wrong rather than as different. Parents who think in these terms find it hard to accept how their former spouses interact with the children. Their disapproval can stem, in part, from the insecurity that parents feel when they are not fully in control of the children. Taking the long view, this insecurity may be rooted in the parents' own childhood experiences, such as trying to exert needed control over their own parents' problematic behavior (for example, drinking, temper outbursts, volatile mood swings) or lack of responsiveness to them.

In order to satisfy this exaggerated need to be in control, parents attempt to tie the children to them and discourage them from being close to the other parent. Their desire to exercise excessive control over their children and their former spouse is masked as being the "right" way to raise them. In fact, these parents may be especially knowledgeable and responsible parents and have legitimate concerns and complaints about the ex-spouse. However, it is difficult for them to stop criticizing the other parent long enough to consider how they may be placing their own needs before the best interests of the children. Many parents who repeatedly litigate against their ex-spouses demonstrate this excessive need for control.

Feelings of Loss

Some parents experience the child's wish to be with the other parent as posing yet another unwanted loss for themselves. Especially during the initial breakup and during the court proceedings, many parents are sensitive to the briefest periods of separation from their children; even small good-byes can evoke bigger feelings of loneliness or loss. The child's desire to be with the other parent can make these parents feel as if everyone has left them or no one wants them. Without realizing it, they may subtly communicate in posture, facial expression or tone of voice that they are hurt when the child wants to be with the other parent. Adults' feelings of loss or rejection are understandable, human responses to divorce. However, parents do not want to protect against their own sadness by giving children the message that they are doing something hurtful or wrong when they miss the other parent or want to be with them.

Not Distinguishing the Child's Feelings from the Parent's

Finally, parents can exert loyalty pressures on children when they cannot separate their own negative feelings toward the former spouse from their children's need for a continuing relationship with the other parent. Let's consider this distinction carefully.

Some parents are able to put aside their differences with their former spouse and support their child's continuing relationship with the other parent. It is not naïve to suggest that divorced parents can do this; about one-third of them do it very well. We don't hear as much about these cooperative parents as we should; they don't appear on TV talk shows, but they do have the most well-adjusted children. When parents cannot support their children's relationship with the other parent, however, children usually suffer. It is highly problematic when one parent criticizes the other parent in order to diminish the child's affection or desire to be with the other parent.

These combative parents are unable to see their children as psychologically separate from themselves—as having feelings and needs that differ from their own. (In adolescent girls, this blurring of personal boundaries is commonly expressed in symptoms of bulimia and other eating disorders.) The ability to see children as distinct from oneself—different in their own preferences and perceptions—is an important part of being a good parent. In contrast, it creates problems for children when angry parents undermine children's relationship with the former spouse by shaping children's feelings to mirror their own. These parents are saying to their children, in effect, that they cannot accept their wishes and feelings if they are not the same as their own. Hence it follows that "if your mother is no good for me, she is no good for you either." The unfair demand to think and feel the same is communicated in parental messages such as, "Your father lied to me for years. You can't trust him. Just wait; you'll see."

The inability to perceive the differences between a child's need for a continuing relationship with the other parent and the parent's need to end the marital relationship is the source of many problems for children. Thinking this viewpoint is naïve, some readers will argue, "If you only knew what my former spouse has done, you'd see why I don't want him to have anything to do with the kids." Some people do act destructively, and occasionally children need to be shielded from irresponsible parents for their own protection. In marital counseling, however, therapists routinely find that there are two sides to every story.

For example, an attorney or therapist sits in his office and hears about all of the awful things his client's wife has done. He empathizes with his client and becomes angry at the man's wife. Somewhere across town, however, that same "awful" wife is telling another attorney or therapist about all of the ways she has been mistreated. That therapist or attorney, in turn, empathizes with her client. When an attorney, mediator, or marital counselor sees a couple together, however, it becomes much more difficult to determine who is at fault. Routinely, counselors find that there are two different truths in every marriage, and both spouses contribute, to some degree, to most problems.

Thus you may be fed up with your former spouse and want nothing more to do with him or her. That may be the right decision for you, but it is not a decision you should make for your children. If children consistently spend time with a parent and don't like the way they are treated, they will want to spend less time with that parent. If children withdraw from the other parent based on their own experience, it is their choice. Do not make it for them.

Understanding Family Alliances

The loyalty conflicts that many children face after divorce are often exaggerations of teams or subgroups that existed in the family before the divorce. The alliances within David's family (the boy with the peptic ulcer in the previous example) are typical. Let's look more closely at this broader issue of family coalitions or alliances.

In nuclear families that function well, there is an emotional bond or alliance between the mother and the father. Both spouses have a loyalty commitment to each other, and the marital coalition cannot be divided by grandparents, children, friends, employers, or others. Parents will still have differences or problems between them, of course, and they will have emotional commitments to others. However, the marital relationship will be a stable alliance that cannot be disrupted by others. Whether in intact or divorced, or in stepparent families, children adjust better when a stable parental coalition exists because they cannot manipulate or play one parent off against the other. Also, children in such families are free to be close and involved with both parents.

By contrast, in most intact families having problems with their children and in most marriages that end in divorce, the mother and father have not been able to establish a secure marital coalition sturdy enough to resist disruption by others. These parents were unable to establish an effective marital coalition in which their emotional needs were met by each other rather than children or others. Typically, they were unable to preserve the marital or couple aspects of their relationship as children were born and the twosome expanded to become a family. Often these parents could not address and resolve the everyday problems that emerged in their relationship, so they avoided problems or embroiled a third person in their marital conflicts to divert them from the issues they needed to address. When parents cannot maintain an effective marital coalition with each other, they often form an alliance or primary emotional bond with one or more of their children. In this situation, one spouse becomes an outsider to this parent–child coalition and usually resents the exclusion. Problems arise for children in such a family constellation because they feel disloyal to the primary parent and guilty if they want to be close to the outside parent as well.

The best way to learn more about family alliances is to draw a map of the patterns of relationships that existed in your family before the divorce. Take a pen or pencil and begin to draw a three-generational map that includes all the members of your family before the divorce: paternal and maternal grandparents, parents, and children (see Figure 8.1). The question here is, Who goes with whom? Based on the bonds of emotional closeness and involvement, what is the primary two-person relationship in the family? Is it between mother and father, or is there some other primary pairing, such as mother and daughter? What other two-person coalitions or alliances exist—for example, grandparent and parent, child and child? Can larger subgroups with three or more members be identified? Circle the members of each of these subgroups. Who is on the outside of this larger group? Is there an outsider who is cut off and does not belong to any subgroup? Do all the children side with one parent and not the other?

In Figure 8.1, the mother and father do not share an effective marital coalition; instead, the primary two-person relationship in the family is between the mother and oldest daughter. The oldest daughter, the mother, and the maternal grandmother also form a three-person subgroup in the family. Therefore, if the oldest daughter wants more of a relationship with her father after the divorce, she may feel guilty about breaking her long-standing alliance with her mother by approaching her father. Often this daughter feels she must sacrifice her relationship with her father to remain loyal to her mother. She is more likely to develop symptoms and problems after the divorce than her younger brother and sister, who are freer to be involved with both their mother and their father.

In some families, all of the children may be allied with their mother, and the father is the outsider. These children feel guilty, as if they are betraying their mother, if they try to develop more of

Figure 8.1. A Three-Generational Map

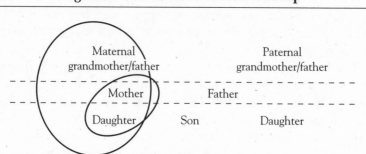

a relationship with their father after the divorce. Whatever the family constellation, children benefit from being as close as possible to both of their parents. Divorcing parents are empowered by becoming aware of cross-generational alliances in the family that have fostered competing coalitions or exclusive loyalty ties for children. If problems that originally contributed to the divorce can be understood and acknowledged, but not used to blame, they are far less likely to cause problems after the divorce.

An Agreement for Parental Cooperation

Often it is difficult for angry ex-spouses to support each other as parents. Many simply cannot do it. Even otherwise responsible parents routinely disrupt the child's relationship with the other parent by undermining his or her parenting authority or by unwittingly encouraging children to take sides. Parents inappropriately vent their own feelings of personal injustice to the children by saying, for example, "Your father is leaving *us* for another woman!" or "You have to change schools and move because your mother is selfish. She cares more about herself than she does about our family." Although hurt and angry feelings are understandable, parents are reminded that children suffer when their relationship with the other parent is compromised. Reaching for the best part of themselves, parents can encourage children to have the best relationship that is possible with the other parent. As hard as this can be, it is the most loving gift divorcing parents can give their children.

In this section, sample scripts and a parental contract to help divorcing parents cooperate more effectively are provided. The scripts and the contract emphasize three points: (1) parents will support the other's parenting role and will not undermine the former spouse's authority with the children; (2) parents will not expose children to parental wrangling or embroil them in parental conflicts; and (3) parents will not make children choose between them but, instead, encourage children to be close to both parents at the same time. I suggest that divorcing parents sit down together and discuss the scripts and the contract that follow. After modifying and rewriting them to better fit your circumstances, agree to follow these guidelines as closely as possible.

Sample Scripts

Script 1: Commitment to Support

Each of you will try to support the other's role as parent. You will not undermine each other by saying such things as, "You don't have to pay attention to your father; he only sees you on weekends. I'm the one who is really raising you" or "Your mother's impossible. You don't have to listen to her." Rather, make the following commitment by speaking it aloud to each other:

> I will support you in your role as [child's name] parent. You have an important part in deciding how [child's name] is raised. I will not make fun of you or disparage you to our child. I will encourage [him or her] to treat you respectfully.

Script 2: Commitment to Child's Relationship

You will encourage your child to be as close and involved with the other parent as possible. Many times parents give off cues, verbal or nonverbal, that make children feel obliged to take sides or choose between their mother and their father. Make the following commitment by saying aloud to each other:

> I will encourage [child's name] to have a close and loving relationship with both of us at the same time. I will encourage [child's name] to spend time with you without making [him or her] feel disloyal to me. I will not pressure our child to choose me over you or to take my side in the disagreements we will have in the years ahead.

Script 3: Commitment to Not Involve Child in Problems

The problems that arise between the two of you will be settled without involving your children in any way. Avoid sending messages to each other through the child, such as, "Tell your mother to stop calling me at work" or "Tell your father he'd better not be late with the support check again." Make a commitment by saying aloud to each other:

I will not use our child when I am angry with you but will try to talk directly with you instead. When there are conflicts between us, you and I can discuss them and decide together what is in our child's best interest. When we cannot solve our problems on our own, we will meet with a neutral mediator to ensure that our children do not get caught in the middle.

Sample Agreement

Each parent should sign an agreement of intent, which reads something like the following:

> I agree to support [ex-spouse's name] parental relationship with our children. I will not undermine your relationship with our children, make the children choose between us, or involve the children in our disagreements. Although I probably will not be able to do this all of the time, I realize this is in the best interest of our children and will try to follow these guidelines as best I can.
>
> Signed _____

The preceding scripts and contract lay down the ground rules that parents need to follow to support their children's development. Both parents can also ask grandparents, attorneys, and others to take a neutral stance toward the other parent. Children need grandparents, relatives, and family friends to be supportive without taking sides or blaming either parent. That is, rather than echo critical comments, other adults should be informed that they are more helpful if they respond to complaints from one parent about the former spouse by making neutral or minimizing comments, such as, "I'm sorry that happened. It sounds like the divorce is hard for everybody in your family."

It is harder for children to feel secure if grandparents, friends, stepparents and others express their love for one parent by criticizing the other. All of the adults and professionals in and around the family can be thoughtful so as not to further polarize parents. Instead, they should act in ways that encourage children to have the best relationship with both parents that is possible. Children will do better in life when they have had permission to be close to both parents at the same time.

Suggestions for Further Reading

The Good Divorce (C. Ahrons, New York: Harper, 1994) and *Healthy Divorce* (C. and S. Everett, San Francisco: Jossey-Bass, 1998) are books that help parents work together cooperatively so they can establish more effective parenting plans and give children permission to be close to both parents at the same time. Although parents may wish to learn more about loyalty conflicts, little is available in the popular press literature on this topic. N. Kalter's book, *Growing Up With Divorce* (Ballantine, 1991) and *Families Apart: Ten Keys to Successful Co-Parenting* (M. Blau, Putnam, 1993) may also be helpful.

Chapter Nine

Parentification: Turning Children into Adults

"My Child Is My Best Friend. What's Wrong with That? She's Very Happy and So Responsible!"

Adults nurture and guide in healthy families and children receive and follow. It doesn't matter what family type or form it is. Parents in families that function well, whether they are single-parent families, intact families, or stepfamilies, have effectively distinguished adult business (roles and responsibilities) from child business. Family therapists refer to this as clearly defining "intergenerational boundaries." By necessity, children in single-parent families usually need to take on more household duties, and children tend to grow up faster, because there is often more sharing between parent and child than in two-parent families. However, even though children in single-parent families may take on more chores and responsibilities, in healthy single-parent families the roles of adults and children are clearly differentiated. The single parent still performs the leadership functions for the family, such as providing a well-organized household with predictable daily routines, making decisions and plans for the family, and setting limits and enforcing rules for children. Further, although parents have legitimate needs for companionship and support, these needs primarily are met in peer relationships with other adults rather than through the children.

This fundamental model for family life often goes awry in the aftermath of divorce. Many single-parent families have problems when adult and child roles are not clearly distinguished, when boundaries between the adult's and the child's generations are blurred, and when adults have too many personal needs met through the children. This can occur in nuclear and stepfamilies as well, but is most likely to develop during the stage of being a single-parent family. In families where this occurs, children take over so many adult responsibilities or try to meet so many of their parents' emotional needs that the roles of parent and child become reversed. Family therapists call this role reversal *parentification*.

Most parents are not familiar with the concept of parentification, and the idea is easily misunderstood at first. This role reversal occurs in several different ways. Children are parentified when they take over so many household responsibilities that, in effect, they become the parent in the family. These responsibilities may include excessive babysitting, cleaning, dinner preparation, disciplining of younger children, and other tasks. More subtly but more commonly, this switching of roles also occurs when children assume a disproportionate sense of responsibility for a parent's emotional well-being. These children, who may try to solve the problems their parents are having with loneliness, alcoholism, depression, or anxiety, take care of their parent at the expense of their own needs.

What is the difference between a child who is put in the position of acting like a parent and a child who is simply asked to be appropriately responsible and helpful? The distinction is a matter of degree. In talking about parentification, I am not suggesting that children should be spoiled or raised to be unresponsive to parental needs and concerns. It is important for children to share in household duties and learn that they can give to parents as well as receive from them. Parentification occurs when a line is crossed and the child meets too many of the adult's needs and responsibilities. These children, who are turned into pseudo-adults and confidants, are often described as perfect or wonderful, but they suffer adverse consequences in the long run.

Three Types of Parentification

Parentification usually occurs in one of three ways: (1) when children provide security or direction for their parent, (2) when they meet parents' needs for closeness or companionship, or (3) when they run the household and become the primary caregiver for younger siblings. These three styles of parentification each merit closer examination.

Providing Security

In response to the stress of divorce and the increased demands of being a single parent, some parents begin to meet too many of their own adult needs through their children. When a boy is parentified and given an adult role in the family, he is often asked to provide stability or guidance for his parent. In this form of role reversal, boys are called on to take care of their parent and help caregivers manage their adult lives. In our first example, a very adult little boy has learned to take care of his mother extremely well, even though he is only nine years old. Although this competence and caring seems positive at first glance, further inspection reveals that it is highly problematic. Let's look at one experience that is typical of how a boy takes care of his mother rather than having her take care of him.

Jeff

Jeff's parents had recently divorced, and he was moving with his mother and two younger sisters to a new city. Jeff was sitting next to his mother in the front seat of the car, and his two sisters were in the back. As they approached the new city, Jeff's mother began to feel anxious and overwhelmed by the prospect of resettling her family and beginning a new life on her own.

Little Jeff had already learned to be highly attentive and responsive to his mother's concerns. He sensed her anxiety and began reassuring her that everything would work out all right. Jeff told his mom she was a good mother, as he often did, and that he just knew she would be able to find a good job soon. Yet, despite his many reassurances, Jeff's mother still felt upset and had increasing difficulty finding the right intersections and exits from the busy freeway. Without being asked, Jeff reached into the glove compartment for a map and started locating the exits and streets they needed! At only nine years of age, Jeff was accurately reading a road map and showing his mother where to go.

What is the meaning of this brief scenario? Jeff is assuming too much responsibility and providing too much control and direction for his mother. He is acting like a parent and taking care of his mother rather than behaving like the child he really is and being taken care of by her.

It is remarkable that Jeff can read a map at such a young age; he can do things that many teenagers can't. Like most boys who have been drawn into adult roles, Jeff has not only learned to be highly capable but he is sensitive to his mother's insecurities. What is wrong with raising such a competent and caring son? Isn't it desirable for a child to be supportive during a time of stress? Of course it is, but only if this type of adult behavior occurs situationally and does not characterize daily interactions.

If, after a period in which a child becomes the "parent," the mother later regains her composure and appropriately resumes that role, the result will be capable, perceptive children who have learned that they can give as well as receive. However, when this way of responding characterizes the parent–child relationship, as it did for Jeff, the child is acting like a parent to the adult. Children like Jeff who do that get along very well throughout childhood. As we will see, however, they begin to deal with the troublesome consequences of switching roles when they reach late adolescence and early adulthood.

Providing Closeness and Companionship

When a marriage ends, adults usually lose whatever friendship and affection they may have shared with their spouse. The second type of parentification occurs when parents begin to meet these needs for emotional support through their children. Parents who describe their children as their "best friend" or their "lifeline," or who characterize their relationship as having "a very special kind of closeness," often are meeting emotional needs through their children that should be met through peer relationships with other adults.

These simple human needs to talk and share, to be listened to and feel understood, are certainly valid. It is essential that parents meet these personal needs for support through other adults, however, rather than through their children. Meeting adult needs for friendship or understanding through children is the form of parentification that is most likely to occur with daughters.

In the example to follow we can see how exciting it is for a daughter to be put in the adult role of mother's friend and confidant.

Mrs. Winter

Before the divorce, Mrs. Winter had always been especially close to her ten-year-old daughter, Joan. Mrs. Winter and her own mother had shared a special kind of closeness that had been very important to both of them, and she now enjoyed that same kind of special connection with her daughter. Following the breakup, however, Mrs. Winter began to describe her daughter as her "best friend" and praised Joan for being a "perfect" child—so responsive emotionally and mature in her understanding.

Joan too was loving this special relationship she was sharing with her mother. Although she wished her parents had not divorced, things were better now. Joan missed seeing her father sometimes but they had never been very close anyway. Joan knew that now she was even more important to her mother than ever, so seeing less of her father was a trade-off she could live with.

Joan and her mother talked over all the significant things in Mrs. Winter's life. Joan knew her mother was mad at a friend at work for gossiping about her, and she even knew all of the untrue things this "friend" had said. Joan also listened to her mother's worries about money and knew they only had $36,000 a year to live on now, compared to nearly $60,000 before the divorce.

The most exciting confidences they shared were stories about what went on during her mother's dates. Mrs. Winter would describe the men she went out with; regularly, she asked Joan whether she should continue dating them. Mrs. Winter also confided to her daughter whether her date had tried to kiss her before she felt she knew him well enough. Soon Joan was asking her mother's boyfriends where they would be going, what they would be doing, and when they would be home! Mrs. Winter would laugh, delighted at Joan's concern, but Joan didn't think this was funny. She worried about her mother when she was out. Joan would wait up, anxiously awaiting her return, and then they would laugh and giggle together as they discussed her mother's love life late into the night. Joan felt so grown up and important because she could talk with her mother about such adult concerns. In fact, her girlfriends at school had begun to sound so boring and childish in comparison.

Running the Household

The third type of parentification can occur with children as young as six or seven years but usually takes place with teenagers, especially if they are oldest daughters. These children are given parental responsibilities for rearing younger siblings and managing the home. In the previous two examples, children met parents' emotional needs that should have been met by other adults by acting as adults and taking care of their parents. In this third form of role reversal, children are not fulfilling emotional needs but are taking over adult responsibilities for child care and running the household when a parent has abdicated.

Boys and girls who are asked to provide emotional support do not resist these attempts; they readily take this role and are very reluctant to relinquish it. It is highly rewarding for children to hold such an important and influential position in relation to their parents. In contrast, children who are required to take over childrearing and homemaking responsibilities may become depressed and, by adolescence, often become angry and defiant. For instance, oldest daughters in single-parent families may take on the role of mother and feed, dress, and discipline their younger siblings every day. With this kind of parentification, the adolescent is not just taking on her fair share of the family workload, she is fulfilling the parent's childrearing obligations. Some fourteen- to eighteen-year-old girls become pregnant or marry early in order to get out of the family and escape this type of parentification.

The following example shows how fifteen-year-old Mike angrily rebels against this parentified role.

Mike

Mike and his divorced mother, Nancy, had been at war for over a year, ever since Mike's father had been transferred overseas. When her former husband moved away, the responsibility for raising their three children fell to Nancy. The children's father used to take them to his house many weekends, and sometimes they would go away on trips with him when they had vacations from school. This relief from the demands of raising three children while working and trying to go to school part-time had been a lifesaver for Nancy.

Once this respite was lost, however, Nancy began to feel overwhelmed by the unrelenting demands of raising three children alone. Irritable and depressed from her mounting fatigue, Nancy began to cope by giving fifteen-year-old Mike more responsibility for taking care of her seven-year-old daughter and ten-year-old son.

Within six months of his father's departure, Mike was practically running the household by himself. Nancy expected Mike to come home and watch his little sister after school and start dinner. Two nights a week, when Nancy went directly from work to evening classes, Mike was expected to cook something for dinner and put the younger children to bed before Nancy returned at 10:00 P.M. Nancy also needed some time for herself on weekends to do homework and required Mike to watch his brother and sister because Nancy could not afford a babysitter. Nancy felt guilty about giving so many responsibilities to Mike. She felt as if she were failing as a mother, but her guilt only served to make her want to stay away from home even more.

Her seven-year-old daughter, Laura, was sad about her father's departure, and now she felt her mother was leaving her, too. She was clingy and demanding, often whining and pleading for Nancy to stay home more. In the unfortunate but common escalating cycle that often occurs, this only tried Nancy further, making her feel even more guilty and more like escaping from the home. The younger brother, Doug, hated that Mike tried to "boss him around" and tell him what to do all the time. As Doug became angrier, it was almost impossible for Mike or Nancy to control him. Soon the constant provocations and mean-spirited competitiveness between the two boys escalated into brawling fistfights. Helpless to make them stop, Nancy knew she had completely lost control.

Mike was angry at everyone. He hated his mother for putting so many demands on him and turned this hostility toward Laura and Doug. But at the same time he resented this parental role so much, it also felt good to be the boss. Mike liked having so much power in the family and did not want to give up the authority when Nancy returned home. Nancy and Mike began quarreling like a married couple over who was in charge. The boys fought more viciously than ever and Laura cried more often as everyone sensed that no one was in charge. At this point Nancy felt defeated and called the psychological clinic for help with her "uncontrollable" teen-aged son.

The Adverse Consequences of Parentifying Children

Why is parentification such a big problem for children? What are the negative consequences for children such as Jeff, Joan, or Mike? To understand the problems that follow from parentification we need to look at both the short-term and the long-term effects. The problems of parentification usually are not evident in childhood; instead, they appear during the transition from late adolescence to early adulthood. Rather than having behavior problems or emotional symptoms, children like Jeff and Joan are exceptionally well-behaved.

Routinely, parents, teachers and other adults interacting with them describe them in idealized terms such as *perfect*. These children are rewarding for adults to be around; they are more mature and responsible than other children their own age. Instead of making demands on their parents and teachers, as normal children do, these parentified children satisfy parental needs and make adults feel better. In the short term, this type of parentification easily occurs because this subtle role reversal is gratifying for both the parent and the child. Adults have their needs taken care of, and the child enjoys the power and importance of having this special status.

The problematic consequences of parentifying children only become evident in the long term. Because the natural flow of nurturing from parent to child is reversed, the child's emotional needs are not met. Although parentified children initially enjoy this special relationship with their parent, as adults they come to resent having been used by their parent and deprived of their own childhood.

The long-term effects of making children responsible for the emotional needs of their parents are significant. Parentified children grow up to feel overly responsible for others, anxious about ever needing help or depending on others, and guilty about having their own needs met. Because the basic model for relationships they have learned is only to take care of others, parentified children often reenact the role of provider or rescuer in subsequent relationships. For example, they often select careers as caretakers and become nurses, counselors, or ministers. Although kind and capable, they feel guilty about saying no, setting limits, and meeting their own legitimate needs. Because they do not draw boundaries well, they tend to overidentify with others' problems and are prone to burn-out. Because they grew up having to be in charge or take care of their parents, they feel threatened by relinquishing this control in their adult lives. It may be hard for them to share work-related responsibilities, for example, although at the same time they resent having to do everything themselves. These control issues may surface in symptoms such as airplane phobias, for example, when they must temporarily relinquish control to the pilot. These parentified children also have problems in love relationships. To be emotionally intimate with someone, they must take the threatening step of relinquishing control and risking shared control or mutuality—uncharted waters that once held real peril.

In these ways the unwanted consequences resulting from role reversal become evident as parentified children grow older and try to establish their own adult lives. The paradox is that children who have acted as adults throughout their childhood have difficulty becoming adults. With this in mind, let's focus on the developmental transition of "leaving home" during late adolescence and becoming an independent adult.

Impact on Emancipation from the Family

During late adolescence and early adulthood, young people pass through a developmental stage of emancipation from the family. At this point, young people physically and psychologically leave their family of origin in some way, becoming more independent adults who are ready to begin their own families. When things go well, loving ties to the family of origin will last a lifetime. However, parent-child relationships become more reciprocal or egalitarian at this time, and offspring increasingly center their lives in their own peer relationships and career goals. Although there are wide cultural differences in this developmental transition, this process of individuation or emancipation involves three complex activities.

First, many young adults move away from home and establish their own separate residence at college, in the service, or in an apartment with friends. At this stage, hopefully, young adults' relationships with friends, mentors at work, and potential mates take center stage, and the family supports these new initiatives beyond the home.

Second, translating their interests and abilities into career goals and achieving success at work become important in the establishment of an adult identity and life structure. Third, young adults may be exploring their own religious beliefs and reexamining their political views. An important part of establishing their personal identity is clarifying their own values rather than merely adopting their parents' beliefs without sorting through their own commitments.

The problem with role reversal is that parentified children are not prepared to leave home psychologically and successfully negotiate these three developmental hurdles. Bound by guilt, they do not have permission to grow up and leave their parent emotionally. Recalling "the ties that bind," it is difficult for parentified children to pursue their own adult lives, as they should be encouraged to do at this age.

Because parentified children have grown up feeling responsible for a parent's well-being, it is difficult for them to leave home, either psychologically or physically. This transition is especially difficult because these young adults feel guilty knowing that their parent still needs them, may be lonely without them, or cannot cope alone. Joan, from the previous example, will feel disloyal when she focuses away from her mother to establish her own close friendships, pursue a career, or marry. The special closeness she has experienced with her mother is a binding closeness. It will prevent Joan from feeling good about herself when she pursues her own goals in life or advocates for herself rather than continuing to orient toward her mother's (or other's) needs.

Impact on Future Relationships

Parentified children such as Joan have difficulty succeeding as adults, in part, because they feel they should keep on responding to their parent's and others' needs rather than defining and carrying out their own plans and dreams. As a young adult, Joan will feel ruled by this binding guilt in several ways. She will be prone to feeling guilty and depressed and will believe that she is selfish and bad when she acts stronger, is more independent, becomes more successful, or asserts what she wants rather than just complying and going along with what others want. Joan may remain uncertain about her career plans for many years and become anxious or depressed rather than happy and proud when she has successes. In particular, it is likely that Joan will have trouble establishing a love relationship with a man who can respond to her needs. She is likely to feel that she must always give because she has never been in a relationship in which it was safe to be taken care of sometimes or acceptable to receive help with a problem.

Finally, without realizing all of this, Joan will probably feel guilty that she is betraying her mother and selfishly forsaking her if she allows herself to enjoy a rewarding love relationship with a man who can give as well as receive. In other words, if a nice guy comes along who treats her well, Joan is likely to find him boring or unacceptable in some other way.

Children who have grown up as pseudo-adults find it difficult to establish egalitarian love relationships in young adulthood. For children such as Jeff, who have taken care of a parent rather than being taken care of, they have always been in control of the relationship. As a result of this role reversal, their appropriate childhood needs have not been met. As adults, it will feel foreign and uncomfortable to relinquish control and have their own legitimate adult needs for affection and caring fulfilled. Receiving from others or being responded to emotionally is unfamiliar and feels unsafe or even inappropriate; they don't know how to respond. Adult intimacy involves giving and receiving love equally. In order to enjoy this balance as an adult, this flexibility must be learned in other close relationships.

Parentified children also have trouble with intimacy because they are afraid of relinquishing control, even temporarily. Often they had to be vigilant in watching over their parent. Perhaps most important, getting close to another may trigger the faulty belief that, here again, they will have to take over and assume responsibility for this person, just as they did with their parent while growing up.

Parentified children often view their own valid human needs to be cared for or helped, even temporarily or in a difficult situation, contemptuously—as unacceptably weak or childish dependencies. In order to avoid the unwanted, shameful feelings evoked by their own needs, children who switched roles with their parent may establish love relationships with needy, problem-ridden partners whom they can "rescue." Others may avoid intimacy and commitment through promiscuity. Either way, it will be hard for a boy like Jeff to have a mutually responsive love relationship with a woman.

Impact on Self-Esteem

In addition, parentified children often cannot ascertain a realistic sense of their own abilities and responsibilities. When children have taken on adult roles, they become too important to the parent and exert too much influence over the parent's well-being. As a result, these children often gain an exaggerated sense of their own importance and of their ability to influence others. Children cannot gain a realistic sense of their own limits and capabilities when they are encouraged in the illusion that they can prop up a parent's sagging self-esteem, maintain the parent's emotional equilibrium, or make important decisions for the parent.

On the other side of their grandiosity, however, these parentified children often suffer with a parallel sense of their own feared inadequacy. This shameful feeling of inadequacy, which is often a continuing but unrecognized source of anxiety permeating their lives, arises because they were never really capable of meeting their parent's needs. It is only an illusion that a child can fulfill a parent's emotional needs. As a result of this family myth, parentified children often suffer from strong performance anxieties as adults and worry about being inadequate to meet the exaggerated demands or unrealistic expectations they place on themselves.

Finally, children who have spent their youth acting like parents have other problems as young adults. Jeff, Joan, and Mike have lost their chance to be a child and, as a result, will probably experience an inner emptiness. For example, parentified children may reflect this depressive void by saying, "I feel as if there is a hole inside of me." However expressed, this emptiness occurs because the natural flow of parental nurturance to a dependent child has not occurred, and these seemingly perfect children have been emotionally deprived.

Why Parentification Occurs

Many parents see their divorce as an isolated event that happened unexpectedly. If we expand this perspective and look at the psychological issues that couples are trying to resolve at different stages of the family life cycle, however, parents can better understand the divorce and why problems such as parentification and loyalty conflicts occur. To gain this understanding, let's leave the topic of divorce temporarily and examine some broader issues of family development.

Becoming a Couple

The birth of the family occurs during the couple's courtship and engagement period. Many of the difficulties parents have during their marriage and following the breakup are problems that were never satisfactorily resolved in this first stage of family formation. Family researchers have identified a number of psychological tasks that the new couple needs to address in order to begin a successful marriage. For example, the couple must establish mutually satisfying routines for making decisions and resolving differences between them: How will they manage money? When will they make love? How will they divide work and other household responsibilities? Will the couple spend their leisure time alone or with friends, visiting family, or developing contacts with business associates? Under what circumstances does the husband, or the wife, make these decisions? Couples do not sit down and overtly devise rules for most of these things, but every couple must establish mutually satisfying patterns for their life together. If the partners do not talk together about their preferences or if one is not responsive to the other's wishes, the groundwork is laid for future problems.

An important task during this stage of couple formation is for both partners to shift their primary commitment from their parents to each other. As observed in Chapter Eight, the couple is trying to establish a stable marital coalition that cannot be disrupted by the competing demands of parents, friends, and work. Chronic marital conflict usually results when one or both partners retain primary allegiance to parents instead of their new spouse.

Shifting loyalty ties from the family of origin to the spouse and forming a successful marital coalition can be illustrated through the familiar ritual of the wedding ceremony. A central purpose of the ceremony is to publicly mark the transition in loyalty from the parents and family of origin to the new spouse. In the traditional Christian ceremony, family, friends, and clergy are assembled, the father walks the bride to the front of the church and, in front of all, the father symbolically gives the bride away. He places her hand in the hand of the waiting groom, steps back from the couple, and sits down beside his own wife. The bride and groom, now symbolically separated from the parental generation, turn toward the clergy person and step forward to be married—publicly announcing themselves to family and friends as an enduring marital couple.

Shifting loyalty bonds from parents to the new spouse is a major developmental task. This transition is challenging for most families, in every cultural context, but becomes especially troublesome in families of origin without a stable marital coalition. The question of who comes first, parent or spouse, may be painfully enacted in conflicts over planning the wedding. For example, young adults who are still embroiled in cross-generational alliances often face a wrenching struggle over whether the ceremony should be conducted the way the couple wants it or the parents' way. The underlying conflict concerns shifting loyalties from the previous generation to the spouse, but it is played out in arguments over who will be invited to the wedding, where it will be held, how it will be conducted, who is financially responsible, and so forth. In contrast, couples who enjoy their wedding day usually have been successful in shifting or rebalancing their primary loyalty from their parents to each other. Such couples are not being pulled apart by guilt-inducing, competing loyalty ties.

In sum, couples who have successfully formed a marital coalition by shifting their primary loyalties from parents to spouse are able to maintain a united front that cannot be divided by parents or others. If they have not established this stable marital coalition, couples usually have far more difficulty in the next stage of family development—having children and becoming parents.

Becoming a Parent

Ideally, the newlyweds will have a few years together to consolidate their relationship before the birth of the first child. This change from a two-person to a three-member family is demanding to say the least. Few couples anticipate how much the new baby will alter their one-to-one adult relationship or how much time and attention the baby will require. Successful couples keep their marriage together by continuing to find ways to spend time together as a couple and continuing to enjoy each other and their own relationship. Unless the marital relationship is nurtured too and given its fair share of attention, it will suffer in the busy years that follow the birth. Thus one of the major psychological tasks for the couple at this stage is to balance the many demands of parenting while still maintaining a marital relationship.

Many couples fail to balance this difficult task, and the marital relationship is lost; it becomes just a parenting relationship. This is especially likely to occur if they have not completed the psychological task of the previous stage—establishing a stable marital coalition. Such couples do not continue to talk and spend time together. Responding to their children, to their work demands, or to others always seems to take precedence over their relationship. Over time, one parent may become resentful and feel unimportant, as if the child (or others) is the only one who matters. Couples who lose their marital relationship to the parenting relationship are more likely to divorce and to embroil children in loyalty conflicts afterward.

Loyalty conflicts are especially likely to occur when the couple was unable to establish a primary marital coalition during the initial stage of couple formation. As a result, problematic cross-generational alliances develop between parent and child to fill the void. Cross-generational alliances established before the breakup usually are exacerbated after the divorce, as parents subtly pressure children to take sides in parental conflict.

Parentification also can result when other psychological tasks in forming a family have not been met. When newlyweds have not psychologically separated from their families of origin or have not communicated well enough to resolve the basic tasks of becoming a couple, they will be less prepared to form an effective marital coalition. With the birth of the first child in the next stage of family life, they will not be able to cooperate and communicate effectively enough to meet the demands of the new baby while still preserving their marital relationship. In this situation, the mother often turns to the child (and perhaps to her own mother) to get her emotional needs met, whereas the father may distance himself from both the mother and the children.

A few years later, the lack of a marital coalition and increasing emotional distance often lead to divorce as children reach preschool and school age. Too often, the already distant father becomes even more uninvolved after the breakup, and the alliance between the mother and the child leads to overinvolvement between them. As the mother tries to cope with the stresses of divorce and raising children on her own, the distinction between the roles of parent and child may become further blurred. Parentification usually begins at this point, as parents begin to have too many of their own personal needs for support or companionship met through their children. Because it may be difficult for single parents to determine objectively whether parentification is occurring, guidelines for assessing this are offered in the following section.

Assessing Parentification

Without realizing what is happening, it's easy to begin relying on a child for comfort as parents try to cope with the stresses of divorce and single parenting. It's fine for children to serve occasionally as listening posts, but the family becomes dysfunctional if this practice becomes habitual. Parents are discouraged from consistently relying on support from sons or daughters or treating them as peers. Even though children love their parents, see their distress, and want to help, they are not equals and are not equipped to deal with adult problems and needs. As we have seen, if children feel they are the glue holding the parent or the family together, they will have a difficult time leaving home and successfully launching a life of their own. By answering the following questions, parents can determine for themselves whether they are parentifying their children.

1. *Are your children assured that you are the one who is in charge of the family?* Even though single parents need more help from their children sometimes, successful single parents communicate in word and deed that they are the adults and they are in charge. It benefits everyone if children feel they have important jobs and responsibilities that contribute to the family. However, if reliance on children interferes with their schoolwork or does not permit time to play with friends, it's too much.

2. *Do you put your child in the role of confidant or emotional caretaker?* Parents are more likely to do this if they do not have adult friends with whom to talk freely and share problems. Single parents have big responsibilities and demanding workloads, and they need friends and a social support system to cope with the stress. These legitimate needs are to be met by other adults, however, not by children. Support groups for parents, such as Parents Without Partners, are available in most communities.

3. *Do your children regularly see you crying, feeling overwhelmed or defeated, or getting too upset when things go wrong?* Most people underestimate how much children worry about their parents and how ready they are to take responsibility for their parents' distress. It promotes growth when children are aware of their parents' concerns, but awareness becomes worry when children see emotional

outbursts. Similarly, "close" becomes too close when children are pulled into adults' concerns that take them away from their own appropriate childhood concerns about school and peers. Parents should establish a buddy system with another single parent and not unburden themselves on their children. In particular, it is usually best to avoid discussing problems with money or financial worries with children.

4. *Do you discuss your dating relationships with your child?* Dating relationships are for adults, not children, and parents want to involve children and adolescents minimally in this aspect of their lives. Single parents are encouraged to keep their children separate from the people they date until it seems likely that this relationship will be ongoing. A parent's love life is adult business and private; children and adolescents will fare better when they are buffered from it.

5. *Do you use your child as an intermediary between you and others?* A parent who asks a child to carry messages to a former spouse or to report on what the former spouse is doing is placing that child in an adult role. The child is being asked meet a parent's needs at his or her own expense. Similarly, having children answer the telephone or door and filter unwanted callers may be steps toward parentifying the child. The adult should be the gatekeeper between the family and others; in particular, children shouldn't be go-betweens between the parent and people who are difficult for the parent to deal with. Although this recommendation will not be apt for many families, putting the adult's voice on the telephone answering machine may be one way to announce to everyone that the parent is leading this family, not the child.

6. *Do you describe your child as your best friend or lifeline, or do you or others characterize your child as perfect?* Although it is gratifying to be so close to such a well-behaved child, it may be a red flag. Sometimes perfect children can be too worried about their parents to act like children. Similarly, it's very rewarding for a child to be a special friend to their parent, but it also burdens them with responsibility for their parent's well-being. Parents in this situation can focus children away from concerns about the parent and toward childhood involvements instead ("You don't have to worry about that, Mary. It's an adult problem and I'll take care of it"). Some parents may want to tell their children that they have only

three jobs to worry about: doing well in school, making good friendships that last, and doing at least one thing to have fun every day.

With only one parent in the family, the boundary line between adults' and children's responsibilities often becomes less distinct because the single parent needs to rely on children more than in two-parent families. If this reliance is not overdone, the increased demands can produce resilient children who are more empathic and capable than many of their peers. However, a clear distinction between the roles of parent and child must be maintained for the family to function effectively. If this line has been crossed, adults need to reclaim the role of leader. Children adjust far better when parents take charge and children are secure in knowing that their parents will take care of them.

Suggestions for Further Reading

As with the previous topic of loyalty conflicts, little is available on parentification outside of family therapy textbooks. A few readers may wish to wade into family therapy textbooks such as *Families and Family Therapy* (S. Minuchin, Harvard University Press, 1974) to learn more about family alliances, loyalty conflicts, and parentification. However, most readers can glean more about parentification and other problematic family roles from the large popular press literature on children who grew up in families with an alcoholic parent (see, for example, *Adult Children of Alcoholics* (J. Woititz, Health Communications, 1990). Readers also may wish to examine a good book, *Becoming Parents: How to Strengthen Your Marriage as Your Family Grows,* by P. Jordan, S. Stanley, and H. Markman (Jossey-Bass, 1999).

For parent support groups or parenting classes, contact the social services department of your local hospital, county department of mental health, or your high school or church.

Chapter Ten

Childrearing Practices

*"How Can You Keep Trying to Tell Me What to Do?
Look How You've Screwed Up Your Life."*

Parents intend to change only the husband-wife relationship through divorce but soon learn that their relationship with their children has changed as well. In particular, the daily business of raising children and heading a single-parent family are usually very different from the life they knew before. Unfortunately, researchers find that in the aftermath of divorce, parents' ability to (1) discipline and effectively control their children, (2) be nurturing and emotionally responsive to them, and (3) provide an organized household with predictable daily routines often declines. In other words, it is not the divorce per se that causes long-term adjustment problems; the culprit is faulty childrearing practices. The bad news is that many mothers and fathers lose control of their children after the divorce and cannot discipline them effectively. The good news is that the marital disruption provides an opportunity for many parents to become more involved in childrearing and more effectively in charge than they were before. Thus the purpose of this chapter is to help parents use the crisis of divorce as an opportunity to become more effective parents.

It's hard for many single parents to enforce rules and consequences when they have no one to back them up. However, it's an entirely different problem to be the responsible parent—the one who is trying to insist on chores and homework—while the other parent undermines that effort and indulges children by offering them vacations or their own phone lines. What can a responsible parent do about this maddening situation? In the short run, some children choose to live with the parent who provides the least supervision and the most lenient rules. Most parents who are serious about enforcing limits hear such threats, especially from preteens and early teenagers ("Listen, I'm going to watch anything I want on this TV, and if you don't like it, I'll just go live with my Dad"). In the face of such commonly occurring threats, parents are encouraged to stand by their convictions and do what their children need, not what they want. Children do not respect parents they can manipulate or parents who cannot say no and discipline effectively because they need the children's approval. Such children do not respect others, either; often they become demanding, selfish, and angry, and especially likely to fail with peers and in friendships. In the long run, however, parents who are coping with an indulgent ex-spouse can be reassured that most children eventually choose the parent they respect the most. Children and adolescents are right in knowing that they are not safe and cannot be protected by a parent who cannot say no to them, cannot tolerate their disapproval, or gives them too much power and control over the parent-child relationship. With this in mind, let's examine four common approaches to discipline and childrearing.

Common Approaches to Discipline

To understand the different styles of childrearing that parents use, consider the two dimensions, Control and Affection, as diagrammed in Figure 10.1.

As is represented on the horizontal axis, parents can vary along a continuum from firm or strict discipline (high control) to permissive or lax discipline (low control). Represented on the vertical axis is parents' variation on a continuum from much warmth, emotional responsiveness, and communication (high affection) to little approval, acceptance, or interest (low affection). Using the high and low points along these two dimensions, parents typically discipline their children using one of four approaches, which could be characterized as (1) authoritarian, (2) permissive, (3) authoritative, or (4) dismissive/disengaged.

Many parents use the *authoritarian* approach, which is strict but harsh (Quadrant II: high control, low affection). This parent issues commands like this: "I'm your Father. Don't ask me why. You'll do what I say or else!"

Figure 10.1. Four Styles of Parenting

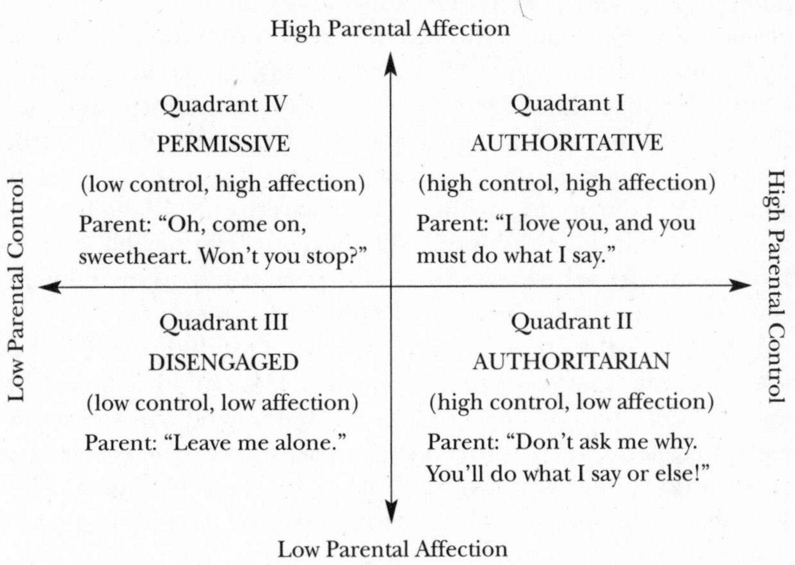

High Parental Affection

Quadrant IV PERMISSIVE (low control, high affection) Parent: "Oh, come on, sweetheart. Won't you stop?"	Quadrant I AUTHORITATIVE (high control, high affection) Parent: "I love you, and you must do what I say."
Quadrant III DISENGAGED (low control, low affection) Parent: "Leave me alone."	Quadrant II AUTHORITARIAN (high control, low affection) Parent: "Don't ask me why. You'll do what I say or else!"

Low Parental Control ← → High Parental Control

Low Parental Affection

In sharp contrast, many parents employ a *permissive* approach that is loving but lax (Quadrant IV: low control, high affection). This parent pleads or negotiates: "Oh come on, sweetheart. Why won't you stop?" Neither of these childrearing strategies works as well as the lesser-known *authoritative* approach (Quadrant I: high control, high affection). This approach combines firm limits with warmth, stresses communication, and provides reasons and explanations for rules (it is unfortunate that the two terms *authoritarian* and *authoritative* sound so similar and are easily confused). The authoritative parent says, "I love you, and you must do what I say." Although many parents erroneously believe they must be either strict or loving, authoritative parents are most effective because they can be both at the same time.

Finally, the fourth parenting style is *dismissive;* parents are disengaged from their children (Quadrant III: low control, low affection). This parent says simply, "Leave me alone." Let's look closely at these four childrearing strategies and contrasting styles of discipline.

Authoritarian Parenting

Perhaps the most common (and ineffective) method of discipline is the authoritarian approach (Quadrant II: high control, low affection). Authoritarian parents give children clear expectations about what behavior is acceptable and unacceptable. Parental rules are clearly explained, and the consequences for violating them are consistently enforced. Authoritarian parents also have high expectations that their children will behave in a responsible and mature manner. Children are expected to perform up to their abilities and to be competent and contributing family members.

However, authoritarian parents do not give their children reasons or explanations for their demands. The child is expected to obey without questioning or trying to understand why the parent has set these limits. Children cannot ask why a rule is set. They must simply obey. As illustrated earlier, children who grow up in an authoritarian household regularly hear their parents make statements such as, "Don't ever ask me *why* you can't go out. I am your father. You'll do what I say or else!" Furthermore, there is no room for compromise or verbal give and take between the parent and child. Children are not encouraged to suggest alternatives or to explain their side of the story. Most important, however, authoritarian parents do not couple their stern directives with much warmth or affection. Children usually experience such parents as cold, distant, and intimidating.

Often the threat of parental power and the fear of rejection keep children in line, especially while they are young. This strict, nononsense approach is far better for children than having no discipline at all, but it has major drawbacks. Children obey, but they do so out of fear. As a result, the insecurity children feel with their parent often generalizes to teachers, coaches, principals, and other adults in their lives. Although most children remain intimidated by their authoritarian parents, some become rebellious and defiant as they grow older and more verbal (or, as we will see, when marital disruption erodes the parent's authority). Either way, these children suffer low self-esteem as adults and lack interpersonal confidence, even though they are often achieving and successful.

Another drawback to the authoritarian approach is that it limits the growth of children's intellectual abilities. When children are not given reasons to help them understand why parents have set certain rules and are not encouraged to suggest alternatives or compromises, they do not learn to exercise language and reasoning skills. Children of authoritarian parents score lower on verbal tests of intelligence than children who are given an opportunity to interact with parents over rules and directives.

In healthy development, children learn to obey but without sacrificing their own initiative and positive self-image. Healthy children become self-controlled and self-reliant without losing their sense of being prized by their parents. For children of authoritarian parents, however, the trade-off between acting on their own wishes and maintaining parental approval is too severe. Because authoritarian parents provide too little nurturance and affection, too much of their children's initiative and positive self-regard is lost in order to secure parental approval. These children are obedient, but they are also anxious because they comply with parents out of fear. These well-behaved, insecure children become harsh, critical, and demanding toward themselves, just as their parents have been toward them. As adults, many children from highly authoritarian families struggle with excessive guilt, depression, unassertiveness, anxiety, and low self-esteem. These personal and emotional problems will be present, even though these people typically are responsible, hard-working, and successful adults.

Permissive Parenting

The authoritarian parent correctly recognizes that children need to know the rules and that the consequences for violating them will be enforced. However, authoritarian discipline is harsh and uncompromising. In contrast, other parents may err on the side of permissiveness, especially in the aftermath of divorce. Although permissive parents provide more affection than authoritarian parents, they are not able to take a firm stance and place appropriate controls on children's behavior (Quadrant IV: low control, high affection). This inability to take charge and discipline effectively may occur for many reasons. Permissive parents may falsely believe that if they are firm they are acting harshly, just like their own parents (who were probably more authoritarian). Or, especially in the aftermath of divorce, some parents fear their children will not love them or stay with them if they say no. Still other parents, perhaps disempowered by their own authoritarian parents in childhood, don't really believe they have the right to be the one in charge and make their children behave or do what they want them to do. For these and other reasons, the balance of power has tipped in permissive families, and children wield too much power and control in the parent-child relationship. Following divorce, these parents often feel disempowered vis à vis their children and may be heard negotiating, bargaining, or even pleading with their children to behave. Parent and child both begin to suffer when control shifts from the parent to the child.

Permissive parents are lax disciplinarians and often indulgent with their children. The children do not know what behavior is expected of them or what will happen if they violate parental norms. Most important, permissive parents do not consistently enforce the few rules they set. As a result, children of permissive parents learn that they do not have to obey because parents will not *consistently* enforce the rules. Thus permissive parents are often loving and communicative, but their children are not disciplined and are not expected to behave in a mature, responsible manner. Without parental expectations that they perform to the best of their abilities, children do not develop the skills or internalize the discipline necessary to succeed on their own.

The children of permissive parents also have problems later in life. Behavior problems may develop involving school authorities for truancy, for example, or with the police for reckless driving, or for involvement with drugs and alcohol. Finally, as adults, they tend to be more self-centered, demanding, and dependent in their interpersonal relations and less capable of making commitments and following through responsibly on obligations.

Why do these problems develop? Children of permissive parents often learn that they can avoid the consequences of their own behavior. They believe that rules and limits do not necessarily apply to them and, whether by demanding, threatening, procrastinating, or manipulating, they find they usually can get their way. Researchers have found these children to be dependent, immature, demanding, and unhappy. They have little self-control and low tolerance for frustration, and they get along poorly with their peers.

Disengaged or Dismissive Parenting

To understand this parenting style, let's look at the interaction cycle that often follows the breakup. Perhaps feeling overwhelmed by the divorce or afraid of the child's disapproval, many previously effective parents become too permissive in the aftermath of divorce. This inability to discipline effectively (especially with boys) is one of the most pervasive problems for single parents. As two or three years go by, it becomes less and less rewarding for permissive parents to stay emotionally engaged with disrespectful children who have become demanding, bossy, and selfish. Over time, this parent may feel increasingly frustrated and helpless and begin to disengage from angry children who are "ruining my life." Now the message from the permissive parent who withdraws becomes, "Leave me alone." In parallel, some previously authoritarian parents who have now lost their authority and can no longer enforce strictness angrily give up on their "impossible" child. Unsupervised and unwanted, the disaffected child with dismissive parents (Quadrant III: low control, low affection) becomes at risk for the peer influences of drugs, delinquency, and early sexual contacts.

Authoritative Parenting

In contrast to the ineffective childrearing of authoritarian, permissive, and dismissive parents, the effective discipline of authoritative parents embodies three principles. The first step is clearly and unambiguously communicating to children what behavior is allowed and what is unacceptable. The second characteristic of effective discipline is that children must be told the consequences or punishment for breaking the rules. Third, and most important, the effective disciplinarian consistently follows through and enforces the rules, without becoming angry and without demeaning the child.

Again, researchers have identified this highly effective disciplinary style as authoritative (Quadrant I: high control, high affection). The authoritative approach combines (1) strict limits and reliably enforced rules, (2) reasons and explanations for parental rules, (3) high expectations for responsible and mature behavior, and (4) parental warmth and overtly expressed affection. Highly effective parents possess a wide range of parenting skills that allow them to *combine* firm discipline with nurturant child care. In effect, authoritative parents are saying to their children, "I love you, and that's why you are going to do what I say."

The authoritative parent believes in strict discipline but, unlike the authoritarian parent, couples this with more physical affection and verbal approval. For example, authoritative parents demand obedience but also tell their children stories, roll with them on the floor, hold them in their lap, praise them when they do well, and look in their eyes and say, "I love you." Children more readily cooperate with requests from an affectionate parent than from one who is threatening or distant.

Although authoritative parents are firm about discipline, they also invite children's participation in the process. They encourage children to offer alternatives or compromise solutions. They also tell their children what they would like them to do and explain why certain behavior is encouraged or discouraged. In contrast, the authoritarian parent provides clearly defined and enforced limits but no room for compromises, alternatives, or explanations. Even very young children may be more willing to cooperate if they understand the reasons for the rules. Adult authority seems less arbitrary or unfair when children can participate in the discipline process.

Authoritative parents consistently enforce the rules they set. Permissive parents may offer reasons and explanations to lessen their children's disapproval, but ultimately they do not take a firm stance and convincingly enforce limits. Children are astute judges of how serious their parents are about enforcing rules. If parents enforce rules inconsistently, children will continually try to break them. Thus, whether or not the child has been able to understand or agree, authoritative parents enforce the rules that have been set.

The authoritative parent exercises a wide range of parenting skills. We have seen that the authoritarian parent sets limits but does so harshly, the permissive parent does not believe in establishing controls on children, and the disengaged parent has given up on attempts to manage them. Although most parents falsely believe they have to be either strict or loving, authoritative parents have the flexibility to be effective in both ways at the same time. Despite the best of intentions, however, balancing these two domains is hard for most people. Authoritative childrearing requires parents to have a broad enough personality to be both nurturing and emotionally available to children, while still being able to set rules and tolerate children's disapproval for enforcing them. In contrast to the dismissive parent who has, in effect, given up on parenting, the authoritative parent is highly engaged and working very hard.

Authoritative parents also make the effort to talk with children and listen to their concerns. They state the rules, explain why certain behavior is encouraged or discouraged, and consider alternatives and compromises before they enforce the rules. These parents also expect mature, responsible behavior from their children. In order to do so successfully, authoritative parents must be able to accurately assess the upper level of their children's abilities. This can be difficult because children are constantly changing, and the demands for mature and responsible behavior that will challenge children must be balanced with their ability to succeed.

One of the most frequent arguments parents have—both before the divorce and after—is how to discipline children. Clearly, authoritative parenting is the solution to polarizing arguments between loving versus strict childrearing. Although it is challenging for parents to provide this authoritative childrearing, it produces the most healthy, well-adjusted children. Researchers have found that these children tend to be independent, self-controlled, successful with friends, and to have a positive outlook.

Discipline After Divorce

The large majority of children are raised by single mothers after divorce, who often struggle with significant childrearing problems. Although children need clearer limits and even more structured households during and after the breakup, too often custodial mothers become more inconsistent in their discipline. Researchers have found that six years after divorce, many single mothers are ineffectual disciplinarians who give many instructions with little follow-through. These mothers tended to nag and complain, but they allowed children to interrupt often and frequently gave in to children's demands. Especially with sons, many single mothers were observed to be angry, short-tempered, and punitive—locked into a power battle with defiant and disrespectful boys that made life miserable for everybody. In addition to problems with discipline and control, these custodial mothers also communicated less with their children and were less supportive and nurturant.

It is these ineffective childrearing practices that lead to child adjustment problems, not "the divorce," as is so often heard. Because boys in particular tend to respond to the stress of divorce with more active, disobedient, and aggressive behavior, children of divorce require effective, authoritative parenting. Parental affection, coupled with firm control, is essential to children's positive adjustment to divorce. Children of divorce, especially boys, also adjust better in authoritative schools with explicitly defined schedules, clear rules and regulations, consistent but understanding discipline, and expectations for mature behavior. Teachers who are nice but disorganized, or unable to manage disruptive children and effectively control the classroom, are problematic.

Single parents need to work toward adopting the authoritative approach with their children. The problems with the authoritarian and permissive modes increase significantly in the aftermath of divorce and sometimes lead to the disengaged or dismissive style that is so problematic. Children are more likely to defy the authoritarian father because they are angry with him for leaving the family and because he no longer holds the same authority in the family that he did before the divorce. A mother may be more apt to be permissive because she has difficulty assuming the disciplinary role the father used to have. It will be especially difficult for her to enforce rules if (1) she needs her children's approval too much during this stressful period or (2) she holds the false belief that if she takes a strong stance and makes her children behave, then she is responding in the same hurtful ways that her own authoritarian parents may have acted toward her years ago. Thus, even though children need authoritative parenting during and after the breakup, it is difficult to provide.

Four factors make effective parenting more challenging after divorce: (1) changes in family interaction patterns and relationships, (2) children's anger, (3) changes in the mother's life, as she becomes the disciplinarian, and (4) the father's becoming less involved with the children.

First, discipline is harder in the first year after the separation because changes in family relationships cause children to be more restless and insecure. To feel safer and more secure, children begin to push rules and limits their parents have set in order to test boundaries and elicit firm controls. Children test to see if their parents are going to remain dependably in control of them. Divorcing parents must keep in mind that firm, consistent discipline is an essential source of security and stability for children as they adjust to new family relations.

Second, children may be less cooperative with parental discipline because they are angry. As noted in Chapter Six, school-aged boys are especially likely to respond to marital separation with anger and defiance. Often, children are angry with the father for leaving but (unfairly) express this anger toward the mother because she is available. Most boys and girls become more demanding and disobedient following the breakup, which makes them harder to discipline.

Third, changes in the mother's life contribute to the discipline problem. As detailed in Chapter Six, the father generally handles most of the discipline of sons. After the marital separation, the single mother often must take on this new role of disciplinarian. Escalating wars often occur between single mothers and sons that make life miserable for both. Mothers are frustrated when they fail to control their angry and disobedient sons and, as a result, become more critical, punitive, and unsupportive of them. In turn, these sons become even more provocative, uncommunicative, and disobedient so that mothers feel more out of control and more like failures as parents. Because this problematic cycle tends to continue—it is not a time-limited phase that children outgrow—it is essential for these single mothers to attend parenting classes, seek counseling, read childrearing books, consult with trusted friends and respected teachers, or find other ways to get the help they need to regain control.

Finally, the father's ability to control his children tends to diminish following divorce because he usually spends less time with his children and, as a result, has less influence over them. Even when he remains actively involved, however, children are often less responsive to his attempts at discipline than they were before the separation. And, if the father becomes more interested in winning the children's approval than in enforcing the rules—as often happens—children receive even less of the discipline and guidance they need.

Thus, several factors converge to make discipline more of a problem following separation: the children are harder to manage; the mother is trying to assume new parental responsibilities; and the father's authority is declining. These circumstances each contribute to less-effective discipline, which in turn leads to behavior problems in the children. As attempts to set limits and establish controls fail at home, children begin to have problems at school with teachers and classmates as well. Often the issue of effective discipline becomes the single most important issue facing divorcing families.

In the following section, we will explore what parents can do to improve their parenting effectiveness in the aftermath of divorce. Because so many problems begin with failed discipline following the divorce, let's begin there.

Effective Discipline

In almost every family—whether intact, single-parent, or stepfamily—discipline is the parents' foremost concern. I once asked forty mothers and fathers attending a seminar to write down their most important parenting problem. Thirty-nine responses focused on the issue of discipline! Many parents report that it is difficult to get their children to mind them and, as we have just seen, these problems with discipline only increase after the breakup. We now know that if parents do not effectively discipline them, children of divorce are far more likely to develop adjustment problems than children who are disciplined effectively.

Giving Warm but Firm Discipline

Positive adjustment in children depends on parental control because children feel safer and more secure when parents effectively discipline them. Children want their parents to take charge of them by setting and enforcing realistic rules; they become calmer and feel happier when parents are in control. Parents often ask the question, If children want their parents to be in charge, why do they push limits and disobey rules? As emphasized earlier, children disobey to test how serious their parents are about enforcing the rules. Children know they are not safe and cannot depend on the adult to take care of them unless they are certain that their parents are in charge.

Communicating Effectively

Effective disciplinarians begin by rewarding children's positive behavior. When children dress themselves, take out the trash, share toys, say thank you, or sleep through the night, parents need to reward this good behavior with smiles, praise, hand-clapping, high fives, winks, and so on. Authoritarian parents, who are reluctant to affirm their children when they behave well, make the mistake of responding only to problem behavior. Children obey better when they are appreciated for what they do well and when they feel loved.

In order to discipline effectively, parents must be able to communicate clearly and directly what they expect of their children. Permissive parents fail to give children clear expectations for what they should and should not do. Their children are not well-behaved, in part, because they do not know what is expected of them. For example, when such a child misbehaves by hitting a younger sister, permissive parents give vague corrections such as, "Why are you hitting your sister again? Come on, that's not very nice." In this vague directive, the child is not told clearly to stop or what to do instead, and does not know what consequence will result if misbehaving continues.

Alternatively, another type of ineffectively authoritarian parent barks commands but does not enforce them. These parents, who are angry and often criticize or embarrass their children, can easily become embroiled in coercive cycles. In the case of the child hitting a younger sister, such parents shout, "Knock it off right now! What's wrong with you? Can't you ever get along with anyone?" In this case, the parent communicates that the child should stop hitting, but this central message is lost in the additional demeaning messages. Because they shout, threaten, and spank repeatedly, these exasperated parents provide a role model of someone who is irrational, upset, and out of control—behavior their children imitate. In particular, negative coercive cycles escalate as children learn that they have the power to agitate their parents. Knowing they do not have to respect or obey, these children often continue purposefully to taunt and provoke parental outbursts.

In contrast, authoritative parents communicate more clearly and directly with the child. They do not make global, nonspecific commands that children cannot readily follow ("Look at this mess. Don't you care what your room looks like? Do you think you're going to watch TV this morning? Give me a break!"). Instead, they make clear, specific requests ("If you have all of these Legos picked up and these clothes put away before the clock says 8:00, you can watch Rugrats for thirty minutes").

Another example of authoritative parenting is when a parent who sees a child hitting a younger sister immediately gives simple, direct commands. The parent walks over to the child, bends over to make close eye contact, has a stern facial expression, addresses the child by name, and in a calm but firm voice gives a single directive with a specific consequence: "John, stop hitting her, or you will have to go to time-out." If the child does not obey, the parent backs up commands with immediate consequences: taking the child by the hand and placing him in the time-out location.

Using Time-Out

Parents must find ways to effectively control their children without resorting to intimidation through physical violence, ridicule and shame, and without threats of abandoning them. Time-out is a highly effective discipline method. It allows parents to be effectively in control and stop unwanted behavior without becoming angry or losing control of their own emotions, which is essential.

How does time-out work? In a nutshell, parents must first select two or three specific behaviors they want to eliminate, for example, having temper tantrums, using profanity, biting, climbing on furniture, hitting, or talking back. Parents then locate the place in the house that is most boring for their child; it should be away from other people, the TV, toys, pets, and other stimulation. For example, a chair in the corner of a quiet room or the bottom step of the staircase may be suitable. Parents should explain the time-out program to their children in advance. When the targeted misbehavior next occurs, the parent places the child in the time-out place. The parent sends the child to time-out using no more than ten words (no arguments, no lectures) and no longer than ten seconds after the targeted misbehavior occurs. It is ineffective to give time-out for misbehavior observed five minutes earlier. Thus, the next time the child hits a younger sibling, the parent responds immediately by saying, "You have time-out for hitting your brother," and taking the child to the time-out location.

Time-out can last one minute for each year of the child's age—two minutes for two-year-olds, ten minutes for ten-year-olds, and so on. Parents can set a portable egg timer when the child goes into time-out and should not interact with the child again until the timer rings (that is, the parent does not respond when the child protests, "But you. . . . "). When the timer rings, children know that time-out is over and must tell the parent why they were sent to time-out. For example, the parent can say, "The timer has rung. Why did you have time-out?" The child might respond, "I hit my brother." The parent can then reply, "Yes, you had time-out for hitting your brother. Time-out is over now." If the child leaves time-out early or creates a ruckus while there, the parent doesn't become upset or threaten but simply restarts the timer. After the timer has rung and the child has stated the reason for being put in time-out, the incident is over. The parent does not scold, lecture, withdraw emotionally, or remain angry with the child; instead, everyone returns to normal activities.

Parents cannot use time-out to make children initiate good behavior or do what they do not want to (for example, clean their rooms or do their homework), but it is remarkably effective in stopping undesirable behavior in a short time. Before beginning a time-out program, parents need more preparation than we can cover in this book to handle complications that may arise (for example, if the child refuses to go to or remain in the time-out location). There are many good books on time-out and other methods of discipline, as well as parent training classes, for parents who are struggling to remain in control of their children.

In addition to time-out, effective disciplinarians employ many other management strategies. At times they may actively ignore children who are misbehaving. For example, if a young child is whining or having a temper tantrum, it is often effective to turn away and act absorbed in another activity or to simply walk out of the room. The parent should avoid eye contact with the misbehaving child and must not look angry or frustrated or the maneuver will not succeed. Children are rewarded when they can provoke parents and will continue to do so as long as they can succeed. As soon as the misbehavior stops, parents must be sure to turn their positive attention back to the child for a minute or two. This final step is essential if the approach is to work.

Using Natural Consequences

Effective disciplinarians also use "natural consequences," although this is more effective for school-aged than younger children. A natural consequence is the result that naturally follows from a child's misbehavior. Some examples of natural consequences are pushing another child and getting pushed back, not sharing with a friend so that the friend goes home, playing rough with a toy and then breaking it, or not getting to school on time and having to stay after. Some parents let children escape the natural consequences of their misbehavior by telling the other child to stop pushing back, allowing another friend to come over, buying a replacement toy right away, or asking the teacher to let the child go out to play. However, parents must not protect children from the real-life consequences of their behavior. Such indulged children are being "enabled," and they often become disrespectful, demanding, selfish, dramatic or attention-seeking, insensitive to others, and less capable of sustained work. Authoritative parents allow children to experience the consequences of their behavior without intervening to rescue them.

Using Logical Consequences

In many situations, of course, parents cannot use this approach. When natural consequences are too serious or dangerous (for example, riding a bicycle in the street), parents can use "logical consequences," which are punishments that logically fit the child's misbehavior. For example, if a child rides a bicycle in the street, it is put away for four days; if a child does not brush his teeth, no desserts or sweets are allowed until brushing is resumed; if a child does not do homework, the television or telephone is turned off until it is completed. In this way, logical consequences follow directly from the child's misbehavior. Parents should communicate these consequences clearly and firmly but without anger or emotional withdrawal. Furthermore, when enforcing these consequences, parents must not become embroiled in arguments that only allow children to escape immediate consequences. Too often parents make idle threats. The child's behavior then escalates, and the parent gets frustrated and overreacts, which the child uses to punish or further provoke the parent ("You're telling me to act my age! Ha! Look at you yelling like that; you should be ashamed of yourself. Come on now, Mom; we all know you can do better than that. Come on now, time to act like a big girl").

Anticipation

Effective parents often avoid the need to discipline by anticipating situations that are likely to arouse problems. For example, when they take children grocery shopping in the late afternoon, parents first give them a snack so they do not feel hungry and demand sweets in the store. Or when they walk in the door after a long day at work, such parents don't talk on the telephone until they have spent time with each child. Or when several children are playing indoors and rough-and-tumble begins, parents intervene at these critical moments before things escalate by providing children with more direction and structure. Initiating projects with blocks, puzzles, or art materials, for example, refocuses children's play. Continuing in the same vein, knowing that siblings often begin to provoke each other as soon as the TV is turned off, parents can use a preventive measure: direct children to separate activities that preclude the likely conflict. For example, Mother might say, "I'm going to turn the television off now because the program has just ended. Johnny, I want you to stand up and feed the dog; Melissa, help me put the groceries away. I do not want you to fuss with each other as the TV goes off now." By anticipating potential problems in these ways, parents can prevent many discipline problems from ever beginning.

The Role of Temperament

Finally, children's temperament is an important aspect of the discipline issue. Every grandmother knows that some children are harder to raise than others. Researchers have given scientific backing to this folk wisdom by identifying a number of biologically based behavioral styles or temperament characteristics that make some children easier to raise and others more difficult.

In the first few years of life, some children are more irritable, more difficult to soothe when distressed, more fearful of new people and places, more active, more intense in their emotional responses, and more irregular in their biological rhythms of feeding, sleeping, and eliminating. These children, who are more often boys than girls, are temperamentally more difficult for many parents. Such children are not "bad" in any way, although frustrated parents may soon begin telling them they are. Some children are simply born with certain physiological characteristics that make them more challenging for most parents to raise.

For example, suppose a new mother has a baby that cries readily and is not easily soothed. Although this mother is just as capable as the mother next door who has a temperamentally easier child, she is likely to feel inadequate because her baby cries a great deal and she cannot do anything about it. And what if her baby is also very intense in his emotional responses? Negative cycles often begin to escalate as the mother's feelings of frustration and inadequacy lead her either to anger and rejection toward the child or to depression and withdrawal. Unfortunately, either response only increases the child's crying. Furthermore, if the baby also has irregular biological rhythms, this mother will have additional troubles because it will be difficult for her to plan her day and carve out time for herself, as she doesn't know when her child will be hungry or want a nap. This exasperated mother will not be able to find much-needed relief from this loud, "demanding" baby, and she may become further frustrated and short-tempered with him—and even more discouraged about her ability to be a good mother. Before too long, many parents in this situation begin to think of their child as "bad" and respond accordingly—a sad outcome indeed.

It is easy to see how children's difficult temperaments can lead to escalating negative cycles between parents and children. Problems in parent–child interaction that start in the first few years of life often are later expressed in behavior problems, as children become school-aged. Researchers have found that the majority of children referred to child guidance clinics for therapy are boys with difficult temperaments. Again, it should be stressed that the temperament itself is not the problem. Some parents enjoy their active and intense children, do not need predictable daily schedules, are patient in helping children warm up slowly to new activities, and are sympathetic rather than frustrated by their children's difficulty making transitions or entering new situations. These parents often think that their child has "character" or a "strong personality" and will grow up to be an interesting person—and they are right. For many other parents, however, the same temperamental characteristics lead to problems in parent–child interaction, so that children are regarded as bad—a characterization that becomes a self-fulfilling prophecy as behavior problems develop that require professional help.

Unfortunately, this problematic sequence does not stop with the parent–child relationship; in most cases, it gradually pulls in the marital relationship as well. Researchers have found that families with temperamentally difficult children have more marital conflict than families with temperamentally easier children. The ongoing conflict between the parent and child creates more stress in the marriage, and researchers have found that parents with temperamentally difficult children are also more likely to divorce.

This unfortunate sequence continues in the years following the divorce, when temperamentally difficult children are more likely to be the target of single parents' frustration than temperamentally easier children. Researchers find that many single mothers in particular are embroiled in ongoing control battles with temperamentally difficult sons. When parents and children become locked in chronic battling, parents need to get help to stop this runaway cycle and regain control. Parents can learn about effective authoritative discipline by reading books, such as those recommended at the end of this chapter. Parent education classes organized by the local YWCA, public school, day-care center, community mental health center, or church also teach parents to take charge more effectively.

Childrearing Problems in Shared-Parenting Households

One of the most common childrearing concerns expressed by divorcing parents is, What will happen to a child who is asked to conform to one set of rules at the mother's house and another set at the father's? As noted in Chapter Eight, it is best if the mother and father can talk together and agree on common rules and childrearing practices. In most cases, however, parents had differing beliefs and values about childrearing before the divorce, and these arguments often continue afterward. However, children can adjust to two different ways of doing things if the rules are clearly communicated and consistently enforced within each household. As long as children know what is expected of them within each home, they are flexible enough to adapt. For example, a mother can say to her child, "It's 8:30 and time for you to go to bed." If the child protests, she can continue: "I know that you don't have a bedtime at your father's house, but you know the rules are different here. Would you like me to read you a story before you go to sleep?"

Sticking to the Rules

As we have seen, however, problems are more likely to arise if one parent enforces the rules and the other is lax. When children are permissively raised and can escape consequences in one household, they will be highly motivated to push the limits to test how much they can get away with in the other household. The parent who is trying to provide a predictable home environment, with clearly defined limits and regularly enforced consequences, will be challenged by these children, especially in the beginning. Parents in this situation can expect extensive testing by children and need to be resilient enough to weather the storm for awhile. Eventually children learn that the parent means business and will stay in charge, even though things are looser at their other home. Gradually, children will stop disobeying and defying the parent when their attempts are consistently met by firmness. These responsible parents may suffer the gauntlet for awhile, but in the long run they are deeply rewarded by seeing that they have indeed earned their children's respect.

Without question, it is difficult for the responsible parent in this scenario to stick to the rules. Initially, most children threaten by expressing preference for the more permissive parent. For example, an adolescent might say, "Fine, if that's how you plan to do things around here, I'm going to just go live with them. I don't need you or your stupid rules anymore. Don't you get it? Things have changed." In response, the effective parent replies, "I would be very sad if you chose to do that, but it doesn't change the rules here. In my house, you have to be home before midnight, and I need to know where you are and who you are with." As hard as it may be, parents need to stand by their convictions and know that, in the short run, some early adolescents may temporarily choose the more permissive household. Over time, however, parents can be reassured to know that most children prefer to be with a firm but supportive parent. Many large junior highs and high schools are scary places to be, even for the cool guys. Preteens and early adolescents feel safer and more cared about with the stronger parent who is not afraid to take charge.

Often the responsible parent resents having to be "the heavy" and begins to give in too often in order to escape this uncomfortable role. It is also fatiguing for responsible parents to hold to their rules and enforce consequences during children's initial period of strong testing. Understandably, many of these parents buckle under the combined weight of the threats and pressures and stop providing the effective discipline their children need. Unfortunately, behavior problems are then likely to begin. Children have no one in either home to provide the much-needed reassurance that comes only from having a stronger adult who is caring enough to remain dependably in control. To help with this problem of a permissive and a responsible parent, the responsible parent should attempt to discuss this parenting problem with the permissive parent and a mediator. Childrearing is easier if this consultation is productive, but even if it isn't, children still adjust far better when one parent remains effectively in charge within one household.

Avoiding Play-Offs

Finally, significant childrearing problems occur in shared-parenting families when children can play one parent off against the other. When divorcing parents are combative, the child uses their conflicts to manipulate them and undermine effective discipline. Problems emerge when children receive support for disobeying the other parent or even when they merely have a supportive ear for complaining about the other parent's rules. For example, the mother will have trouble enforcing limits with her daughter if the child can successfully appeal to her father for support. If mother insists that daughter pick up her room at 8:15 P.M. and go to bed at 8:30, but father scoffs at these rules and tells the daughter that she is old enough to set her own bedtime, the father has, in effect, given the daughter permission to disobey her mother.

In their readiness to continue their conflicts with the former spouse, combative parents undermine the parenting authority of the other parent and allow children to escape the consequences of their behavior. Commonly, these parents do so by drawing a parallel between their own conflicts with the former spouse and the discipline-related problems the child is having with the other parent. For example, whenever eleven-year-old George complained to his mother that his father insisted he do his homework every night at the same time, his mother sighed and said reassuringly, "Yes, I know exactly what you mean; your Dad was always rigid and controlling with me, too." In turn, of course, his father complained to George about his mother's lack of standards and tried to control what George did at her house. George quickly learned how to get the responses he wanted at both his mother's and his father's house and, consequently, had no effective discipline in either one.

What happens to children like George who can play their parents off against each other and escape the consequences of their behavior? In a word, they become manipulative. Such children learn that rules apply to others, not to them, and they will disobey teachers and other authority figures whenever they think they can get away with it. These children may become opportunistic and learn to please those in power for their own immediate gains, thus ingratiating themselves with teachers or popular peers. Oriented to power, prestige, and appearances, these children may be verbally skilled, well-dressed, and top performers in high-status activities such as dance or student government. Despite having such popularity, however, their relationships often are superficial; they have short-lived friendships without enduring or close friends.

As adults, their manipulativeness, self-centeredness, and reluctance to accept limits are especially likely to lead to problems in the world of work, where adults must be able to conform to rules, accept responsibility, and cooperate with others. Their ability to manipulate others and avoid consequences also leads to impulsive acting out. As a result, they are more likely than others to become involved with drugs, especially alcohol. Combative parents who allow children to avoid discipline by playing one parent off against the other are not looking ahead to the significant problems that are likely to follow.

Meeting Children's Needs for Affection and Attention

We have already seen that children have heightened needs for love and affection in response to the breakup of the family. They try to cope with their initial anxiety and insecurity by eliciting reassurance from other adults in their lives. They want to be held and read to, have their hair brushed, and have endless questions answered. These are predictable reactions to divorce, and parents can help their children cope by responding to their bids for involvement.

Boys as well as girls have these heightened needs. Some divorcing parents may be more comfortable responding to their daughters' bids for affection than to their sons'. Cultural norms and traditional sex-role stereotypes can lead us to downplay the reality that little boys feel sad, want to be held, and suffer from the same insecurity as girls when parents part. For boys, these feelings can be discounted or shamefully derided as dependent or weak, which is one of the reasons young boys tend to have more trouble adjusting to divorce than young girls. In the culture of boys, it is hard to overstate the dread evoked by the potential threat of being called a sissy—leading some dads to be afraid of being emotionally responsive.

Although divorcing parents want to be emotionally responsive to their children, what about parents' ability to respond to these increased needs? Previous chapters have already emphasized that divorce is a highly stressful time for parents. Mothers and fathers must cope with new living arrangements, financial worries, and their own personal losses. It's often hard for newly single parents to find enough time or emotional energy to respond to their children's heightened needs. Thus, just at the time they need it most, children often receive less affection and attention in the first year following the breakup. Many parents feel guilty about not being able to meet their children's needs—guilt that may intensify doubts about the decision to divorce and create an unproductive cycle of self-recrimination and depression.

How can this two-fold problem of increased child need and decreased parental availability be resolved? First, parents must establish their own support system. It's hard to respond to your children if you are not doing anything for yourself. Realistically, the demands of single parenting are too great to fulfill without the support of others. Parents can begin to create a support network for themselves through friends and family, as well as community organizations such as Parents Without Partners, church groups, the YMCA, or play groups that form in connection with child-care programs.

Making Time

Having established some ways to take care of themselves, parents can begin to provide three- to eight-year-old children with a regularly scheduled "special time." Parents can set aside specific times every week to be alone with the child. For example, every Monday and Thursday night from 7:00 to 7:30 and every Saturday from 4:00 to 4:30 Johnny is scheduled to have his mother all to himself. They will still be together at many other times during the week, but Johnny knows that he can have his mother's complete attention during these special periods. Children like having these predictable half-hours with their parent, and this special time will have a stabilizing effect on them.

Once children learn that they can always rely on having the time that has been set aside for them, they will be better able to accept those times when parents must put them off. For example, when Johnny is demanding his mother's attention as she is leaving for work, his mother can respond, "I know you would really like me to be with you right now, but I have to go to work. Today is Monday and we will have our special time tonight at 7:00. We can be together then. Let me give you a hug for now and tonight will be our special time just for you and me." Special time can lessen many conflicts over the need for more time and affection.

Parents can use this period as an opportunity to do several important things with their child. Some "special time" ground rules follow:

- *Parent–child time should be spent in a room with the door shut to prevent all interruptions.* Do not answer the phone or turn on the television during this special time. Instead, read a favorite story together or play a game of the child's choosing. The idea is for the parent to give the child undivided attention and *follow the child's lead* as much as possible. For example, the parent might say, "What would you like to do together now?"

- *Parents can use this special time as an opportunity to tell children how much they love them and enjoy being with them.* For example, "I am really glad we have this time when just you and I can be together. I've been looking forward to it all day. I like it when we can just be close and talk and play together like this. Do you know how much I miss you when I am away at work?"

- *The parent can praise the child for at least one thing he or she has done recently.* For example, a parent might say, "I was really proud of you for helping your sister with her homework last night." Even when, for example, a mother is thinking about the six things the child has just done that she didn't like, she can use this time to acknowledge what she has appreciated. If nothing comes to mind, it may suggest that she is depressed or too critical of her child and should keep searching until she finds something positive.

- *Discussion of discipline problems or other causes of parental unhappiness should be saved for another time.* This period is a time for affection, sharing, and play.

- *The parent should offer to hug or hold the child during every session and welcome the child's bids for physical affection.* If this seems awkward or unnatural at first, the parent should try it anyway. The child will be hungry for affection, and such gestures will soon feel more natural. If not, the parent may want to discuss this feeling of reserve with a trusted friend or counselor.

This kind of affectionate and attentive parent–child interaction can do much to alleviate a young child's distress and reduce parent–child conflict. Parents who reliably provide their children with special time and carry out the guidelines I have suggested will have fewer behavior problems to cope with. A parent could try it for one month, two times per week, and evaluate the results. They are often surprising.

Of course, special time is not enough by itself. Parents also need to find frequent opportunities to be with their child, such as reading together, playing games, coloring or building, playing make believe, and so forth. There is no substitute for putting in the time together, with no TV or e-mail and no phone conversations, and with plenty of time spent getting down on the floor to play. This type of affectionate and playful contact goes a long way toward meeting the child's emotional needs of a parent.

Finally, some parents feel awkward telling their children that they love them, are uncomfortable with close physical contact, or cannot think of positive things the child has done. These are problems that stem from parents' relationships with their own parents. All too often, parents unwittingly repeat the limitations of their own parents with their children. I encourage parents who have difficulty expressing affection or approval (or setting limits and enforcing rules) to seek help and learn how they can be a better parent to their own children than their parents were with them. As problems in their own childhood are better understood, it is easier for parents to learn new and better ways to nurture and discipline their children. Although the process may require acknowledging some painful feelings, and parents may feel guilty—as if they are being disloyal to their parents or ungrateful for realistically acknowledging limitations—this relearning makes life richer for parent and child alike.

Giving Structure and Organization to Children's Lives

Young children of divorce adjust better if parents structure their lives with predictable daily routines. As adults, most of us find it boring to have the same schedule every day. We look forward to weekends and vacations when we don't have to plan what we are going to do next, but children are different in this respect. Younger children find security in a predictable routine, and they are made anxious by too much freedom.

Researchers have found that children of divorce who have a more organized home environment are better adjusted than those living in less structured homes. A theme we have touched on before merits mentioning again, that is, some single parents are so stressed by the pain and disruption of divorce and the enormous demands of being a single parent that their ability to provide a predictable family environment is diminished. It is hard to plan a family's activities and make sure that this schedule is followed when you are feeling overwhelmed. Most divorcing parents take a year or more to regain control of their lives and effectively organize daily family routines after the separation. The longer this adjustment takes, however, the more difficulty children have.

It is hard for young children to make sense of their world and understand what happens to them. Because young children do not have the emotional or intellectual capacity to take control of their environment and order their own world, they depend on adults to filter their experiences and make the world manageable. When adults fail to provide structure and predictability, children are confused by their experiences. If parents can provide an orderly and predictable environment, children are calmer and secure enough to explore and learn. It is a romantic notion to think of children as carefree and creative beings who can effortlessly float through a day's activities. Especially in response to the many changes and stress of divorce, children welcome a predictable daily routine and a smoothly organized household.

Divorcing parents can create this routine by organizing their children's day. Children should know where they are going, what they will be doing, and who they will be with each day. Breaks in this schedule should be minimized; when they occur, children should be informed of the changes in advance. As much as possible, children should also know when they have to go to bed, when dinner will be served, and what time parents will be coming and going from the home. It also helps if children know what they can and can't watch on TV and what they have to do to prepare for school each day. Children of all ages should have household responsibilities they are regularly expected to perform, such as setting the table, carrying dishes to the kitchen, emptying trash, sweeping walks, and completing homework. If organizing and planning isn't your strength, hold on to one essential cornerstone: have dinner together (no TV, no telephone, everyone at the table).

All of these activities can be used to establish a predictable daily schedule. Although this structure may sound rigid to some parents, most children of divorce feel more comfortable within an orderly, familiar routine. It empowers children and helps them feel more in control when they know what to expect. This predictable home life, coupled with effective discipline and affectionate caring, helps ensure children's healthy adjustment.

Suggestions for Further Reading

Many books are available to help parents discipline more effectively. Especially good are *The New Dare to Discipline* (J. Dobson, Tyndale, 1996) and *Parenting the Strong-Willed Child* (R. Forehand and N. Long, Chicago: Contemporary Books, 1996). A useful reference for parents interested in child temperament and parenting is *The Difficult Child* by S. Turecki and L. Tonner (Bantam, 2000).

Chapter Eleven

Stepfamilies: Forming New Family Relationships

"You're Not the Boss of Me. You're Not My Mother!"

Stepfamilies are the fastest-growing type of family in the United States. Although the divorce rate is high, people have not given up on marriage. Approximately one-third of all adults who divorce remarry within one year, and about three-fourths of men and two-thirds of women eventually remarry, most within three years. Despite somewhat lower remarriage rates for adults who have children, most people continue to seek a partner in life. As a result of this high remarriage rate, about one out of every four children will spend some time living with a stepparent; stepfamilies now make up nearly 20 percent of all two-parent families with children under eighteen.

Important differences are embedded in these statistics, however. Couples with remarried wives are twice as likely to divorce as are couples with remarried husbands. Why? Remarriages in which children from previous marriages are present have a 50 percent higher divorce rate than remarriages without children. As we will see, couples forming stepfamilies face additional challenges to maintain their marital relationship. In this final chapter, we look ahead to the problems and opportunities children face when their parents remarry.

The Bias Against Stepfamilies

Stepfamilies have an undeservedly bad reputation as problem-ridden families that are not as good as "real" or nuclear families.

This attitude is probably an extension of the stigma of divorce. Prejudice against stepfamilies is clearly seen in the wicked stepmother myth that still flourishes. Cinderella and Snow White taught us long ago that stepmothers are selfish, cold, and cruel. However, it is unfair to see stepparents as villains; it is time they received the support they need.

Stepchildren, too, are sometimes viewed as living in second-class families that are imperfect copies of the idealized nuclear family. One of the tasks of forming a successful stepfamily is to overcome these unfortunate stereotypes and create a positive family identity. The stepfamily can be a rich and satisfying family form that holds the opportunity for marital happiness and rewarding step-relationships. For example, the well-being of both men and women increases after the formation of a mutually caring, intimate relationship such as remarriage. However, life in a stepfamily is very different from the original, nondivorced or nuclear family. To illustrate, consider the household that children may live in if both divorced parents remarry. Children have to negotiate the transition to a complex kin network that may include stepsiblings, half siblings, and stepgrandparents, as well as stepparents and biologically related kin. Clearly, growing up in this household is far different from growing up in a nuclear family, and stepfamilies using a traditional nuclear family as its ideal are headed for disappointment. In this chapter we will clarify the problems that commonly occur and show how they can be addressed in order to build a successful stepfamily.

Children's Reactions to Stepfamily Formation

Children entering stepfamilies face two basic problems. First, it is hard for many children to accept that a new spouse is joining their family. Children often feel as if the new spouse is replacing their other parent; of course, they resist this change. In particular, school-aged children and adolescents are usually very cool toward this "substitute" for their natural parent. Thus loyalty conflicts are aroused by the remarriage, which become especially intense when the natural parents do not get along. Even if their natural parents are cooperative, however, *children still fear that they are betraying their other parent if they accept the new spouse.* Parents and stepparents must keep in mind that, regardless of how infrequently children see the other parent or how irresponsible that parent has been, most children do better when they can keep alive some type of connection to their biological parents. Wise parents accept this need. Adults should not pressure children to acknowledge problems with their natural parent or to accept a personal relationship with the new stepparent within the first two years.

Out of allegiance to the other parent, most children initially reject new spouses and prevent stepparents from feeling that they belong to the family. Children do this, for example, by calling a biological parent at work for permission, even when the stepparent is at home. The child might tell a stepparent that only a "real" parent can sign a school permission slip, or inform the stepparent that their real parent does something a different (better) way, or tell stepparents about good times when the biological family was together and they were a "real" family. Most blatantly of all, the child might make direct verbal accusations such as, "You're not my Dad!" Further, if there has been a high level of parental conflict during and after the divorce, the children are far more likely to reject new stepparents and evoke more conflict with them. In the face of persistently hostile and rejecting behavior by stepchildren, even stepparents with the best intentions may give up.

It is easier for those outside the family to appreciate why children feel threatened by the new spouse. However, it is not as easy to be so understanding when you are the one receiving the brunt of children's anger and rejection. It is hard for most adults when children only speak to the natural parent, constantly intrude on adult conversations, and refuse the overtures of the stepparent.

The second problem for stepchildren is the fear of losing their parent to the new spouse. Children have already suffered a loss through the marital breakup, and they will be highly sensitized and reactive to further losses, whether real or perceived. From children's perspective, the remarriage may pose a threatening loss of their parent rather than the gain of a stepparent. This is especially likely between single mothers and daughters because such close relationships often develop during the period of being a single-parent family. The remarriage brings another adult into this tightly woven team and changes the strong alliances that developed while parent and child lived alone together. In the beginning, children often feel displaced by the intrusion and try to keep their parent for themselves. Children may not feel there is "enough" of mother or father to go around if they have to share their parent with a new spouse. Reluctant to give up any of their parent's attention and affection, many children are jealous, competitive, and rejecting toward the new spouse. This is especially likely in the early stages of a remarriage when children may exhibit more behavior problems than do children in stabilized, divorced families.

Largely because of these two factors, there is often a high level of family conflict during the first two years of the remarriage. Some researchers suggest that it may take up to five years to resolve these significant issues and fully restabilize with a more harmonious equilibrium. As we have seen in other situations, however, age and gender differences play an important part in determining how children adjust to remarriage.

Although boys often have more trouble adjusting to divorce and to life in a single-mother home, with remarriage the picture changes. Girls usually have more difficulty adjusting to the introduction of a stepparent than boys. Why is remarriage easier for boys? Sons can gain something from a stepfather if he is warm and supportive. As described in Chapter Six, many sons have little contact with their natural fathers in the years following the divorce. In addition, many sons are embroiled in angry, coercive control battles with their mothers while living as a single-parent family. If their stepfathers are emotionally responsive, most sons gradually accept their interest, and a mutually satisfying relationship develops. Researchers have found that several years after remarriage, sons with nurturant stepfathers are better adjusted than sons in single-mother homes, and they are as well-adjusted as sons in intact families.

Unlike sons, however, daughters usually have something to lose from the addition of a stepfather. Girls tend to cope with the initial marital breakup better than boys and function better in single-mother homes. Powerful mother–daughter ties often develop in such households, and these close ties are threatened by the remarriage. The daughter is often especially close to her mother and may have become her mother's confidant and friend. Most daughters are reluctant to share this close relationship with their mothers; if it has progressed to parentification, they will be highly resistant to relinquishing their special status and accepting a new stepfather. As a result of the displacement that the remarriage threatens, the level of conflict between parents and stepdaughters becomes as high as it was between divorced mothers and sons in single-mother families. Unfortunately, whereas the high level of initial conflict between sons and stepparents usually diminishes, the level often remains high for stepdaughters years after the remarriage. As a result, most stepfathers will eventually be able to adopt an active parenting role with sons but will continue to be rejected by stepdaughters.

What can we do to reduce tension and increase family cohesion in stepfamilies with girls? As we will examine later, many stepparents need to take on parenting and discipline roles slowly; in some families, they will have to leave these roles to the biological parents. In particular, biological mothers and fathers need to continue to monitor and supervise their daughters, especially during adolescence, and not allow themselves to become discouraged and disengage (see Quadrant III in Figure 10.1).

In addition to these significant gender differences, age is also an important factor in stepfamily formation. In general, the younger the children are at the time of remarriage, the more easily they adjust to the new stepparent. Researchers find that preadolescence is an especially difficult age for remarriage. Almost all stepparents are less likely to be accepted by ten- to thirteen-year-old stepchildren than by younger children and older adolescents. In particular, children's concerns about their own awakening sexuality seems to make even modest displays of affection between the new couple unacceptable. In contrast, older adolescents, who are future-oriented and preparing to leave home, often adjust more easily to the new stepparent.

As with the divorce, however, children's adjustment to remarriage depends greatly on how parents respond to stress and parents' well-being or distress during this transition. Adjustment problems are most likely to occur for stepchildren when signs of parental distress (irritability, anxiety, depression, alcohol use) lead to inept parenting.

Three Styles of Stepparenting

Largely in response to children's ages, most stepparents fall into one of three styles of stepparenting: (1) a primary parent, (2) the other parent, and (3) an older friend.

Primary Parent

Parents with young children who remarry can establish a stepfamily that is similar to the traditional nuclear family, and the stepparent can become one of the primary parents. Young children can readily develop a close attachment to a responsive stepparent. As a result, a stepparent can take on a traditional parent role with children under seven or eight years of age. Stepparents can often nurture and discipline stepchildren as if they were a close aunt or uncle in only a few months. If young children do not have a close relationship with their other natural parent, they may choose to call these stepparents Mom or Dad and fully accept them as parents. Such primary stepparenting is more common when the other biological parent is uninvolved and when children are younger. This is usually the most harmonious stepfamily.

Other Parent

The most common form of stepparenting and the most difficult is that of being the "other parent." This style usually occurs when children have a continuing relationship with their other biological parent, and they are nine to fifteen years old. Children at these ages are likely to reject or antagonize the new stepparent, especially during the first one to two years of the remarriage. As a result, most children who are nine to fifteen years old when their parent remarries do not accept mothering or fathering from a stepparent. Daughters in particular often have a difficult time accepting the authority of a new stepmother or stepfather.

In the beginning, most natural parents need to retain primary responsibility for parenting; stepparents should only move into the parent role gradually, if at all. Some children will be able to accept the new stepparent's authority over time; some will not. Much conflict ensues when the natural parent tries to leave parental responsibilities for nurturing or disciplining children to the new stepparent. In particular, assuming a strong disciplinary role in the beginning is usually fraught with problems for stepparents. Children can be responsive and adjust well when stepparents are warm and involved. However, family life will be more harmonious when stepparents support both biological parents' discipline rather than make their own attempts to control children.

In most cases, stepparenting in the role of the other parent is challenging. Being effective in the role requires effective family communication, the patience to develop a relationship with children, and most important, unambiguous support from the stepparent's spouse to exert authority with the children. It is the job of the natural parent to communicate to the child about showing respect and being obedient to the stepparent. If the ex-spouses remain entangled in overt conflict, however, it is almost impossible for children to develop a close relationship with the stepparent.

Older Friend

In contrast, the third stepparenting style of "friend" is easier. Stepparents who are friends may become important influences in children's lives, but they do so through the personal relationships they develop with children over time, not by filling a parental role. Preteens and adolescents usually prefer this role of older friend and often call stepparents by their first names. These stepfamilies are relatively harmonious because children's ties to the noncustodial natural parent are not threatened, and control battles with the stepparent over power and authority are by-passed.

The roles that stepparents play with stepchildren often change over time. An adult may fulfill all three stepparenting styles with one child over time or enact different roles with different stepchildren. Clearly, *flexibility* is the operative word.

With these three general stepparenting styles in mind, let's look more specifically at the issues confronting stepmothers and stepfathers.

Becoming Stepparents

Men and women face differing challenges as they assume the roles of stepmother and stepfather. Let's explore their experiences as they remarry and enter stepfamilies.

Becoming a Stepmother

Honestly stated, it is difficult to become a stepmother. A woman who marries a man with primary or shared custody of his children will probably encounter significant pressures that often place the stepmother in a frustrating bind.

To begin with, many stepmothers have unrealistic expectations of themselves. Initially, many kind and well-intended women want to make up to the children for the pain they suffered from the divorce. New stepmothers also want to prove that they are not the wicked stepmother portrayed in all of the fairy tales. And all too often they try fruitlessly to create happy, close nuclear families— working hard and sacrificing themselves to try to please everyone in the family.

These self-imposed pressures are intensified because others often hold unrealistic expectations for stepmothers as well. The traditional female gender role dictates that she automatically love her husband's children, even though she is almost certain to be rejected by her new stepchildren. As a woman and wife, she is also supposed to nurture and provide daily care for her husband's children. If she cannot meet these socially sanctioned prescriptions, she is considered to be inadequate—failing as a wife or as a mother. Clearly, these expectations are unrealistic for most women; they cause much pain for many stepmothers and serve only to heighten conflict in stepfamilies.

How do older children respond if their new stepmother tries to assume a mothering role? Out of loyalty to their natural mother and competition for their father, most children reject the stepmother's attempts to be close, to take care of them, or to fill any of their mother's old role. In the process, children tend to idealize their natural mother and actively attempt to make the stepmother feel inferior by comparison.

What happens to stepmothers when children rebuff them? Most keep trying to prove their affection and good intentions but continue to be rejected. A stepmother is placed in a no-win situation. If she complies with cultural expectations and attempts to become a good mother and win the children's love and approval, she will have to submit to rejection and ridicule. At the same time, she will be putting her stepchildren in a position of power and control over her. *Substantial problems result for children and adults alike whenever this occurs.*

Eventually, the children's rejection produces hurt and anger. This stepmother often goes through a period of anger at everyone: her new husband's former spouse, whose influence continues despite the remarriage; her husband, who may spoil or indulge the children because he feels guilty about the divorce; and especially the stepchildren, who reject her and are impossible for her to manage. The stepmother is now in a worse bind. Not only does she not like the children she is supposed to love, she resents them because they are ruining her life and making her fail as a homemaker and perhaps as a new wife as well.

This unhappy scenario occurs with great regularity. Soon after the marriage, many stepmothers who try to assume a primary parenting role begin to feel powerless, angry at the children, and abandoned by their new husbands. As they begin to question their decision to marry ("What am I doing here?"), the level of conflict in the family starts to rise even higher. What is the solution to this unwanted scenario? Relationships between stepparents and stepchildren need to develop naturally over time. There is no instant love. Stepparents must be patient and have realistic expectations for how much acceptance can occur in the first year or two. Before examining this point further, let's look at the issues facing the new stepfather.

Becoming a Stepfather

It is usually easier to become a stepfather than a stepmother because men do not have the same cultural pressures to love and care for children. However, stepfathers have their own parallel set of problems. Stepparents enter the picture with little power or authority as far as the children are concerned. However, men are often expected to discipline children, and the frustrating attempt to assume this role often becomes the single biggest problem in many stepfamilies.

Life will be very difficult for most new stepfathers if they try to assume a disciplinary role with older children within the first two years. Adults (especially the other natural parent) will hear constant complaints of injustice from the children, no matter how fair he is. In most cases, even the most sensitive and effective disciplinarian will be faced with outright defiance of his authority. A power struggle between stepfather and children routinely ensues whenever stepfathers try to take on a disciplinary role soon after joining the family, and this control battle can make life miserable for everyone. In response to this initial failure to discipline children, and to children's reluctance to accept their friendly overtures, too many stepfathers give up on the children altogether and disengage. Soon many begin to ignore the stepchildren, claiming "I married her, not the children." This withdrawal is unfortunate because most stepfathers can become integrated into the family and develop meaningful relationships with children. This usually takes more time than everyone expects, however. Even with young children, researchers find that it often takes stepfathers up to two years to fully enter the family and achieve a co-manager status with their wives.

There are many reasons why older children do not tolerate the stepfather's attempts to discipline them. First, they resent his assumption of their natural father's disciplinary role. As with natural mothers, the biological father is idealized, and the stepfather receives the brunt of children's anger over the divorce and other problems he had little or nothing to do with.

Second, children do not want to obey someone they do not know or care about. Authority over children grows out of investing time in the effort to develop a caring and mutually respectful relationship. Many stepfathers can eventually assume a disciplinary role, but they do so over a period of years as they gradually develop personal relationships with the children. After about two years, most sons accept—even welcome—the stepfather's parenting role, although many daughters do not. Adolescents almost always resist the stepfather's discipline, however, and most mothers must keep this responsibility.

Part of the discipline problem in some stepfamilies is that the stepfather receives conflicting messages from the mother. On the one hand, she may want him to share in the disciplinary role that she has had to carry alone. On the other hand, she may have become so closely allied with the children during her years as a single parent that, without fully realizing it, she may be reluctant to give up any of her special relationship with them. Even mothers who are very tired of being the only one who is responsible for discipline may find themselves resisting their new spouse's attempts to help. These conflicting messages commonly occur and are upsetting for everyone. For the stepfather to eventually succeed at parenting, however, the mother must support him in the actions he takes and communicate convincingly to children that she wants the stepfather to be in charge when she is away.

Complex changes in family roles and relationships are taking place in the first two years after remarriage. Family members need to be patient during this challenging family reorganization.

Finding Solutions

The difficult transitions involved in creating a blended family can be eased in several ways. First, stepparents should not expect to love their new spouse's children. There is no need to feel guilty about not loving someone else's children. It is a bonus if these positive feelings develop over time—and they often do—but they should not be expected. Stepparents should treat children fairly and respectfully, but that is all that can realistically be asked. Once the onerous expectation to love each other has been shed, stepparents and stepchildren alike are free to enjoy each other's company.

Similarly, there is no need to try to earn children's affection. Problems often develop when stepparents feel they have to compete with the natural parent for the stepchildren's love. Instead of spending more money or trying to be more fun, be yourself and do not attempt to outdo the other parent. Courtesy and respect for the other parent is one of the best ways to end this competition.

Second, a stepfamily is formed because of the adults' interest in marrying each other, not because of the new spouse's interest in the children. The new spouse should not be expected to take on a parental role with the children—certainly not in the beginning and, with older children, perhaps never. Too many stepparents feel they have to fulfill traditional childrearing roles, but they will face a great deal of conflict with older children and failure with adolescents if they attempt to do so.

In the most harmonious stepfamilies with older children and adolescents, the new spouse does not attempt to be a parent to the children; he or she leaves this role to the natural parents. Although stepparents can try to develop friendly relationships with children, they acknowledge the fact that their interest in the marriage was in the relationship with the spouse. Although this attitude may sound insensitive, it is honest and alleviates many stresses that occur in stepfamilies: the children do not suffer from loyalty conflicts concerning their other natural parent, and they are not worried about their natural parent being replaced. Further, the stepparent is not placed in the untenable position of needing the children's acceptance as a parent and is not entered into a losing battle over trying to make them obey.

I want to emphasize that one of the riskiest situations for stepfamilies is when the natural parent wants the new marriage partner to take over parental responsibilities that he or she is having difficulty with. For example, a custodial father may expect his new wife to make sure that his adolescent daughter stops cutting classes and gets to school every day after he goes to work. Or a mother who has never been comfortable taking a firm stand to make her twelve-year-old son do what she wants may expect the stepfather to discipline him. These expectations are unrealistic. Natural parents can use this life transition as an opportunity for growth and resolve their own parenting problems rather than hand over the conflict to stepparents. Unless the children are young, the natural parents should keep the parental role to themselves. For many stepparents, older friend is a better role than parent toward adolescents and toward all children in the beginning. When new spouses want to take a more active role, they should move slowly from the role of older friend to that of parent.

Many parents who are remarrying do not want to hear this. Initially, it may seem to dash the hopes and dreams they hold for the new family and the better life they are working to establish. Without realizing it, however, many parents are trying to recreate the new blended family on a model of the traditional nuclear family. Despite the best of intentions, this usually leads to heartbreak and anger. Parents can have a second chance for love in their lives, and they can provide their children with a secure family life. In many stepfamilies, however, adopting the role of older friend rather than parent may go a long way toward diminishing conflict and building relationships.

Finally, effective childrearing practices are essential if stepmothers and stepfathers are to succeed. Authoritarian stepfathers (and stepmothers) are doomed to fail. Stepchildren will reject their attempts to control. In parallel, permissive stepmothers (and stepfathers) will be dominated by disrespectful stepchildren. In stepfamilies, parents who have employed either of these ineffective parenting styles often give up and disengage from children and childrearing altogether. Successful stepparents, in contrast, use the authoritative childrearing approach as they begin to adopt a parenting role (see Figure 10.1). Combining the warmth and firmness described in Chapter Ten, they neither dominate children nor allow children to control them.

Forming a Successful Stepfamily

Couples are able to establish a marital coalition in successful stepfamilies, and they have the flexibility to determine the parenting roles that fit best for their family. Let's examine both of these far-reaching topics.

Establishing a Marital Coalition

The marital relationship is the pivotal axis in the blended family, just as it is in two-parent families. The two biggest differences between well-functioning and problem-ridden stepfamilies lie in (1) the quality of the stepparent–stepchild relationship and (2) the nature of the marital partnership. The stability and cohesiveness of other family relationships is shaped by the adults' ability to establish a marital coalition in which each partner feels supported by the other. We have already discussed the need for a marital coalition that cannot be disrupted by the demands of children and others. That need takes priority in stepfamilies, too. However, the heightened divorced rate for remarriages that include children (60 percent end in divorce, usually within the first five years) reflects that is harder to establish a strong marital coalition in stepfamilies than in nuclear families. Because the marital relationship is so important to successful family life and childrearing, we should examine these difficulties closely.

The biggest obstacle for the new couple is having the children already present while they are trying to establish their own relationship. In effect, they are trying to have a honeymoon in the midst of a crowd. Unlike the couple in a nuclear family, the remarried couple does not have an exclusive spouse-to-spouse relationship before the children arrive. In Chapter Eight we examined the developmental period of couple formation and saw that a newly married couple has a great deal of psychological work to do in building their relationship. Newlyweds need to establish mutually agreeable goals for their life together, agree on big decisions about how money will be earned and spent, and seemingly smaller decisions about who does the dishes and who takes out the trash. How will the couple resolve differences of opinion and conflicts between them? What kind of balance will be struck when one spouse wants one thing but the other wants something different? The presence of children makes it harder to conduct the psychological business of building a relationship as a couple; too often, children become inappropriately involved in the marital relationship, resulting in a higher divorce rate. It is essential for the re-married couple to keep children and child-related concerns from interfering with their relationship. In stepfamilies that function well, remarried parents realize that their children still need them, but they also accept their own need to enjoy the security that comes from a stable and supportive marriage. These parents recognize that children benefit from experiencing a successful marital coalition that is happy and working well together as a model for their own future marriages.

Bob and Laura

The Martins are a blended family made up of "his, hers, and ours." The parents, Bob and Laura, are in their late thirties and have been married for four years. Bob was previously married and has two children—John, age ten, and Emma, age eight. John and Emma live with Bob and Laura three days a week and with their mother, who lives nearby, the rest of the week.

Laura has been divorced from her first husband for seven years. Her son, Ron, is nine, and her daughter, Leah, is seven. Both of her children live with her and Bob. Her former husband moved out of the state following the remarriage and has had little contact with his children. Together, Bob and Laura also have one child, an eighteen-month-old toddler named Ross.

When Bob and Laura first began dating they found that they had a reasonable amount of time to enjoy each other, even when their children were present. The four older children were close in age, played well together, and soon became friends. After the wedding Bob and Laura were able to spend a week alone together before beginning their life as a family of six. Not long after their honeymoon, however, the couple found that some problems with the children that had been manageable before were now escalating.

After Bob and Laura married, Bob tried to take more of a fathering role with Laura's children, but they resisted his attempts to discipline them. Bob's daughter, Emma, also became increasingly negative and critical of Laura. Although the couple had always had some difficulty being close at home, now it was impossible for the newlyweds to have an uninterrupted moment. The children intruded whenever Bob and Laura tried to lock themselves away to get some privacy, and the two older children "erupted" whenever they were affectionate with each other. The children seemed to be joined in a conspiracy to keep them apart. As the level of conflict in the family rose higher, the tension in the new marriage increased as well.

Bob and Laura were determined not to let this continue, however. Unlike most couples, they had anticipated that their children might feel insecure and try to disrupt their relationship once they were married. Rather than let things get entirely out of hand, Bob and Laura redoubled their efforts to support and communicate with each other. They set aside regularly scheduled times to be alone together and faithfully held to them (fifteen minutes of quiet time to talk together every day and a date every Saturday night). They were committed to not allowing the children to come between them and talked about this with the children at the family meeting they held every Sunday night.

Tensions ran high in the new family for several months, but gradually Bob and Laura's efforts paid off. They were able to maintain their relationship as a couple, despite their children's attempts at disruption. As it gradually became clear to the children that they could not come between Bob and Laura, or reestablish the old alliances that existed before when they were single-parent families, family conflict began to subside. Bob and Laura were also effective in communicating overtly to the children that they would not lose their relationship with their other natural parent because of the new marriage, and they affirmed the need for children to spend time alone with their biological parent on a regular basis. There were more ups and downs than they had expected, but things gradually improved throughout the first eighteen months of the marriage. By the end of the second year, the Martins were enjoying a harmonious family life and hoping for a new baby.

Children may place a direct obstacle in the path of the new couple's relationship by disapproving of the marriage and trying to come between the newlyweds. This opposition makes it harder but even more necessary for the marital pair to carve out a separate sphere for their own relationship and preserve their marital coalition with each other. Parents should not expect their children to share their happiness over the new relationship because, as discussed in Chapter Three, children often want their original parents to reunite. From their point of view, when one of their parents remarries their original parents are prevented from reuniting. Parents should anticipate children's resentment, and they can give children opportunities to talk together about their disappointment, anger, or other worries they may have about the remarriage. Although parents should make it safe for children to talk forthrightly about these concerns, children's disapproval of the marriage is not a reason to cancel it.

Some single parents involve their children in approving the people they date and may even solicit their children's approval of their marital partner in the belief that they help themselves and their children by sharing this part of their life. A few parents may even go so far as to base their decision to remarry on the children's approval of the new spouse. When this occurs, parents are giving children too much responsibility for an adult decision. As we have already seen, it is not in children's best interest to be able to exert so much control over adult relationships. The decision to remarry should be left to the adults.

Another problem in establishing the marital coalition is the issue of loyalty bonds. Stepfamilies struggle with the question, Who comes first, the children or the new spouse? Routinely, there are accusations that too much time, attention, or cooperation is being given to the former spouse or even to the parent's own parents. It is especially hard for single parents to rearrange existing loyalties with their children to include the new spouse, and new spouses often complain that they are being left out of the parent–child unit. Legitimate responsibilities to children must be met, of course, and it is important to maintain the most cooperative parenting relationship that is possible with the former spouse. However, it is also critical for spouses to be committed to each other and to meet each other's emotional needs—each partner feeling that the other is available and supportive. This responsiveness is made more difficult in stepfamilies, however, because there are so many competing demands and responsibilities. In particular, spouses frequently complain that "the children always come first; there is never time for me." In stepfamilies, this feeling of always coming second is a significant marital problem. Stepparents who feel displaced by the children often begin to wonder, "What am I doing here?" When that feeling doesn't change, they begin to say, "I'm out of here."

Couples must set limits on their obligations to others and regularly set aside time to be with each other. If that doesn't happen, parent–child relations will suffer along with the marital relationship.

Understanding That Stepfamilies Are Different

Stepfamilies are not the same as nuclear families. Because the nuclear family is the basic model for parental roles and family relations that most of us have, too many adults try to recreate this traditional family style in their remarriage. As we have seen, adults can often approximate this model if children are under eight years of age or so when the adults remarry. With older children, however, initial attempts to share the parental role with the new spouse often create conflict, which is why most stepfamilies have more arguments and tension than nuclear families. Stepfamilies with older children should not even try to be like a nuclear family but should determine which parenting roles and family relations will work best for them. For example, one sibling may accept some guidance and discipline from a stepparent; another accepts none. One stepparent may want to take on parental responsibilities with children; another may not. Stepfamilies blossom when they respond to their own preferences and make the family what each member wants it to be rather than try to force it into the traditional nuclear family model.

Stepfamilies also have more *ambiguity* than nuclear families because they need to establish more of their own roles and rules. The guidelines for what to do are not as clear. For example, even something as basic as what to call another family member must be decided. There is no convention for addressing stepparents to fall back on. Should children call Mother's new husband Jim, Dad, Mr. Jones, Stepdad, Father? In response to this ambiguity, children should be encouraged to talk about this decision and find their own names for family members. It doesn't need to be an awkward topic that can't be joked about and explored together. We don't want to tell children how to address others but to encourage them to find what is comfortable for them. Further ambiguity occurs as the stepparent's role in the blended family often changes over time and has to be repeatedly redefined. The blended family will change significantly, especially during the first two years, and stepparents may assume, relinquish, and then resume again discipline and other child-care responsibilities during this transition. To succeed, parents need to foster in themselves the flexibility necessary to adjust to these ambiguities.

Another characteristic of stepfamilies that parents should be aware of is the issue of belonging. Membership in the family and sharing a collective identity with other family members is not the same in stepfamilies as it is in nuclear families. To function successfully, every family member must share in a group identity, and each family develops its own rituals and traditions for demonstrating how each member belongs to the family (for example, ways of decorating the Christmas tree every year or celebrating birthdays). Families also demonstrate their shared identity with each other by attending a Fourth of July picnic together each year or by taking pictures during Hanukkah that are kept in photo albums year after year. Some families set places for absent members at the Thanksgiving dinner table as a way of acknowledging everyone who belongs to the family. These are examples of the many different traditions families use to define themselves as a family group: "We are the Harris family."

Membership in the stepfamily is different from in the nuclear family because it is more "open." For example, noncustodial parents may regularly participate in the stepfamily. They make decisions about the children and often take an active role in determining the direction of the children's lives. This situation, which brings an outside person—a third parent—into the stepfamily, does not occur in nuclear families. Also, children of divorce usually belong to two families. They often have strong ties to their other parent and feel a part of the other parent's family as well. Further, grandparents as well as stepgrandparents may now play an important part in extended family life, special events, and holidays. Thus the stepfamily is not their whole world; often they must find a way to balance a sense of loyalty and shared family identity with two families. In parallel, perhaps some can appreciate the challenge of identity formation that confronts a biracial child who is trying to integrate a coherent sense of self. The mixed-race child grapples with the complex question, How do I honor and include aspects of both of my parents and the two different cultural worlds they represent into my own sense of self? The challenge is significant but, when met, the outcome can be especially rich.

Finally, blended families differ fundamentally from nuclear families because there are frequent comings and goings that are an enduring feature of family life; 50 percent of children leave the stepfamily on a regular basis to be with their other natural parent. If that parent has also remarried, stepbrothers and stepsisters may enter into the equation in that household as well. It is easy to see that the question of family membership is central for these children: "Who is in my family? Who belongs and who doesn't?" Children do not feel settled in their families or secure in themselves until they have answered this profound question to their satisfaction. This is no simple task; children must think and feel and talk about this question over and over and revisit it at different points in their development.

Children often have trouble feeling that they can belong to two different families while maintaining ties to both of their biological parents. Parents help children resolve this problem by (1) giving them spoken permission to belong to both families at the same time, (2) reassuring children that they do not have to choose between them but can be close to both parents at the same time, (3) affirming the positive characteristics they enjoy with their other family, and (4) helping them solve or put into perspective, rather than inflame or punctuate, the problems they complain about with the other parent.

Guidelines for Parents

In summary, I would like to emphasize four guidelines for parents in blended families:

1. *Appreciate the importance of children's relationship with their natural parent.* Children will see the stepparent as less of a competitor if adults can affirm and overtly support the children's relationship with both of their natural parents. This spoken appreciation and the acknowledgment of children's need for private time with their natural parents should be repeatedly expressed.

2. *Love isn't necessary.* Partners in a remarriage should drop the expectation that stepchildren and stepparents love each other. This expectation puts an unrealistic burden on both children and stepparents. Further, when older children are involved, stepparents

should move into the parenting role slowly, if at all. An older friend is a more workable role than parent in many cases.

3. *Remember that children have no choice.* It is important to remember that parents choose to remarry, whereas children simply become part of a stepfamily. Parents are to take full responsibility for the decision to remarry. Children should not be given the power to decide whether their mother or father remarries (divorces, has new children, and so forth). Although parents want to talk with children about the new marriage and reassure them about the concerns they may have, the responsibility for the decision to marry should be left to the parent, not shared with the children.

4. *Establish a coalition.* The remarried couple needs to establish their own marital coalition. This does not mean that the natural parent is supposed to love the spouse more than the children or place the needs of the spouse before the children. Nor does it suggest that the parents should never argue or disagree in front of the children. It means that the couple needs to be able to put other demands on hold, find time to be alone, and prevent children and others from repeatedly coming between them and disrupting their relationship or their ability to communicate. Establishing a successful marital coalition also means that each feels secure that the other is looking out for him or her and will be available and responsive if called upon. Many competing demands impinge on the new marital relationship, but there will be more cohesion in all stepfamily relationships when the new spouses can preserve their own relationship as a couple.

Conclusion

I wish to end this book by acknowledging once again how painful divorce can be. Many of us have grown up believing that most change and conflict are relegated to our youth. We often expect that once we marry, we are grown up and life will settle down and proceed at a steady pace. Divorce shatters this myth of stability and well-being, along with our ready assurance of who we are and where we are headed. During the crisis of divorce, many responsible parents feel far more distressed than they had anticipated, and for a much longer period of time, as seemingly everything in their lives is changing. More significant, they worry about whether they are doing the right thing and are saddened by the pain their loved ones are suffering.

It sometimes helps to be reminded that divorce is not the end of the line. It is the end of a marriage and the beginning of a new phase of life. The unfolding sequence of family transitions that follow the breakup leads most of us to see ourselves in new ways. These far-reaching changes to our sense of self and life plan is even more difficult when we are not only responsible for ourselves but for our children as well.

Although it may take a year or two to fully regain your equilibrium, you can create a new and meaningful life for yourself and your children. This period of adjustment can also be a time of growth as an individual and as a parent. The upheaval of the divorce may be a wrenching crisis, but it offers you a chance to become more independent, flexible, and tolerant. As you learn that you are able to cope with life's problems, you may also find that you are capable of becoming a better parent. The promise that accompanies the pain of divorce is that you can learn to listen better to your children and really hear them, become more accessible and emotionally present when you are with them, and earn their respect and help them feel secure by taking charge and disciplining them effectively.

As you struggle to manage your life in a period of self-doubt and turmoil, your children are coping with their own distress evoked by all of the changes that are occurring. They look to you for love and reassurance, which you can provide by taking their concerns seriously and helping them to solve the problems that trouble them.

By explaining children's fears, concerns, and misconceptions, I have tried to help you understand some of the things your children cannot communicate very well on their own. I offer this with the hope that you will use this understanding to help your children successfully cope with divorce.

Suggestions for Further Reading

How to Win as a Step-Family by E. Visher and J. Visher (Bruner/Mazel, 1991) is an especially helpful guide for parents who are remarrying. The authors are reassuringly knowledgeable about life in a stepfamily and help parents anticipate the problems they are likely to encounter and provide practical guidelines to help solve them. These authors are experts who can help you form a more successful stepfamily.

Why Marriages Succeed or Fail . . . And How You Can Make Yours Last (J. Gottman, Fireside, 1994) helps marital partners learn how to communicate more effectively, recognize the interaction patterns that lead to divorce, and make the most of marriage. Clear, practical, and highly informative for all.

Help! A Girl's Guide to Divorce and Stepfamilies by N. Holyoke (American Girl, 1999) helps stepparents talk with their stepchildren about their new family. Finally, stepparents can benefit greatly from developing a support network. Readers are encouraged to learn more by contacting, The Stepfamily Association of America, 650 J Street, Ste. 205, Lincoln, NE 68508.

About the Author

Edward Teyber is professor of psychology and director of the psychology clinic at California State University, San Bernardino. He received his M.A. and Ph.D. degrees in clinical psychology from Michigan State University. He is also the author of two counseling textbooks: *Interpersonal Process in Psychotherapy: A Relational Approach* and coauthor, with Faith McClure, of *Casebook in Child and Adolescent Treatment: Cultural and Familial Contexts*.

Teyber has published research articles on the effects of marital and family relations on child adjustment and contributes articles on parenting and postdivorce family relations to newspapers and magazines. He also enjoys clinical supervision and training and maintains a part-time private practice.

Index